£12.50

689

COMMUNITY AND CONFLICT IN THE SOCIALIST CAMP

Community and Conflict in the Socialist Camp

The Soviet Union, East Germany and the German Problem 1965–1972

by GERHARD WETTIG

Translated by Edwina Moreton and Hannes Adomeit

 C. Hurst & Company, London

First published in the United Kingdom by
C. Hurst & Co. (Publishers) Ltd., London

© 1975 by Gerhard Wettig

This study was written in the Bundesinstitut für
ostwissenschaftliche und internationale Studien, Cologne

ISBN 0–903983–36–2

Printed in Great Britain by
Billing & Sons Limited
Guildford and London

Contents

Acknowledgments

This book could not have been written without the help and advice of many colleagues and institutions. I am particularly indebted to the stimulating exchange of views with Fred Oldenburg at the Bundesinstitut für ostwissenschaftliche und internationale Studien in Cologne, with Dr. Peer Lange at the Stiftung Wissenschaft und Politik near Munich, and with Professor Dr. Heinrich Machowski at the Deutsches Institut für Wirtschaftsforschung in Berlin. I have been greatly stimulated by the ideas and concepts presented by Professor Dr. Richard Lowenthal from the Free University of Berlin in many discussions. The responsibility for any errors in my study naturally rests with me.

I have to express my gratitude to the Bundesinstitut für ostwissenschaftliche und internationale Studien in Cologne, where I work, for having given me sufficient leisure to write the book and for supporting my project in every way possible. In particular, my thanks go to the Director of the Bundesinstitut, Dr. Hans-Walter Poll, and to the personnel of the library and the press archive. Untiring help has been given me also by the librarians of both the Gesamtdeutsches Archiv and the Bundestag in Bonn. I am indebted to the Federal Ministry for Intra-German Relations in Bonn which has regularly sent me the newest publications on GDR problems. The Federal Press and Information Office in Bonn has made possible the translation of the study into the English language by bearing the costs. Last, but not least, I want to thank the translator, Miss Edwina Moreton, and Hannes Adomeit who has given his valuable advice in the course of translation. The credit for having published a scholarly book, not without financial risk, goes to Christopher Hurst. I am very glad that his initiative has made my study available to a wider world public than could be reached by a German-language edition alone.

Cologne
April 1975   G. W.

Preface

When Chancellor Brandt and Minister President Kosygin signed the Moscow Treaty on 12 August 1970 and this put an end to the sharpest of the controversies between the states of East and West, there was widespread belief that a fundamental change in East–West relations had occurred and that international conflict in Europe was waning never to return. To many it seemed that lasting peace with no serious tensions had been realized. At the same time, however, there were apprehensions that *Pravda* might be right in predicting that the West Germans would take the opportunity to loosen their ties with the West, and thereby evoke the final dissolution of the Western Community.

Neither estimate was to prove right. The Federal Republic of Germany, it is true, has reduced its conflict with the USSR and the latter's allies. But that did not mean that the conflict had been eliminated altogether. There was still to be much argument with the Warsaw Pact countries on many issues, such as the arrangements concerning Berlin or the regulation of intra-German relations. Agreements which, after much debate, were finally concluded soon became subject to controversial interpretations; new differences of opinion and attitude came to the fore when East–West negotiations successively touched upon ever new subjects. Under these circumstances, the West German government had as much reason as ever to act in solidarity with its partners both in the European Community and in the Atlantic Alliance. The Soviet policy-makers, who increasingly oriented their words and deeds in conformity with the postulate of anti-capitalist 'ideological struggle' made it clear that, in their opinion, the former East–West conflict had undergone a process not of elimination, but of transformation.

Brandt's seemingly spectacular 'new *Ostpolitik*' and Brezhnev's positive reaction to it were also not fundamental changes, if one examines their genesis. As early as March 1969, the Soviet leaders had come to the conclusion that some kind of political rapprochement with Bonn was necessary. The decision was prompted largely by domestic needs, among which the pressing desire for Western – and to a considerable extent West German – help for economico–technological modernization was most prominent. It was quite clear from the beginning that any West German government taking office after the elections of September 1969 would respond to the conciliatory moves of Moscow in one way or another. After all, since December 1966 the 'Grand Coalitions' formed by Christian and Social Democrats (CDU/CSU and SPD) alike had continuously tried to find a *modus vivendi* with the Kremlin, even though it had been discouraged by Soviet confrontation policies.

Under the auspices of détente, a new interaction pattern between the Soviet Camp and the Western countries began to emerge in Germany and Europe. Until 1968–9, the Soviet offers to the West under the catchword of 'European security' were little more than propaganda slogans designed to appeal to the Western public, in order to induce it to exert pressure on their governments in conformity with demands voiced by the USSR. Much of what was being said then (like 'all-European reconciliation' or 'elimination of the barriers between the Europeans'), was intended for Western consumption only while, at the same time, such rhetoric was carefully avoided wherever Soviet control was effective in Eastern Europe. It was fairly obvious that the Soviet leadership was not keen on the negotiations with Western governments which it was advocating in public: unacceptable pre-conditions were voiced, and Soviet statements argued that no Western regime, not even de Gaulle's government (which was given much credit for its anti-NATO policies), was living up to the standards of 'European security'. The Soviet line was therefore détente rhetoric, and confrontation action towards the West – particularly towards West Germany until, in autumn 1969, new considerations began to prevail.

The 'Prague Spring' of 1968, which in Soviet eyes was a great disaster, had convinced the Soviet leaders that it was impossible simultaneously to preach reconciliation and approximation to West European audiences and to suppress all tendencies towards East–West reconciliation and approximation within the East European societies. For this reason, the practice of détente propaganda was being increasingly perceived as dangerous for domestic stability in the Socialist Camp. Nevertheless, the Soviet leaders did not want West European hopes of East–West détente to be disappointed, as such hopes opened up the prospect for unilateral erosion of community and solidarity in the West. An impression of spreading détente was to be created in Western Europe, despite the Soviet suppression of all the conciliatory tendencies which had arisen within East European Communism in 1968. The Soviet leaders chose to present an appearance of co-operation at the inter-governmental level. From then on, it was the collective effort of Eastern and Western governments (particularly in the form of negotiations and agreements) which was to lay the basis for peace in Europe.

The new Soviet policy concept was co-operative in form, but not in substance. It implied that, for the time being, the USSR refrained from pressing its objectives by means of open and extended confrontation. But there was no intention of giving up those policy orientations which were obviously incompatible with Western needs for political self-preservation. The Soviet leaders did not, for example, refrain from the attempt to substitute some kind of (Soviet-dominated) 'All-European security system' for the Atlantic Alliance and the European Economic Community. In their view, Soviet hegemony all over Europe (to be realized, of course, only cautiously and gradually) was the 'natural' state of affairs which was only artificially blocked by American interference in Europe. As Soviet statements put it, the West Europeans would be wise to drop their hopeless efforts to form a politico-military counterweight to the USSR and entrust their security to the strong and peaceful might of the Soviet Union. It is wholly consistent with this policy that Soviet representatives continuously stress the growing importance of military power in a period of détente and that the Soviet forces have been greatly strengthened since 1967–9 (while NATO's efforts have been reduced).

The fact that, during the present period, the leaders in the Kremlin seek to attain their objectives by negotiation with Western governments is not without importance, even though these objectives imply the attempt to expand Soviet influence. The Soviet concept, it is true, calls for the exploitation of Western weaknesses (lack of realism, wisdom and/or strength). But it depends on the actions of the Western countries – in particular, whether they allow themselves to be exploited by the USSR. If Western statesmen recognize the situation and its issues clearly, if they can mobilize their societies for the common interests *vis-à-vis* the USSR, and if they can muster sufficient political and military strength to counter Eastern pressures, they may well be able to take advantage of the formally co-operative Soviet policies.

To a certain degree, Western governments have already made use of the changed East–West interaction pattern. In 1969, the Soviet proposals for 'European security' envisaged the immediate calling of an all-European Conference. This would have implied that some of the East–West conflicts in Germany would be decided according to Soviet policy without a *quid pro quo* for the Western side (particularly by a *de facto* recognition of East Germany, without any concessions to West German wishes for an increase in intra-German contact), while others would have remained unresolved to the advantage of the USSR (as in the case of Berlin, where both local power superiority and unconditional recognition of East German sovereignty made Soviet recognition of Western rights highly desirable for the Federal Republic and the Three Powers, in order to restrain future pressure). Therefore, the West German government took the stand in late 1969 that it was willing to support the Eastern conference project in principle, but the pre-conditions for the success of such a conference had to be created by eliminating the conflicts in Germany. Thus the Soviet leaders were confronted with the choice either to see their hopes for the conference wrecked or to accept the necessity to bargain at least on certain aspects of the German problem. In the beginning, the Kremlin was only willing to trade a force-renunciation agreement (which Bonn sought in order not to be any longer subjected to Eastern polemics) for the fixing of the East European frontiers (which Moscow sought in order to have the 1945 annexations of the USSR and its allies formally accepted). But later on the West German government, with energetic support from its Western allies, also managed to make a satisfactory Berlin agreement an unavoidable condition of détente. Similarly, other Western objectives had to be taken into consideration by the USSR and its allies, Of course, the USSR was also in the position to demand fulfilment of important wishes from the other side: what matters, however, is the fact that, as long as the Western governments acted together with resolve and strength, the USSR was prevented from carrying its points unilaterally, and was dragged into a process of mutual give and take instead.

For the USSR the détente of 1970 implies a marked change of behaviour *vis-à-vis* the Atlantic Alliance in general and the Federal Republic of Germany in particular. Until then, it had been the recipe of the Kremlin to assure Soviet dominance in the Socialist Camp and to mobilize anti-NATO feelings in West Europe by pointing to the alleged danger of 'West German revanchism'. The argument had been that the alleged West German aspirations towards forceful expansion were an immediate threat to the East Europeans (who, for this reason, had to look for Soviet protection) and created the possibility of un-wanted war for the West Europeans (who were therefore well advised to unite with the East against Bonn). This campaign had been based by the Soviet leaders on the assumption that it was the Federal Republic which was the decisive Atlantic power on the European continent. If West Germany left NATO, there would be, according to the Soviet estimate, only a truncated Western alliance between the United States, the United Kingdom and Canada. The Soviet decision not to play the card of 'West German revanchism' any longer implied that the old mode of anti-NATO policy had been dropped. In fact, the Soviet leaders had realized after the invasion of Czecho-slovakia that the West German bogey had lost its credibility and that it did not work either in Eastern or Western Europe. Therefore, the prospect of a future all-European security arrangement was regarded in Moscow as a better instrument of anti-NATO appeal.

There was, however, a revision of former policies, not only on the Soviet side. The SPD–FDP government in Bonn was also rethinking political concepts. During the years of the Grand Coalition (1966–9), the West German leaders had made considerable efforts to come to terms with the East European countries. Their aim was to reach agreement with all Warsaw Pact states including the USSR and, with some legal reservations, the GDR. Soon, however, it had become clear that the GDR, the USSR and some other countries were unwilling to respond. Under these circumstances, the West German government began to normalize its relations with those East European states which, despite Soviet opposition, were prepared to accept its offers. The *Ostpolitik* of the Grand Coalition had thus obtained an anti-Soviet image which had not been intended.

In the autumn of 1969 Brandt and his advisers felt that the concept of starting the normalization process with Eastern Europe from the periphery and waiting for the USSR to join in later had no chances of success. The Soviet military action in Czechoslovakia, which had taken place one year before, seemed to indicate that no political development was possible in Eastern Europe without Moscow's wholehearted approval. Brandt and his advisers concluded that there had first to be agreement with the USSR if the Federal Republic of Germany was to come to terms with its Eastern neighbours. Acceptability in Moscow therefore, became the first priority for Bonn's 'new *Ostpolitik*'. Brandt and his advisers were even prepared (as the Moscow Treaty was to show) explicitly to concede to the USSR the role of protector and advocate for the other Warsaw Pact countries. This new concept also had, in one respect, an advantageous side for the West German policy: it opened up the prospect that East Germany, which was the toughest opponent to deal with, could be induced through the USSR to accept normalization.

The new emerging patterns of interaction could not but deeply affect the relations between the USSR and its allies. The new round between East and West was begun on Soviet initiative, and the other Warsaw Pact states were expected to follow suit. The policies of West Germany, which in the ensuing period was the most important partner in the West, aimed primarily at agreement with the USSR. Under such circumstances, the restricted room for political manoeuvre, which the Soviet allies had possessed till then, was likely to be narrowed even further. At first, however, it seemed as if there could be more room for national interests. Romania had the triumph that her policies *vis-à-vis* Bonn, which had been severely criticized in 1967, were justified at last by the Soviet policy change. Poland allowed itself to offer and to start negotiations of its own with West Germany. Within a short time, however, the Soviet leaders managed to establish full control over their allies' efforts to negotiate agreements with Bonn. Poland could only move forward after the relevant points had been settled in principle between Moscow and Bonn. Hungary and Bulgaria, let alone satellitized Czechoslovakia, were allowed to start negotiations with West Germany only after the basic agreements had been reached. Even then they had to act in strict conformity with the USSR's wishes of the moment.

The situation of the GDR was somehow different. East Berlin's interests were not directed at an early normalization of relations with Bonn. On the contrary, the East German leaders were extremely apprehensive of such a normalization, whether it were their own or that of their allies. In their eyes, a position of strict enmity towards the Federal Republic was an absolute necessity. Such enmity provided the GDR with the role of a 'peaceful and democratic' counterweight against 'West German revanchism'. The GDR was then able to claim that it was the indispensable guarantee against a future rise of the West German danger. As long as that claim was accepted by the East European allies, the GDR was able to demand full support for its policies from the Warsaw Pact members. East Berlin's vested interests, therefore, lay with the type of *Westpolitik* which had been followed by the USSR until 1968-9. At the same time, the GDR had to be a part of any Soviet-West German normalization almost from the outset. In particular, the Berlin Problem-which was necessarily a stumbling-block on the road to Soviet-West German agreement – could not be regulated without the GDR.

The following analyses will deal with the various processes which mark the way from former East-West confrontation to present East-West détente in Germany and Europe. Their purpose is to make clear how the policy changes came about and what they imply for the present political situation on the Continent of Europe. The perspective will be different from the usual one: the problems will be seen not with Western, but with Eastern eyes and in the context of converging or diverging national interests. The author feels that this unconventional perspective will help to see the détente situation in a broader and clearer light than is customery. His hope is that this will open new insights both into the nature of East-West relations and into the patterns of Eastern intra-bloc interactions.

I

Definition of the Problem

According to Soviet ideology, there can be no 'antagonistic contradictions' between states belonging to the 'socialist community' – although the quarrels with Yugoslavia, China and Albania and the use of military force against Hungary and Czechoslovakia contradict this assertion. Where conflicts have arisen, it is claimed, they have been of a trivial nature and have in no way disturbed fundamental political harmony. Soviet publications usually ignore these 'non-antagonistic contradictions' as far as possible, in order to create an impression of monolithic unity not only for domestic consumption but also for the benefit of the 'imperialist class enemy'. In this way the mass media in the East deliberately set out to create the impression of unbounded solidarity and complete agreement between the USSR and its allies. Conflicts are aired only behind closed doors. Where a particular leading group wishes to give emphasis to its point of view publicly, it usually does so by innuendos meant as a signal for other Communist élites but designed to escape the notice of wider sections of the population. This practice, where the cipher is known only to the initiated, is referred to by Western experts as 'esoteric communication'.[1]

In relations between the USSR and the GDR special care is taken in cultivating the image of complete harmony. Even in times where it has seen its own vital interests jeopardized by Soviet policy, the SED leadership has repeatedly concealed its anger and opposition under a cloak of unanimity. For example, this was the case when Khrushchev, in July 1964, sent his son-in-law, A. Adzhubey, to Bonn to bring about a political rapprochement between the USSR and the Federal Republic. Numerous Soviet journalists began paying visits to West Germany; their relatively objective and sympathetic reports[2] contrasted sharply with the undifferentiated polemics which continued to be voiced by the GDR. Not until after the fall of Khrushchev was it learned how strenuously the SED leaders had opposed the change of policy. On 17 October 1964 the Politburo of the SED expressed its 'firm conviction that the unanimous resolutions of the Central Committee [CC] of the CPSU are inspired by the CPSU's deep awareness of the responsibility it bears in the consistent pursuit and

1

implementation of the general Leninist line'. This statement did not simply represent deference to the new rulers in the Kremlin. The SED Politburo was specifically engaging in criticism of the ousted leader, and in doing so contrasted his earlier achievements in the implementation of the Marxist–Leninist policy formulated by the CC of the CPSU with assertions that he had 'failed in the end' and 'proved himself no longer equal to his duties'.[3] Since the new men in the Kremlin had expected formal approval, but certainly no detailed justification for their coup, the additional remarks sprang essentially from pent-up displeasure which could now find its release.

Can the tension between Moscow and East Berlin in the later period of Khrushchev's rule be attributed to the personal high-handedness of the Soviet leader, or is it to be seen as the expression of a latent objective conflict of interest between the USSR and the GDR? Subsequent events must hold the answer. And the period from 1965 to 1972 seems particularly suitable for a closer examination of the network of interests between the two states. Initially the political state of affairs in Germany was still determined by the tensions of the 1950s. However, a new trend gradually emerges which brings about a fundamental change in the constellation of forces, characterized by the East–West treaties of 1970 to 1972. During the course of this process, changed situations are brought about in rapid succession requiring that unforeseen decisions be taken and thereby again and again demanding new efforts at harmonization from the USSR and the GDR. Of course, the discontinuities in the flow of events accentuate the element of conflict: the less efficient the functioning of the well-tried mechanisms of coordination, and the greater the pressure to make decisions in foreign policy, the more difficult it becomes to achieve a harmonious balance of interests. Consequently the conclusions drawn from a period of upheaval can only be applied with reservation in times where relations follow a fixed pattern.[4] A period of upheaval, however, does reveal more clearly submerged points of conflict in mutual relations.

The reactions of the USSR and the GDR, whether coinciding or differing, to the behaviour of third states provide insights into relative positions on points of mutual interest; the areas in which there is reciprocal coordination or non-coordination of interests; the methods by which harmonization of interests is achieved, and finally the extent to which one side or the other is able to assert its own interests.

The central concept is that of interest. By that is meant expectations of a positive or negative nature which motivate behaviour designed to promote or respectively to counter those expectations. The interests of two actors in relation to each other can be congruent, unrelated or opposed. These interests can be either central or peripheral, which naturally affects the weight attached to the respective relationship.

It is of considerable importance to discern how attempts are made to render the pursuit of congruent interests more effective by joint action; to see how the reciprocal handicap of conflicting interests is resolved by equitable compromise, or rendered ineffective by tacitly leaving it out of consideration. The actors have at their disposal various means of emphasizing their respective standpoints. The particular choice of methods by which to conduct the conflict can, therefore, favour one side or the other. Mutual efforts at coordinating interests and behaviour usually produce results which do not correspond in equal proportion to the wishes of both participants. One side may assert itself more strongly than the other. Where the outcomes over a long period of time do not vary from case to case, but work out overwhelmingly in favour of one side, this can be interpreted as an indication of a one-sided relationship of dependency.

Unfortunately, the Western observer has little insight into the political constellations operating within the leading circles of the Warsaw Pact states. Therefore, in general, analysis must be based on the interests advanced by influential foreign policy spokesmen in the respective countries and put forward as official policy. Differing views put forward by other groups within the respective government apparatus, which have failed to gain acceptance, do not then become apparent. Thus, if of necessity the official external line in foreign policy is taken to be the true expression of a state's interests, only a distorted picture is obtained. In particular, this excludes the interesting question of the extent of interest convergence and behaviour coordination between proponents of the official line on the one side and their opponents on the other, when conflicts occur at an official level. The present study avoids this distortion only at one, albeit decisive, point – namely the crisis in the relationship between the USSR and the GDR in 1970–1 – by giving a more detailed presentation of the internal political constellations.

The German Question seems especially suitable for the purpose of distinguishing the interests of the two states from each other. This whole issue area is of primary importance to both Moscow and East Berlin. Since the Second World War, Soviet policy on Germany has continually been set in an all-European framework. As for the GDR, decisions concerning Germany eclipse all others in importance. The greater intensity of interest displayed by the USSR and the GDR is accompanied by a higher probability of conflict between the two states. Increased political commitment may lead to an increase in congruent as well as opposing expectations. However, it is more difficult for the SED to integrate itself into bloc policy laid down by the Soviet Union when, in addition to the idea of joint action against the 'imperialist enemy', there is also a need to put forward its own special interests.

3

The GDR, therefore, is more likely to act independently of the USSR's in respect of the German question than on almost any other issue.

The relative power considerations conditioning the relationship between the two states are of a very varied nature. The USSR is a nuclear superpower with global political influence. The GDR, on the other hand, can hardly be described even as a medium-sized power, and its independent activity is largely restricted to the Central and East European region (this applies particularly to the period prior to international recognition in 1972–3). Thus it cannot hope to come anywhere near offsetting the USSR's military and economic potential. However, the East German state does enjoy the advantage of a considerably higher *per capita* income. This is a reflection of a generally much higher stage of economic and technical development. Within the 'socialist community', that is, within the Warsaw Pact Organization and Comecon, the USSR enjoys the role of undisputed leader. Thus, the GDR is integrated politically, military and economically into the Soviet hegemonial sphere; the twenty Soviet divisions stationed in the GDR provide an additional guarantee that this state of affairs will continue, as does the Soviet doctrine of 'socialist internationalism', which dictates a collective definition of sovereignty for all 'socialist states'.[5]

It would be a mistake to assume that the SED leaders regard the incorporation of their state into the USSR's hegemonial sphere as an unwelcome imposition. Quite to the contrary, they see their position both internally and externally as so exposed that close alignment with the leader of the Communist movement is regarded as an essential guarantee of continued existence and prosperity. Despite the progress achieved in East Germany since 1961 in terms of regime consolidation this dependence in the functionaries of East Berlin has not declined so far. It would appear that influential circles within the SED continue to perceive latent dangers in their situation as long as the Federal Republic continues to exist as a large and prosperous polity within Germany outside the political influence of the East German Communists.

The attitude of SED leaders is clearly reflected in official statements. The declarations of loyalty to the USSR by far exceed the norm for the rest of Eastern Europe. The first and so far the only Party Programme of the SED makes the attitude towards the USSR the 'touchstone for the policies of the Communist and Workers' Parties and the socialist states'. The 'wealth of experience of the Soviet Union in foreign policy and the struggle for peace' is to be the guideline for the foreign policy of the GDR. The acknowledgement of the 'leading role of the USSR on the path to Communism and the preservation of peace' is linked to the idea that the 'fraternal friendship with the USSR' and

4

East Germany's position 'firmly within the socialist camp' form the foundations of foreign policy and are considered a 'vital necessity'.[6] Here the leading circles of the SED are putting forward the notion that state sovereignty is inextricably linked with good relations to the USSR.[7] Soviet supremacy is seen as an indispensable guarantee of the solidarity of the 'socialist community', which the party functionaries in East Berlin see as the political basis of their activity. The GDR is the only state in the world to have bound itself by its constitution to foreign countries. According to the constitution 'all-round friendship and cooperation' and 'close comradeship in arms' with the USSR and other Communist states are the primary objectives.[8]

In economic affairs too the SED leaders are striving to bind the East German states as closely as possible to the USSR. This serves the economic as well as the political purposes of the USSR. As a more highly developed industrial state, the GDR is in a position to supply the USSR with modern and urgently needed machinery and production plant. Thus, from the USSR's point of view the GDR is a most important trading partner.[9] However, Soviet import needs can also be detrimental to the GDR if they exceed certain limits; excessive demands can only be met at the expense of its own direct and indirect needs.[10] In the mid-1960s there was considerable opposition within the top leadership of the SED to the practice of neglecting domestic interests in favour of those of the USSR. On 3 December 1965 the head of the Economic Commission attached to the Politburo of the SED, Erich Apel, committed suicide rather than sign what he considered an unacceptable trade agreement with the USSR, his objections having failed to impress Ulbricht. The First Secretary of the SED set aside all economic considerations in his efforts to make the GDR an indispensable partner to the USSR. For a time the Soviet leaders seem to have made a serious attempt at using the GDR to resolve their problems of economic and technological modernization. However, by 1969 at the latest it had become apparent to the USSR that the GDRs capacity in this respect would not suffice and that extensive reliance on Western economies was difficult to avoid.

The relationship between the USSR and the GDR is marked by inequality of status under international law. According to a treaty concluded between Moscow and East Berlin on 20 September 1955, the GDR would in future be 'free to make its own decisions concerning domestic and foreign policy, including its relations with the German Federal Republic'. At the same time both states gave mutual assurances of their readiness to participate in any international actions 'aimed at the preservation of peace and security in Europe and the whole world'. In doing so the GDR bound itself to the long-term perspectives of Soviet foreign policy, which typically claims to be peaceful. In addition, each side agreed to consult the other 'on all important international matters'.[11] Although the GDR was thereby bound to priorities of Soviet policy, the USSR in addition preserved supremacy, maintaining its status as an occupation power. The Soviet Government declared that the 'rights and duties of the USSR in respect of Germany as a whole contained in the corresponding resolutions of the Four Powers' continue to apply.[12] Also, when the USSR transferred control to the GDR on the transit routes to West Berlin, this was not done unconditionally. The USSR would continue to exercise 'control over the movement of troops and goods of the garrisons stationed in West Berlin', and committed the GDR to 'settle all questions' relating to civilian transit traffic with the Federal German authorities.[13]

The GDR was also obliged to accept discrimination within the framework of the Warsaw Pact. This was reflected in the wording of the clause on mutual assistance. According to the treaty of 14 May 1955, each member-state is obliged to render assistance to an ally in the event of attack. According to the original Russian, Polish and Czech texts, assistance was to be effected with all the means 'it' – i.e. the state in question – considered necessary. The original German text replaces the 'it' by 'they' – i.e. the other member-states of the Warsaw Pact.[14] Also, prior to their formal inclusion in the structure of the pact, an upper ceiling was placed on the East German forces.[15] Thus the National People's Army (NVA) is relatively smaller than the military units of other East Central European states.[16] Unlike the military units of its allies, the armed forces of the GDR were put under direct command of the Warsaw Pact Organization in 1956.[17] In its treaty with the USSR on the stationing of troops (12 March 1957) the GDR came off worse than the other East Central European countries in corresponding agreements.[18]

Along with the USSR's other allies, the GDR has had to dispense for the most part with the idea of producing its own armaments. The only exception is in the manufacture of ammunition, where the GDR has played a role for some time. Obviously this corresponds to Soviet interests in establishing short supply lines in the event of war. Since the end of the 1950s the armed forces of Poland, Czechoslovakia and the GDR have been allotted an active combat role in the plans of the Warsaw Pact; since 1963 they have constituted the 'first strategic echelon' of the alliance, in other words they would be the first units to be deployed in the event of war.[19] This change was accompanied by a complete modernization of weaponry, although dependence on Soviet deliveries still remained. At the same time Soviet influence over the allied armies was increased. Organizational changes made in the Joint Supreme Command of the Warsaw Pact in March 1969, supposedly designed to improve the status of the smaller allies, seems to have had the effect of tying them even more closely to the Soviet-dominated alliance structure.[20] This met the SED leadership's marked interest in bringing about as close an integration as possible within the sphere of Soviet hegemony.

Power relationships, provisions of international law, the organizational structure of the alliance and, not least, the East Berlin functionaries' need of integration all combine to form the background which decisively influences the relationship between the USSR and the GDR. Case studies which are to illuminate relative interests, processes of coordination, instruments of exerting influence and outcomes cannot always refer expressly to these matters. However, they must always be borne in mind if a complete picture of the events under consideration is to be gained. The first three case studies deal with specific events on which there is relatively little information available, and must therefore be discussed systematically and in detail. The five subsequent case studies form an integrated whole. In these latter case studies there is no need to deal separately with background, decision-making and motivation. These become sufficiently clear from the context.

References

1. See M. Rush, 'Communist "Esoteric" Communication', *World Politics*, Vol. XI, No. 4 (July 1959), pp. 614–20.

2. A. Buchholz and J. Dietrich, *Die Bundesrepublik Deutschland in der sowjetischen Publizistik*, Cologne, 1964.

3. *Neues Deutschland*, 21 November 1964.

4. This became apparent in 1973 when Moscow and East Berlin found it much easier than in previous years to coordinate their actions to their mutual satisfaction.

5. According to this doctrine, known in the West as the 'Brezhnev Doctrine', the 'socialist states' are obliged to treat important foreign and domestic policy decisions as matters of joint concern and must therefore treat sovereignty exclusively in the light of their joint interests. In practical terms this means that the East European allies must resolve their problems multilaterally – in other words in accordance with the wishes of the USSR. The 'Brezhnev Doctrine' is thus an instrument of Soviet hegemony. As the action taken against Czechoslovakia in 1968 shows, the USSR is prepared to back up its doctrine with military force if necessary. See the documents in Boris Meissner, ed., *Die 'Brezhnev-Doctrine'*, Cologne, 1969, and the article in *Osteuropa*, No. 9, 1969, pp. A189–97.

6. *Programm der Sozialistischen Einheitspartei Deutschlands*, (East) Berlin, 1963, pp. 60, 63 and 124.

7. This was particularly apparent in 1968 when reform communist tendencies

in Czechoslovakia gave rise to the prospect of an internal emancipation of the East European states from the Soviet model of government and society.

8. According to the Constitution adopted on 6 April 1968. See *Aussenpolitische Korrespondenz*, No. 15 (1968), pp. 123–34.

9. Compare W. Bröll, 'Die ökonomische Bedeutung der DDR für die RGW-Staaten', *Osteuropa-Wirtschaft*, No. 1 (1969), pp. 24–41.

10. Indirect in the sense that an expansion of trade with the West would be in the economic interests of the GDR. It was only with the aid of increased imports of industrial equipment obtained in this way that the GDR could narrow the gap in modernization of the economy as compared with the developed industrial countries of Western Europe.

11. Treaty between the USSR and the GDR of 20 September 1955, in E. Deuerlein, ed., in collaboration with H. Schierbaum, *Dokumente zur Deutschlandpolitik*, Series 3, Vol. I, Frankfurt/Main and (West) Berlin: Bundesministerium für gesamtdeutsche Fragen, 1961, pp. 371–4.

12. Resolution of the government of the USSR concerning the abolition of the office of German High Commissar of 20 September 1955, ibid., p. 377.

13. Correspondence between the Deputy Foreign Minister of the USSR and the Foreign Minister of the GDR, ibid., pp. 375–7.

14. Warsaw Treaty of 14 May 1955 (in German and Russian), ibid., pp. 37–44.

15. Declaration and law enacted by the government of the GDR concerning the formation of the NVA of 18 January 1956, in *Dokumente zur Deutschlandpolitik*, op. cit., Series 3, Vol. 2/1, Frankfurt/Main and (West) Berlin, 1963, pp. 41–6.

16. Only the Hungarian armed forces were reduced to a similar status after 1956. Admittedly, in the meantime, the GDR's troop strength was greatly augmented indirectly by the formation of paramilitary units.

17. Th. M. Forster, *NVA: Die Armee der Sowjetzone*, Cologne, 1967, p. 65.

18. Unlike in the USSR's corresponding treaties with Poland and Hungary, the question of troop movements outside their garrisons was dealt with in the treaty with the GDR. Only the treaty imposed on Czechoslovakia on 16 October 1968 makes similar provisions. What is more, the GDR was given no jurisdiction over the movements of Soviet military personnel into and out of the country (Hungary after 1956 was the only other country which had to accept such a provision). See M. Csizmas, *Der Warschauer Pakt*, Berne, 1972, p. 73.

19. See the statements of the Czech General J. Sejna concerning the discussion which took place at the decisive Prague session in autumn 1965, in *Paris Match*, 14 August 1971, pp. 59–61.

20. See D. Holloway, 'The Warsaw Pact in an Era of Negotiation', *Survival*, No. 6 (1972), p. 278; M. Csizmas, *Der Warschauer Pakt*, op. cit., p. 30; J. Erickson, *Zum Frühstück in München*, Düsseldorf, 1972, p. 244. The problem was brought to my attention by Peer Lange.

II

Actions against West Berlin.   April 1965

Background

The geographical location of West Berlin inside the USSR's sphere of hegemony has meant that the lines of communication between the city and the West have been susceptible to disruption, particularly since the Western powers in 1944–5 failed to insist that the USSR unambiguously recognize rights of access.[1] However, civilian traffic continued more or less without hindrance for sixteen years following the lifting of the blockade of 1948–9, with the exception of one instance in 1957 (at the time of the currency change in the GDR).[2] In 1955 the USSR transferred control of civilian traffic to and from West Berlin to the GDR authorities. The Western powers reacted by declaring that this action did not absolve the USSR of its responsibilities 'with respect to transport and traffic between the different parts of Germany, including Berlin'.[3] The division of Germany made it necessary for the Western sectors of Berlin to develop close ties with West Germany. Although the three Western powers refused to accept a total incorporation of West Berlin into the Federal Republic,[4] the city became part of the Federal Republic's legal, economic and currency system. Moreover, Committees of the Lower House of Parliament, the *Bundestag*, had been meeting in West Berlin since 1949; in 1955, 1956, and 1957 the city also played host to plenary sessions of the West German Parliament. In 1954 and 1955 the GDR leaders welcomed the holding of sessions of the *Bundesversammlung* and *Bundestag* respectively in West Berlin.* However, since the Soviet Berlin ultimatum of November 1958, the East Germans have protested the convocation of the *Bundesversammlung* in West Berlin. The meetings of *Bundestag* committees escaped the attention of East German polemics for a whole longer.[5]

During the Berlin blockade of 1948–9 and the protracted Berlin crisis of 1958 to 1962, Soviet attacks had been directed at the presence of the Western powers in Berlin.[6] Following the Cuban crisis, however, Moscow shifted the direction of its attack. Whereas West

* The Bundesversammlung (Federal Assembly) is convened for the purpose of electing the President of the Federal Republic (transl. note).

9

Berlin's protecting powers were spared, polemics and protests were now directed against the ties between the Federal Republic and the city. It would appear that the Soviet leaders were trying to avoid the risk of conflict with the adversary superpower. Making the 'illegal interference' of the Federal Republic in West Berlin the object of attack presented a double advantage. On the one hand, Soviet propaganda aimed at separating the Federal Republic from its Western allies by claiming that protests were directed solely at West German infringements and were thereby defending the rights of the Western powers too. On the other hand, it is evident that if a point were reached at which the ties between West Berlin and West Germany were decisively disrupted, the rights of the Western powers to maintain their presence in the city would also be undermined. Without its vital support from the Federal Republic, West Berlin could not survive, and could therefore no longer serve as a basis for the presence of the three Western powers.[7] It was consistent with the modified strategy of the USSR that, using the pretext of 'illegal and provocative' activities of the Federal Republic in West Berlin, the USSR and the GDR should put pressure on the city by interfering with the access routes.[8]

Course of events

As soon as the plenary session of the *Bundestag* had been scheduled for 7 April 1965 in West Berlin, the USSR and the GDR reacted by issuing menacing protests. The Soviet government declared in a note to the three Western powers on 23 March 1965 that the *Bundestag* session served 'revanchist claims on this city by the German Federal Republic'. Therefore, it reserved the right 'to take such measures . . . as would meet the obligations undertaken with respect to guaranteeing the inviolability of the borders of the German Democratic Republic'.[9] At the beginning of April the GDR sent letters of protest to the Foreign Minister of the Federal Republic of Germany, the Mayor of West Berlin and the governments of the three Western powers. There was a threat implied in references which gave a warning of 'serious consequences for negotiations on a possible extension of the border pass agreement' and stating that the Western powers should consider themselves jointly responsible for any 'consequences' which would result 'should the planned provocation be carried out'.[10] On 4 April 1965 the government of the GDR decreed that 'for the period of the planned plenary session' participants would be refused permission to cross East German territory.[11] By issuing this decree the SED leadership was claiming that it could grant or refuse transit rights as it saw fit. This was a direct challenge to the West on a matter of principle, as it had always maintained that not only military but also civilian transit traffic between West Berlin and the Federal Republic was based on the allies' rights as the victorious powers and was therefore to be respected by the GDR.

The GDR decree was less significant from a practical point of view. It applied only to those taking part in the *Bundestag* meeting, who in any case normally used the air corridors. Moreover, the ban applied only to the week in which the *Bundestag* and its Committees were meeting in West Berlin. However, the decree was reinforced by additional measures directed against the transit routes. The most harmless of these was the demonstrative refusal to allow the Mayor of West Berlin to pass through. Manoeuvres, which were originally to have taken place at Frankfurt-am-Oder, were shifted to the transit routes west of Berlin. Under the pretext of military exercises, the GDR authorities completely stopped all West Berlin traffic six times for periods lasting many hours; in addition, the clearance of vehicles proceeded very slowly. Thus, waiting time at the border checkpoints lasted for anything up to thirty-six hours. Traffic on the waterways between West Berlin and the Federal Republic was halted for almost a week. Even Western air traffic in the three air corridors was affected: Soviet air force planes violated the air space and posed a threat to safety. East German civil aircraft flying low over West Berlin and sonic booms from high-flying air force planes jarred the nerves of the population.[12] Immediately after the *Bundestag* session Brezhnev claimed in a speech that the members of the West German Parliament had arrived in West Berlin 'illegally' and that by their 'provocation' the Bonn 'revanchists' were attempting to lay claim to the city, which did not belong to them.[13]

As the disruptions reached their peak on 7 April 1965 the Americans began to send small convoys of troops – initially without armed protection – from Helmstedt to West Berlin. As these were not always given speedy clearance by the Soviet authorities, the Americans on 10 April began moving armed units for the first time. This time the Soviet border authorities let them pass without delay. An hour or two afterwards the Soviet High Command announced the termination of the manoeuvres,[14] although according to the GDR they had not been due to end until the following day. Disruption of transit traffic ceased; the long queues of lorries at the border check points were quickly cleared. A few weeks later the Soviet government repeated its declaration to the Western powers that should the 'provocations' be stepped up, it would be obliged to take effective counter-measures to safeguard the inviolability of the GDR's borders and prevent illegal activity in West Berlin.[15]

The Central Committee of the SED made it clear at its X Plenum on 24 June 1965 that it did not consider the events of April as a bygone episode. On the contrary, this was to be the starting point for further far-reaching claims. These were directed primarily at achieving GDR control over Western air traffic in the air corridors. The newly-appointed Foreign Minister, Winzer, demanded for the GDR 'full and unrestricted sovereignty . . . on land, on water and in the air'. According to him the Soviet Union exercised 'control over the flights necessary for communication purposes and the supplying of the three Western powers in West Berlin' only by virtue of the fact that this had been conceded to it by the GDR. What is more, the GDR had sovereignty over its air space, and foreign planes could cross it 'only with special permission of the government' in East Berlin. Winzer declared that 'the old Western propaganda fairy-tale' – namely 'that the four powers supposedly had unrestricted right to air traffic over Germany' – collapsed in the face of the 'sovereign rights of the GDR in its own air space'. Thus, 'all assertions' that 'the Western powers could fly over the GDR whenever they like' were invalidated. The Western powers were therefore obliged to make corresponding application to the GDR whenever they wanted to make use of GDR air space.[16]

Process of decision-making

Some information concerning the decisions on the measures taken in April 1965 found its way into the West German press via East Berlin. Judging from this information, it would appear that the initiative was taken by the GDR government, which is said to have demanded Soviet approval and support for the following retaliatory measures: (i) preventing *Bundestag* deputies from using the land routes to West Berlin; (ii) introducing transit visas for all movement of persons between West Berlin and the Federal Republic; (iii) abrogation of the border pass agreement permitting visits to relatives in East Berlin; and (iv) stopping visits by GDR pensioners to the Federal Republic.

The Soviet authorities are said to have adopted a reserved attitude toward these demands. According to the report in question, the limited duration of the ban on *Bundestag* deputies crossing to West Berlin can be attributed to Soviet influence. In order to placate the SED leadership, the USSR caused the disruption of West Berlin's lines of communication by holding manoeuvres. At the same time, the GDR is said to have concluded an agreement with the USSR for the future, according to which (i), in the event of future plenary sessions of the *Bundestag*, meetings of the *Bundesrat* (the Upper House of Parliament) or the Federal Cabinet in West Berlin, there should be further disruptions of transit traffic, and transit visas would be introduced; and (ii) concerning future visits by the Federal President and meetings of individual *Bundestag* Committees or the Federal Assembly in West Berlin, only verbal protests should be lodged. In addition the SED leaders reserved the right, if necessary, to break off the visits by relatives.[17]

How much credibility is to be attached to this report? As the source remains unknown (it is not even known whether or to what extent the details originate from the GDR or the USSR), the only possible path open is to ask whether the account of circumstances and events is plausible. It is safe to assume that the impetus for the actions against West Berlin originated with the GDR and that the Soviet Union advocated restraint. There are numerous indications that the SED leaders thought that Soviet policy towards West Berlin did not go far enough in the selection of goals or the utilization of means.

The Treaty of Friendship and Mutual Assistance of 12 June 1964 between the two countries simply attributed to West Berlin the status of an 'autonomous political entity'.[18] The incorporation of the city into West Germany was simply declared inadmissable. All other questions were left open to broad interpretations, which corresponded with a clear Soviet interest in avoiding more serious conflicts over Berlin with the Western powers.[19] Statements made in the GDR emphasized that basically West Berlin belonged to the GDR – a position supported in principle by the USSR.[20] Thus, from the point of view of the GDR the formula on the status of West Berlin agreed upon with the USSR apparently represented an unwilling concession of an existing right.[21] The SED leaders tried everything possible to circumvent, or at least qualify, this renunciation. West Berlin was to be subjected to extensive control by the GDR by means of far-reaching demands for good conduct.[22] Such ambitions contradicted not only Soviet circumspection in dealing with the Western powers in Berlin, but also Soviet conceptions concerning the status of West Berlin.[23] In accordance with its Party Programme of 1963,[24] the SED stuck to the demand, dropped by the USSR, for the status of a West Berlin to be that of a demilitarized free city, i.e., for withdrawal of the Western military presence.[25] In doing so it expressly called into question the occupation rights of the Western powers.[26]

There were also clear differences of opinion over the question of traffic between West Berlin and the Federal Republic. While the USSR claimed that it alone was responsible for controlling the military traffic of the three Western powers,[27] the GDR also claimed that in principle it had overall sovereignty in this area too. The fact that, in practice, Soviet military authorities were exercising this control was explained by the East German government as having

13

temporarily given the USSR permission to act on its behalf.[28] The GDR's claim to full control over the civilian traffic to and from West Berlin was supported by Moscow, but the broad practical conclusions to be drawn from this met with no response from the USSR. This applies particularly to the idea that the GDR could, at any time, restrict or revoke the transit regulations already in operation if it considered this necessary.[29]

In claiming GDR sovereignty over the Western air corridors on 24 June 1965, Foreign Minister Winzer was calling into question the legal position of the Western powers,[30] which not even the USSR had dared assail during the Berlin blockade of 1948–9. Nor was the GDR demand directed solely against the West. By explicitly attacking the air traffic rights of the Four Powers, the USSR was affected too. Also, from the point of view of conflict control in relations between East and West, it could not be in the USSR's interests to allow the GDR decision-making powers over the air corridors, thereby potentially giving it the opportunity of sparking off or exacerbating crises with the Western powers. It was not coincidental that the Soviet authorities in April 1965 used only their own military aircraft for all actions in the flight paths of Western aircraft. In this way they could be sure that the conflict did not exceed predetermined limits. It is not surprising, therefore, that the Soviet reaction to Winzer's trial balloon was negative.[31]

The information concerning individual events connected with the measures taken by the East in April 1965 should be evaluated against this background of generally differing views and interests of the USSR and the GDR over the Berlin question. The USSR was primarily concerned with avoiding a political confrontation with the three Western powers.[32] However, at the same time it agreed with the GDR representatives that something should be done to counter the activity of 'West German revanchism' in West Berlin. Any action directed exclusively against the parliamentary presence of the Federation in West Berlin seemed to involve hardly any risk, because the USSR calculated that in holding the *Bundestag* meetings in West Berlin for a week Bonn would manoeuvre itself into a vulnerable position and would not be able to count on Western support.[33]

Given these circumstances, it was consistent with Soviet policy to agree to measures designed to put pressure on West German politicians (announcement of the ban on crossing East German territory; holding of manoeuvres; hold-ups of West Berlin traffic; and threatening gestures in the air corridors), but on the other hand to restrict these measures in such a way that they involved no challenge to the Western powers, by casting fundamental and lasting doubts on their rights of access (limiting duration of the ban; and not agreeing to changes in procedure). It seems equally plausible that the Soviet leaders wanted to avoid creating the impression of having renounced the gestures towards détente made over the previous few years, and switched back completely to a policy of tension in Central Europe (maintenance of existing 'alleviations of hardships').

The SED leaders, on the other hand, were clearly interested not only in procedures demonstrating the validity of the principle of international sovereignty, using the West Berlin access routes (by the introduction of transit visas), but also wanted to restrict as far as possible the opportunities for contact and communication between the people in the two German states (by cancelling the border-pass agreement and revoking permission for pensioners to visit West Germany). In the former case the aim was to demonstrate that the GDR was a state with full sovereign rights, and in the latter the SED leaders were worried that even after the construction of the Berlin Wall the GDR was still too exposed to West German influence. In fact, the GDR leaders did introduce transit visas during the next Berlin crisis in June 1968;[34] and the border pass agreement had not been renewed two years earlier after the calling off of the SED–SPD dialogue.*

It seems quite possible that, even though the Soviet Union had stopped short of an introduction of transit visas and the termination of 'alleviations of hardship', it had kept both measures in mind as reactions against possible serious West German 'provocations' in West Berlin in future. From a Soviet point of view it was essential that the idea of the 'autonomous' existence of West Berlin alongside the Federal Republic would not be weakened in the future by any conclusive act such as the convening of plenary sessions of the *Bundestag* in particular, meetings of the *Bundesrat* or the Federal Government.[35] Certainly the question can be asked why the election of the Federal President by the Federal Assembly was not considered the kind of conclusive 'infringement' the USSR was trying to prevent the Federal Republic from perpetrating in West Berlin.[36] If, as is to be assumed, the USSR initially did not agree to endorse specific measures but retained them for exercising future options, it may be possible to adduce a further consideration: a completely different impression is created when certain steps are undertaken without prior warning, as compared to instances where reactions occur automatically, as a 'necessity'. Responsibility for causing a sequence of actions and counter-actions is then shifted to the adversary.

---

* In the spring of 1966 the East German Communists and West German Social Democrats corresponded, among other things, on the possibility of an exchange of speakers. This plan was aborted by the SED. See below, Chapter 3 (transl. note).

Motivation

Three assumptions can be made regarding the USSR: (i) It was imperative that the measures taken should not lead to a basic confrontation with the three Western powers.[37] In a crisis situation it would be the USSR which would suffer the risks and disadvantages accruing from a Berlin conflict. It seemed highly undesirable to allow such an eventuality to become a reality. (ii) At the same time, it would be a great advantage if the Soviet leaders by limited but, for the West Germans at least, painful actions could in future prevent major demonstrations of the legal and political cohesion of the Federal Republic and West Berlin. This could be interpreted as activity consistent with the idea of the 'autonomous political entity of West Berlin', especially if the USSR, after forestalling gross 'encroachments', concerned itself with the prevention of lesser 'provocations'. (iii) Finally, it was in the USSR's interests to provide proof to the East German leaders of its support for their cause. This idea suggested itself especially in those areas where the views of the two states on Berlin coincided.

Seen from the GDR's point of view, the situation looked different. Even after the construction of the Berlin Wall, West Berlin was still a hostile enclave – and therefore an unpleasant anomaly – right in the middle of GDR territory. It was understandable that the SED leaders should want this problem resolved once and for all. However, the East German state lacked the political and military means to assert its claims in the face of West Berlin's three protective powers. It could only initiate conflicts by virtue of its presence on the access routes, which its powerful ally would then have to tackle. In these circumstances there was an incentive to add fuel to the conflicts over Berlin. For the chances of a local success would primarily benefit the GDR, whereas the risks of a global conflagration would have to be borne overwhelmingly by the USSR.

The same state of affairs which suggested to the SED functionaries the adoption of a conflict strategy in Berlin, induced the Soviet leaders to display caution and restraint. It could not be in their interests to allow themselves to be embroiled by an impatient GDR in a battle which corresponded less to Soviet interests than to those of the GDR. These factors led the Soviet leaders to draw the practical conclusion that, as far as Berlin was concerned, the GDR would have to operate within a framework acceptable to the USSR.[38] For this purpose they could rely not only on overwhelmingly superior power against their East German ally but also on their responsibilities as occupying power.[39] It also rested on the logical argument that in cases of conflict and crisis the power obliged to deal with the situation which has arisen should also have control over the situation from the beginning as it develops.

References

1. Summary in G. Wettig, 'Berlin in den interalliierten Vereinbarungen der Kriegszeit und im Potsdamer Abkommen', in E. Deuerlein, A. Fischer, E. Menzel and G. Wettig, *Potsdam und die deutsche Frage*, Cologne, 1970, pp. 93–111.

2. See the Four-Power communiqué of 4 May 1949, in Forschungsinstitut der Deutschen Gesellschaft für Auswärtige Politik, ed. in conjunction with the West Berlin Sentate, *Dokumente zur Berlin-Frage 1944–1962*, Munich, 1962, p. 109.

3. *Das Viermächte-Abkommen über Berlin vom 3 September 1971*, Bonn: Federal Press and Information Office, September 1971, p. 141.

4. Ibid., p. 123. The aim was to maintain the status of Berlin as an occupied city and thereby preserve fully the legal basis for access to West Berlin.

5. Ibid., p. 136.

6. Ibid., pp. 142–5 and p. 149; *Dokumente zur Berlin-Frage, 1944–1962*, op. cit., pp. 77–81, 296–9 and 301–35.

7. For this reason Federal support of West Berlin in essential areas stems not only from West German inclination but also is intended to meet Western demands.

8. This is explained in more detail in *Das Viermächte-Abkommen über Berlin*, op. cit., p. 152.

9. German text in *Dokumentation der Zeit*, No. 33 (1966), p. 39. The note was not published in the Soviet press.

10. Texts in ibid., p. 40.

11. Text in ibid., p. 41.

12. For references to individual measures see *Das Viermächte-Abkommen über Berlin*, op. cit., p. 153.

13. Brezhnev on 8 April 1965 in Warsaw, as reported in *Pravda*, 9 April 1965.

14. *Izvestiya*, 11 April 1965.

15. Note from the Government of the USSR to the Governments of the Western powers, 14 May 1965, *Neues Deutschland*, 15 May 1965.

16. Text: *Dokumentation der Zeit*, No. 359 (1965), p. 10. Winzer claimed that the Allied Air Safety Commission was merely a technical body without decision-making powers.

17. *Der Spiegel*, 21 April 1965, p. 31.

18. Text: *Pravda*, 13 June 1964; *Neues Deutschland*, 13 June 1964 and *Europa-Archiv*, No. 13 (1964), pp. D325–8.

19. See also the opinion by H. H. Mahnke, 'Der Beistandspakt zwischen der Sowjetunion und der DDR vom 12 Juni 1964', *Europa-Archiv*, No. 14 (1964), p. 508: Berlin conflicts above all had seriously upset American–Soviet negotiations on arms control agreements linked by the Soviet leaders, following the Cuban crisis, with their increased interest in joint management of conflicts and crises. Moreover Berlin was a showplace where conflicts directly carried the unacceptable risk of a (nuclear) war between East and West.

20. R. Arsinger and W. Poeggel, *Westberlin – selbständige politische Einheit*, (East) Berlin, 1965, pp. 29, 31, 35, 43 and 61.

17

21. J. H. Stein, 'Bonner Regierung bedroht den Status quo in der Westberlin-Frage', *Deutsche Aussenpolitik*, No. 10 (1965), p. 1156; Ulbricht's remarks at the VII SED Party Congress on 17 April 1967 can be found in *Aussenpolitische Korrespondenz*, No. 17 (1967), p. 134.

22. R. Arzinger and W. Poeggel, *Westberlin-selbständige politische Einheit*, op. cit., pp. 42–9. As a precaution it was declared that the GDR claims to West Berlin took precedence over the right to self-determination of the West Berliners and provided the framework in which this could be expressed. See H. Kröger, 'Das Potsdamer Abkommen und die Westberlinfrage', *Dokumentation der Zeit*, No. 338 (1965), pp. 33–5.

23. Soviet policy was designed to stress the rights of the USSR as an occupying power as against the Western powers and thereby affirm its status as a power with joint responsibility for the city. See Yu. Rschewski, *Westberlin – ein Gebilde sui generis*, Moscow (1966/7), p. 76.

24. *Programm der Sozialistischen Einheitspartei Deutschlands*, (East) Berlin, 1963, p. 58.

25. R. Arzinger and W. Poeggel, *Westberlin-selbständige politische Einheit*, op. cit., pp. 34, 56, and 72–91.

26. Ibid., p. 28; H. J. Stein, 'Bonner Regierung bedroht den status quo', op. cit., p. 1157; remarks by Foreign Minister O. Winzer on 24 June 1965 in *Dokumentation der Zeit*, No. 339 (1965), p. 10. See also the remarks by W. Ulbricht on 7 September 1967, *Neues Deutschland*, 8 September 1967; of 1 December 1967 in *Neues Deutschland*, 2 December 1967; and 22 March 1969, *Aussenpolitische Korrespondenz*, No. 13 (1969), p. 101.

27. Yu. Rschewski, *Westberlin*, op. cit., p. 10.

28. R. Felber, 'Völkerrechtliche Probleme bei der Sicherung der DDR Staatsgrenze', *Deutsche Aussenpolitik*, No. 3 (1966), p. 284; O. Winzer to the Central Committee of the SED on 24 June 1965, *Dokumentation der Zeit*, No. 339 (1965), p. 11. Similarly the later remarks by G. Görner, *DDR gewährleistet friedlichen Westberlin-Transit*, (East) Berlin, 1969, pp. 48, 66 and 99.

29. R. Arzinger and W. Poeggel, *Westberlin-selbständige politische Einheit*, op. cit., p. 80. Even more so G. Görner, *DDR gewährleistet friedlichen Transit*, op. cit., pp. 34–43 and 68–73. Compare the cautious remarks by B. M. Klimenko, *Pravo prokhoda cherez inostrannuyu territoriyu*, Moscow, 1967, pp. 7–33. For all practical purposes Yu. Rschewski, *Westberlin*, op. cit., does not deal with this problem.

30. Background information in *Dokumente zur Berlin-Frage 1944–1962*, op. cit., pp. 42–58.

31. The Soviet leaders certainly took care not to make their annoyance public, but for anyone familiar with East European mass media the absence of any references to Winzer's remarks in the reports on the X Plenum of the Central Committee of the SED was an indication that these were sharply rejected (see *Pravda* and *Izvestiya*, 26 June 1965). The fact that the SED made no mention of the subject for the next three years is a further clear indication of Soviet objections.

32. It is characteristic that the USSR terminated its actions as soon as the danger of a serious conflict became evident with the sending of armed units by the United States.

33. According to the diplomat in the Soviet Embassy in the GDR responsible for questions relating to West Berlin, V. N. Beletsky (using the pseudonym 'V. N. Boldrev' as explained in *Deutschland Archiv*, No. 4 (1974)); see *Dokumentation der Zeit*, No. 1-2 (1969), p. 10.

34. Measures decreed by the Volkskammer of the GDR concerning civilian transit traffic between the Federal Republic and West Berlin, 11 June 1968, *Neues Deutschland*, 12 June 1968. Accompanying declaration: *Neues Deutschland*, 12 June 1968 and *Aussenpolitische Korrespondenz*, No. 25 (1968), p. 211.

35. See Rschewski, *Westberlin*, op. cit., pp. 33, 57, 65, 78, 87 and 90.

36. In fact in 1969 – in contrast to 1964 – the USSR took a firm stand against the Federal Assembly. Admittedly, in the meantime Soviet bloc attitudes to West Germany had hardened as compared with those in 1965. For the background see: Wettig, 'Die Berlin-Krise 1969', *Osteuropa*, No. 9 (1969), pp. 685-97.

37. Apart from control and limitation of the measures taken this motive would also seem to be behind the fact that the Soviet press made as little fuss as possible about the events concerning Berlin. Contrary to previous practice, the two notes sent by the Soviet Government on 23 March 1965 and 14 May 1965 to the governments of the three Western powers were not published or even mentioned in the Soviet press. (They were only published in translation in the GDR.) *Pravda*, on 9 April 1965, published an article and on 10 April two articles on the Berlin question, which were all relatively short and only attacked the Federal claim that West Berlin belonged to the Federal Republic. *Izvestiya*, on 10 April 1965, published a TASS announcement concerning the condemnations of Bonn's 'revanchist policy' by the *Staatsrat* of the GDR; it also included a casual reference to the measures taken.

38. See also the account and evaluation of later Berlin decisions by G. Wettig, 'Ost-Berlin im Schatten der Moskauer Deutschland-Politik', *Aussenpolitik*, No. 5, 1969, pp. 267-72 and 'Der Einfluss der DDR auf die Deutschland-Politik der Warschauer-Pakt-Staaten', *Aus Politik und Zeitgeschichte*, No. B49 (1969), pp. 17-19.

39. From time to time GDR statements showed evidence of covert opposition to the occupation rights of its Soviet ally. See R. Arzinger and W. Poeggel, *Westberlin-selbständige politische Einheit*, op. cit., p. 24; R. Felber, *Völkerrechtliche Probleme*, op. cit., p. 273. Remarks by Foreign Minister Winzer to the X Plenum of the Central Committee of the SED on 24 June 1965, in *Dokumentation der Zeit*, No. 339 (1965), p. 10. Especially revealing are the later remarks by Ulbricht during his press conference on 19 January 1970, which – possibly in view of Soviet objections – were not included in the published text.

III

The SED–SPD Dialogue in the Spring of 1966

Background

Towards the end of the Khrushchev era the Soviet attitude towards Social Democracy changed. This became evident at an inter-Communist Conference on the Social Sciences in September 1964, where the Director of the Moscow Institute for World Economics and International Relations, A. Arsumanyan, stated that the social struggle of the working class in the Western countries was of necessity political because the state apparatus in those countries has assumed functions of economic control. The movements for social and political reform, which had arisen in conjunction with this, could be considered a basis for 'revolutionary changes'. The decisive factor was said to be the 'establishment of the unity of all sections of the working class'. In Arsumanyan's view the Communists should not attempt to solve this task alone as long as the Social Democratic parties in many Western European states exercised decisive influence over the working class. Thus the speaker demanded that the Social Democrats, despite the 'bourgeois' policies of their leaders, should not simply be rejected as enemies of socialism. Wherever possible, efforts should be made to engage Communists and Social Democrats in joint activity. Admittedly, if reference was made here to the progressive role of Social Democracy, it was addressed primarily to the broader party membership; the leaders, inasmuch as they refused to go along with this, were to be mercilessly 'unmasked'.[1] The following day Ulbricht dealt with this concept in detail, applying it to the relationship of the SED to the SPD.[2]

Particularly from late autumn 1965, this theme became more pronounced in the speeches of SED functionaries. Albert Norden called for an 'all-German peaceful arrangement' with the SPD. The SPD, in turn, was to develop a 'political alternative' to the policies of the ruling Christian Democratic party – the CDU/CSU.[3] Following a *Pravda* article calling for unity of action between all 'sections of the working class' as the only effective form of struggle against the class

20

enemy in the Western countries,[4] the SED made repeated exhortations to the West Germans to engage in all-German solidarity and help build a front against the anti-national policies of the CDU/CSU.[5] These were accompanied by occasional remarks to the effect that the workers expected the SPD to provide an alternative to the CDU/CSU and the Erhard-Mende government.[6]

The appeals reached a climax with the Open Letter of 7 February 1966, addressed by the SED Central Committee to the delegates of the forthcoming SPD Party Congress and to the members and supporters of the SPD.[7] This action was not out of the ordinary: since 1949 the GDR leaders had addressed a dozen similar letters to the West German Social Democrats. The SPD party executive had regarded them as propaganda manoeuvres and had therefore left them unanswered. Although this time there were no direct polemics against the policies of the Social Democrat leaders, it seems doubtful that the senders expected a reply to this particular letter – even more so as their remarks had not even been addressed directly to the party executive.

Course of Events

The Open Letter demanded that the West German Social Democrats should agree to work for three basic objectives: (i) negotiations and an understanding between the governments of the two German states with a view to achieving détente and creating the basis for cooperation and gradual unification; (ii) conclusion of a German peace treaty; and (iii) a united Germany 'really democratic' in nature i.e., a Germany that had rid itself of 'brown [Nazi] officials', of 'militarism and neo-Nazism', of the 'dictatorship of the armaments millionaires' and of the 'capitalist opinion factories'.

The 'vital question' was to be: 'What kind of Germany do we want and what character should it have?' More precisely, who should exercise power in a future united German state? From a Communist point of view there could only be two alternatives: power could be with 'the working class and its allies as the strongest class in society', as in the GDR; or it could be in the hands of the 'hundred multi-millionaire families', as in the Federal Republic. At the same time the letter made it quite clear that any move towards German unity was only conceivable in terms of the former alternative. Moreover, 'the one-sided attachment of West Germany to the USA and its interests' would have to be dropped because it was incompatible with the process of reunification. A united Germany could become 'a factor contributing to a stable peace in Europe', but 'only as an independent state free of any external, non-European influences'.

The Open Letter contained a concrete proposal in the form of a two-stage action programme. First of all, it said, the SED and SPD 'together' would have to 'seek new paths', 'establish good relations with one another' and, following discussion of their many and, for the time being, opposing views, 'come to an agreement on some joint proposals'. The end-result should be an all-German united action front between Communists and Social Democrats, which would include a 'negotiated peaceful understanding' and 'reconciliation'. To this end it was proposed that 'a meeting of representatives of the SED and SPD' be held. If agreement could be reached, it should include, according to the Central Committee, several specifically Communist ideas, such as the Social Democrats breaking away from the 'misguided CDU policy' on the German question and making better use of the 'right to national and social self-determination' in the Federal Republic. This demand was expressed even more clearly in subsequent commentaries in the GDR: again, the Social Democrats should develop a 'political alternative' to the CDU/CSU and join the SED in the 'struggle' against the West German government. Once the SED and SPD had reached agreement concerning joint action, the Open Letter continued, a 'body for open discussion between Germans of East and West' – an 'all-German deliberative forum' – should be set up. The political parties and social organizations which were specifically mentioned in the letter should be represented on a basis of parity between the two German states. If, as demanded, the SED and SPD had come to a prior agreement on joint policies, they would be in a strong majority position from the outset. As was expressly stated, this political agreement between the two workers' parties was an indispensable precondition without which there could be no guarantee that all-German deliberations would take place.[8]

This time the SPD executive decided to reply. In an Open Letter on 18 March 1966 it rejected the proposal of a united action front with the SED, but suggested that 'conditions be created throughout Germany in which the spokesmen of the parties represented in the [West] German *Bundestag* and the [East German] *Volkskammer* can freely state, advocate and discuss their views on the German question.'[9] In this the SED Central Committee saw itself confronted with a situation fraught with risks and opportunities. If the Social Democrat leaders, contrary to their practice over the previous two decades, were no longer rejecting the idea of talks with the East German Communists, this could indicate that their previous policy had come to a dead end, that they were under pressure from their own party and that perhaps, as a consequence, they could be induced to undertake corrections of course in the desired direction.[10] But, at the same time, the leading party functionaries in East Berlin were of the opinion that the Open Letter from the SPD executive 'in part contained provocative and offensive language'.[11] This referred not only to the building of the Wall and the order to shoot at the border, matters which had been touched upon by the Social Democrats, but also the demand made by the SPD that the SED leaders consent to an all-German political dialogue and thereby accept the breaking of their monopoly on the dissemination of information and opinion in the GDR.

In its Open Reply of 25 March 1966 the SED Central Committee did not reject the Social Democrats' proposal outright. Instead it formulated proposals taking up some ideas contained in the SPD's reply. Certainly, there was to be no general political dialogue taking place in Germany, but it was suggested that two joint meetings be held with speakers from the SED and SPD – one in the GDR and one in the Federal Republic. The decision as to what steps might then follow would depend on the 'experiences of this first step'.[12] Thus the proposal made by the SPD executive was restricted in two respects: (i) only the SED and SPD and not all parties were to take part in the political dialogue; and (ii) it was envisaged that there would be only one opportunity for political dialogue in each of the two parts of Germany.

As subsequent commentaries showed, the SED leaders wanted the two proposed speakers' meetings to be interpreted not merely as a technical matter of simultaneous appearances of the speakers, but also as a matter of substance – as a manifestation of the process of forming common viewpoints.[13] The East Berlin functionaries were obviously not sure whether their concept could be realized. Accordingly, they wanted to be in a position to weigh the results of the two proposed meetings and then decide how matters should proceed.

Their doubts seem to have increased during the course of April. In the second half of the month the SED representatives, at the preparatory talks with the Social Democratic negotiators, insisted that the speakers' meetings, which had been set for May, be postponed until July – in other words until after the SPD's Party Congress in Dortmund at the beginning of June. At the beginning of May the GDR began a campaign against the draft of a West German law on 'safe conduct', a legal device whereby the SPD hoped to forestall any possible proceedings against GDR speakers in the Federal Republic. East German commentators completely distorted the purpose of the bill, by claiming that it was designed to place 'GDR citizens' under threats of prosecution in West Germany.[14] Also, authorship was falsely attributed to the CDU/CSU-led government instead of to the SPD. It was claimed that the purpose of the law was to prevent the SED–SPD dialogue taking place; the speakers from the GDR were to be deprived of all protection under the law, thus making it impossible for them to come. The campaign reached a first climax on 10 May 1966 with a protest issued by the official East German news agency ADN.[15] The SED leaders were apparently building up a case to justify their retreat from the dialogue should the need arise.[16]

The theme of the Dortmund Party Congress of the SPD, which took place from 1 to 5 June 1966, was of an 'orderly coexistence' between the two German states.* The idea of some kind of political alliance with the SED found no response. This line brought the SPD leaders extensive and strong support from the party. The response in the GDR to the SPD Party Congress was negative. By 6 June the central organ of the SED was claiming that the SPD offered no political alternative to the CDU/CSU. From 8 June onwards the GDR mounted a campaign against the Dortmund resolutions, which were depicted as being a triumph for the CDU/CSU and a defeat for the working class, brought about by the SPD leaders. From the following day voices could be heard questioning whether the official SPD was capable of participating in an all-German dialogue, cooperation and understanding.[17] On 10 June the GDR issued a declaration via ADN repeating its protest against the proposed law of safe conduct and demanding that numerous Federal German legal provisions based on the idea of a single German citizenship be revoked.[18] On 15 June Prime Minister Stoph sent a letter to this effect to Federal Chancellor Erhard.[19]

The next day Ulbricht severely criticized the SPD leaders, accusing them of hiding the truth from their followers and declaring their solidarity with CDU policy. He hinted that the political programme which the SPD apparently intended to make the basis of the dialogue was presumptuous and could not possibly be acceptable to the GDR. The tenor of these remarks implied that, given the circumstances, it would be pointless to hold the speakers' exchange. However, also implied was the question whether the Dortmund Party Congress really represented the SPD's last word on the subject, as there were so many members holding differing views.[20] On 22 June Ulbricht sent a letter to SPD Chairman Brandt condemning the Social Democrats' idea of a political showdown with the SED and declaring that in present circumstances a speakers' exchange was 'hardly conceivable'. He insisted that there should be a meeting between representatives of the two parties to 'examine how a rapprochment could be brought about'.[21] On 27 June Brandt rejected this demand.[22] Two days later the SED leaders withdrew their consent to the speakers' exchange,[23] pointing to the law on safe conduct as passed by the Bundestag on 23 June and officially condemned by the GDR on 26 June.[24]

* '*Nebeneinander*' is the German original, not '*Koexistenz*' (transl. note).

Even before the Central Committee's Open Letter of 7 February 1966, when only the basic attitude to Social Democracy and – stemming from that – the general line towards the SPD were being discussed, there was noticeable coordination between Moscow and East Berlin. Judging from the chronological sequence of statements it would appear that the USSR had provided the initial stimuli.[25] As the scene opened on the 'dialogue between the German Workers' Parties' the two Warsaw Pact actors had disproportionately greater occasion to coordinate their policies with one another. As far as can be ascertained from the incomplete source material available, this was the case throughout. The Open Letter of 7 February 1966, published two days later, received the unqualified approval of the central organ of the CPSU. *Pravda* not only fully endorsed the proposals made by the SED, but even adopted the theme that the division of Germany should be overcome.[26] After the reply from the SPD executive had confronted the East Berlin party officials with a difficult choice, Soviet and GDR representatives conferred on how to proceed.[27] The immediate publication in *Pravda* of the statement by ADN of 10 May 1966 can be taken as an indication that this move too, preparing for the possible breaking off of the SED–SPD dialogue, had been cleared previously with the USSR.[28] It is also characteristic that the SED's anti-SPD campaign following the Dortmund Congress was launched only after the central organ of the CPSU had already sharply rejected the Social Democrat line.[29]

During the phase immediately preceding the final breaking off of contacts with the SPD, despite all the mutual coordination, there appear to have been certain differences in attitude between the Soviet leaders and the most influential group in the SED leadership. Presumably Brezhnev and Ulbricht used the opportunity of their joint attendance at the XIII Congress of the Czechoslovak Communist Party from 31 May to 4 June 1966 in Prague to discuss the policy which should be adopted towards the SPD. However, the two top party officials did not draw entirely congruent conclusions from the course of the Social Democrat Party Congress, which ended on 5 June. Judging from the comments in *Pravda* from 7 June onwards, the Soviet leaders immediately reached the verdict that no great hopes could be attached to the SPD and, therefore, to the proposed speakers' exchange. Discussions held between the Soviet Ambassador to East Berlin, P. Abrasimov, and Willy Brandt, the SPD Chairman, seem to have strengthened this conviction.[30] It was apparently during this conversation that the Soviet diplomat pointed out to Brandt that the USSR would press the GDR to call off the speakers' exchange.[31]

In the days and weeks that followed, Soviet officials hinted to representatives of the West Berlin Senate that their country feared that given present circumstances, an "all-German dialogue' between the SPD and the SED would result in a dangerous growth of reunification tendencies among the whole German people.[32] By that time those forces in the GDR opposed to contacts with the SPD had increased in strength;[33] but even so Ulbricht, despite all doubts about the West German Social Democrats, was reluctant to relinquish irrevocably all ties with the 'other German Workers' Party' and, along with them, hopes for a Communist infiltration of West Germany. Even the talk he had with Ambassador Abrasimov on 8 June did not make him change his mind. Only on 27 June, after the SPD Chairman had unequivocally rejected Ulbricht's appeal for a rapprochment, did the SED officially break off the agreed speakers' exchange.[34]

Motivation

Up to the beginning of June the USSR and GDR appeared to be following a jointly agreed policy over the SED–SPD dialogue. Even the terms used to define the aims and intentions of the action for the benefit of the rest of the population coincided. Soviet experts and commentators identified themselves with the slogans of national community and unity on which the SED based its appeal to the West Germans in general and SPD circles in particular. The propaganda in favour of workers' co-determination in industry and the polemics against the draft emergency legislation, both of which the GDR party officials deemed useful as crystallization points for a broad movement of solidarity against the CDU/CSU, also found a favourable reaction in the USSR. If both the ideas on all-German action and the domestic themes received less coverage in the USSR than in the GDR, this can be explained by the fact that it was the GDR which essentially bore the responsibility for propaganda and agitation on West Germany. Party *apparatchiki* of both the CPSU and the SED attached considerable importance to the idea that attacks on the CDU/CSU-led German government should extend to the Atlantic orientation of the Federal Republic and thereby, by implication, the viability of NATO.[35]

Despite all outward appearances of unanimity, there were indications as early as February 1966 that the aims pursued by the USSR and the GDR diverged. All-German aspects were of central importance for the GDR, but the USSR avoided making any official statements on the subject. This was quite noticeable in the context of efforts made by the GDR, with the support of the USSR and other Communist states, to gain admission to the United Nations. In the corresponding memorandum of the GDR Foreign Ministry of February 1966, particular emphasis was put on the continued existence of national unity between the two German states and the demand for eventual reunification of the German people. At the same time the claim was made that the GDR exercised 'unconditionally all sovereign rights', having fulfilled all obligations ensuing from the Potsdam Agreement.[36]

On the other hand, the letters from the USSR, the Ukrainian Soviet Republic and the Byelorussian Soviet Republic in support of the application contained no reference to common all-German interests and the desirability of German unity. In the first two documents notice was also given that the accession of the two German states would in no way affect the continued validity of Article 107 of the UN Charter.[37] As this proviso affected the GDR as well as the Federal Republic, it meant that the GDR was not to be released from control by the USSR as a victor-nation, notwithstanding any previous political achievements of the GDR. What is more, the provisions of Article 107 would still apply to the GDR in the event of its no longer continuing, at some future time, to fulfill Soviet demands based on the Potsdam Agreement. When, in August 1966, the GDR Foreign Ministry formulated yet another memorandum on the question of UN membership, there was only a passing and vague reference to the bridging of the division of Germany. The proposition that the GDR, as the German state which had met the requirements of the Potsdam Agreement, had achieved complete sovereignty was omitted.[38] Clearly, the Soviet view on the subject had been taken into account.

Following the SPD's Dortmund Party Congress differences between the Soviet leadership and the Ulbricht group at the head of the SED became more apparent. After the realization had dawned in the East that the Social Democrat Party executive could not be persuaded to adopt a course of confrontation in domestic and foreign policy with the ruling CDU/CSU and that not even the broader mass of members and supporters were prepared to press for such a strategy,[39] the men in the Kremlin lost interest: there was no organized force in the Federal Republic advocating fundamental change in West German policy, and therefore no one worth collaborating with in opposing the government coalition. All hopes that the opposition party in the struggle for power would abandon all positions which it shared with the weakening Erhard-Mende government proved illusory – as did hopes that Social Democracy must automatically draw nearer to Soviet policy, opening up the prospect of a Federal Republic corresponding more closely to the wishes of Moscow.

On the other hand, Ulbricht and his followers entertained rather different expectations. From their point of view the most important consideration was the degree of influence the SED could gain at an all-German level. It is quite immaterial whether one should assume that the Ulbricht group, despite all past setbacks, still entertained hopes of being able in the end to guide developments towards reunification according to its preferences. It can be assumed with equal justification that the slogans of national unity were meant solely as a propaganda instrument designed to win West German sympathies and support. In any event, it was imperative for the SED leader to use all possible means to win over political allies and sympathizers in the Federal Republic and thereby secure the strongest possible SED influence over West German affairs. It could be of little use to him if the Federal Republic merely corrected its foreign policy course in the desired way, without at the same time opening up increased opportunities for the SED leadership to influence events at the domestic level.[40] As soon as it became evident that hopes of changing the political orientation of the Social Democratic party members were unfounded, measures were called for which necessarily had to conflict with the aims of the Soviet leaders if the original objectives were to be secured.[41] But if the SPD executive could be persuaded to reject open confrontation – the idea of a 'political exchange of blows' – the East Germans could still use the dialogue as a means of exerting direct influence on groups within the Social Democrats, in other words for creating a 'united action front from below'.[42] Not until the reply of the SPD Chairman on 27 June 1966 finally precluded this possibility did Ulbricht and his followers realize that the contacts established with the Social Democrats at an official level were no longer worth pursuing. Characteristically, when the SED withdrew from the speakers' exchange it claimed that the dialogue was continuing – with members and supporters of the SPD in open confrontation with the executive.

References

1. A. Arsumanyan, 'Itogi mirovogo razvitiya', *Mirovaya ekonomika i mezhdunarodnye otnosheniya*, No. 11 (1964), pp. 81 ff. and No. 12 (1964), p. 81.

2. Speech by Walter Ulbricht on 25 September 1964, *Dokumentation der Zeit*, No. 321 (1964), pp. 34 ff.

3. The acronyms CDU and CSU stand for Christian Democratic Union and Christian Socialist Union. The speech by Albert Norden to the Nationalrat session of 15 November 1965 as published in *Dokumentation der Zeit*, No. 347 (1965), pp. 5 ff.

4. 'Liniya, proverennaya zhiznyu', *Pravda*, 12 December 1965.

5. Resolution of the 22nd German Workers' Conference of 29 December 1965, *Dokumentation der Zeit*, No. 351 (1966), pp. 9 ff. Ulbricht's New Year Address of 31 December 1965, *Aussenpolitische Korrespondenz*, No. 1 (1966),

pp. 1–3; Statement by the head of the State Secretariat for all-German Affairs (founded on 18 December 1965), Joachim Herrman, on 13 January 1966, *Aussenpolitische Korrespondenz*, No. 3 (1966), p. 19.

6. Speech by Herbert Warnke to the 22nd German Workers' Conference on 29 December 1965, *Dokumentation der Zeit*, No. 351 (1966), pp. 6–9.

7. Text: *Dokumentation der Zeit*, No. 353 (1966), pp. 20–3; *SBZ-Archiv*, No. 7 (1966), pp. 105–7.

8. Hermann Matern explained in *Pravda* on 7 May 1966 that it would be worth devoting attention to other matters after the formation of a united action front with the Social Democrats.

9. Text: *SBZ-Archiv*, No. 7 (1966), pp. 107–9.

10. See, for example, the address by Walter Ulbricht on 21 April 1966, *Dokumentation der Zeit*, No. 358 (1966), pp. 3 ff. W. Ulbricht, 'K 20-letiyu ob'edineniya KPG i SDPG', *Kommunist*, No. 6 (1966), pp. 103 ff. M. Voslensky and Ostrov in discussions broadcast by Radio Moscow (German Programme), 24 April and 1 May 1966; V. Kelin and V. Lomeyko in *Izvestiya*, 22 May 1966; E. Novosel'tsev, 'Zapadnogermanskie diskussii', *Mezhdunarodnaya zhizn*, No. 6 (1966), pp. 109 ff.

11. H. Matern in *Pravda*, 7 May 1966. See also V. Kelin and V. Lomeyko in *Izvestiya*, 22 May 1966.

12. Text: *Dokumentation der Zeit*, No. 356 (1966), pp. 1–4; *SBZ-Archiv*, No. 7 (1966), pp. 109–12.

13. See, for example, W. Ulbricht in *Pravda*, 20 April 1966; Address by Walter Ulbricht on 21 April 1966, in *Dokumentation der Zeit*, No. 358 (1966), pp. 4–7; W. Ulbricht, 'K 20-letyu ob'edineniya KPG i SDPG', *Kommunist*, No. 6 (1966), p. 104; S. Doernberg in a discussion broadcast by Radio Moscow (German Programme), 1 May 1966; H. Matern in *Pravda*, 7 May 1966.

14. In fact, theoretically, the mechanism had existed for some time in the Federal Republic for the prosecution of lawbreakers of German citizenship who had committed their offences in the GDR. Inasmuch as the SED regime employed means in contravention of the laws of the Federal Republic (for example, the shooting of refugees at the borders of the GDR) these procedures could conceivably be instituted against responsible SED functionaries (such as those responsible for the order to shoot). In order to prevent any possible use being made of this by a West German court, thereby torpedoing the SED speakers' exchange, the SPD introduced a bill into the *Bundestag* temporarily exempting the East German guests from legal proceedings.

15. Text: *Dokumentation der Zeit*, No. 359 (1966), p. 1.

16. The official GDR case cannot be taken at face value. The sequence of events clearly contradicts this. The two protests of 10 May and 10 June each came in the wake of increased doubts concerning the readiness of the Social Democrats to engage in a united action front with the SED. Even the final 'No' from the SED on 29 June was obviously a reaction to Brandt's reply of two days before; the passing of the law on safe conduct on 23 June had prompted the SED leadership to issue a protest on 26 June (Text: *Dokumentation der Zeit*, No. 363, p. 12) but not to break off the speakers' exchange. Moreover it would be inconceivable that the SED leaders would allow themselves to be prevented from making a political appearance in the Federal Republic by the

passing of a law designed precisely to protect their speakers from any possible legal proceedings in the Federal Republic. Common German citizenship, which put inhabitants of the GDR basically on the same legal footing as those of the Federal Republic, had never before prevented SED agitators and propagandists from entering West Germany when it suited their purposes. In 1966 the SED would quite definitely not have let this get in the way of developing contacts with the West Germans if these had shown any prospect of success. East Germany's real reasons are better expressed by the argument of a Soviet expert: the majority of Social Democractic parties in the West, and above all the SPD, had 'become "integrated" in the political machine of present-day capitalism', they were recognized by the ruling class as being 'part of the bourgeois order', and they had 'ceased to regard themselves as political representatives of the working class movement'. This applied particularly to the SPD Chairman and other leading West German Social Democrats, who saw everything in the light of the struggle against Communism. (A. Chernyaev, 'Sotsialdemokratiya pered litsom mezhdunarodnkh problem', *Mirovaya ekonomika i mezhdunarodnye otnosheniya*, No. 8 (1966), pp. 14 and 17–21). According to the GDR, the SPD leaders were taking on 'the role of avantguarde of a more flexible imperialist policy of revanchism towards the GDR' in the interests of the CDU/CSU (W. Lamberz, 'Der Dialog geht weiter', *Deutsche Aussenpolitik*, No. 8 (1966), p. 908); they were 'in close collusion with the imperialist system' and had 'adopted its policies in all decisive questions' (H. Schaul, 'Der Dialog und der Dortmunder Parteitag der SPD', *Einheit*, No. 8 (1966), p. 1032). In this context the law on safe conduct was probably an indication to Moscow and East Berlin that the SPD was not prepared to allow itself to be manoeuvred into confrontation with the CDU/CSU. At any rate, this assumption is suggested by a Soviet statement according to which the Social Democrat leaders were not able by themselves to guarantee the personal security of the SED speakers and so, having got cold feet, latched on to the CDU/CSU (commentary by V. Michailov in *Pravda*, 6 July 1966), the conclusion being that only if the SPD had been prepared to risk breaking with the CDU/CSU for the sake of the safety of the SED speakers, instead of jointly formulating legal provisions with them, could the SED have had confidence in the West German Social Democrats.

17. It opened with a commentary by Karl-Eduard von Schnitzer on GDR television on 9 June 1966: 'The SPD leadership is anti-communist, it is filled with burning hate for the GDR. Would there be any real point in conducting a dialogue, an exchange of speakers with such a leadership?'

18. Text: *Dokumentation der Zeit*, No. 361 (1966), p. 9.

19. Text: ibid., p. 10.

20. Text: ibid., No. 362 (1966), pp. 1–5.

21. Text: *SBZ-Archiv*, No. 13 (1966), p. 204.

22. Text: ibid., pp. 204–6.

23. Text: ibid., p. 12; *SBZ-Archiv*, No. 13 (1966), p. 206.

24. Text: *Dokumentation der Zeit*, No. 362 (1966), p. 12.

25. The conclusions are based on the previous section 'Background'. The fact that it was Soviet theorists and commentators who first broached the change of perspective makes it probable – though not inevitable – that the

initiative came from the USSR. It is also conceivable that joint consultations had been held and simply that the results were first made public by the Soviet side – in accordance with the USSR's leading role in the Communist movement. But it is hardly likely that the CPSU would allow the SED to take part in this way in the making of decisions affecting internal strategy not only in the Federal Republic but also in all West European countries.

26. *Pravda*, 12 February 1966.

27. According to information reaching Otto Frei from several sources in East Berlin (*Neue Zürcher Zeitung*, 28 March and 18 April 1966). This was corroborated indirectly by the report of V. Kuznetsov from East Berlin concerning a Plenum of the Central Committee of the KPD. The report, published prior to the Open Letter from the SED Central Committee of 25 March 1966 (in *Pravda*, 24 March 1966), contains references to the course to be adopted by the SED.

28. The ADN statement was published by the GDR press on 11 May 1966. *Pravda* published the contents in detail on 12 May 1966. As the process of deciding what can and cannot be published in the USSR is relatively long and complicated, the ADN statement could not have been published so quickly if it had not had prior approval. It was also unusual for such a declaration to be reported so extensively in *Pravda*. Quite often such statements are not published at all.

29. P. Naumov in *Pravda*, 7 June 1966.

30. This seems to be implied from the sharper tone of the remarks by Yu. Zhilin and A. Chernyaev in *Pravda*, 10 June 1966.

31. A report by Ellen Leutz in the *New York Times* (international edition) of 20 June 1966, quoting sources close to Brandt on Abrasimov's remarks, gives the conversation as taking place simply 'earlier this month'. However, it is highly probable that there was not another discussion after that date.

32. Ellen Leutz in *New York Times*, 20 June 1966. See also P. Naumov in *Pravda*, 7 June 1966.

33. See, for example, the commentary by K.-E. v. Schnitzler mentioned in note 17.

34. It was no coincidence that Ulbricht did not announce the decision himself on 29 June 1966 but left it to one of the 'hard-line' party officials (A. Norden).

35. See the Open Letter of the SED Central Committee of 7 February 1966 (note 7); W. Ulbricht in *Pravda*, 20 April 1966; H. Matern in *Pravda*, 7 May 1966; E. Novosel'tsev, 'Zapadnogermanskie diskussii', *Mezhdunarodnaya zhizn*, No. 6 (1966), pp. 113 ff.; P. Naumov in *Pravda*, 7 June 1966; Yu. Zhilin and A. Chernyaev in *Pravda*, 10 June 1966. Apparently this view was deliberately not expressed to the West Germans.

36. Text: *Dokumentation der Zeit*, No. 355 (1966), pp. 34-7. (This was included in UN Document S/7192 of 10 March 1966, UN Security Council, *Official Records: Year 21 (1966), Supplement Jan.–March 1966*, New York, 1967, pp. 233-40.) See also the remarks by W. Ulbricht to the Volkskammer on 16 March 1966, *Aussenpolitische Korrespondenz*, No. 12 (1966), pp. 82-92 and pp. 101 ff.; *Dokumentation der Zeit*, No. 355 (1966), pp. 37-40. The declarations naturally made it clear that only a quite specific form of reunification would

be considered – serving the interests of 'peace' in accordance with the Potsdam Agreement (interpreted in a manner corresponding to Communist demands).

37. Documents S/7184 of 7 March 1966, S/7314 of 23 May 1966, S/7474 of 22 August 1966 and S/7599 of 28 November 1966, UN Security Council, *Official Records, Year 21 (1966), Supplement, Jan.–March 1966*, New York, 1967, pp. 194–6; *Supplement, April–June 1966*, pp. 102–4; *Supplement, July–September 1966*, pp. 100–2; *Supplement, October–December 1966*, pp. 100–1. At the time when the two last-mentioned documents were drawn up the GDR was no longer pressing its case. Article 107 of the UN Charter provides that measures taken against World War II enemy states be not affected or excluded by the guarantees included in the Charter.

38. Text: *Aussenpolitische Korrespondenz*, No. 40 (1966), pp. 323–5; UN Document S/7508, 26 September 1966, op. cit., *Supplement, July–September 1966*, pp. 139–43.

39. This view was shared by the leaders in both Moscow and East Berlin. See, for example, the reports on the Dortmund Party Congress in *Dokumentation der Zeit*, No. 361 (1966), pp. 19–30; A. Chernyaev, 'Sotsial-demokratiya pered litsom mezhdunarodnykh problem', *Mirovaya ekonomika i mezhdunarodnye otnosheniya*, No. 8 (1966), pp. 14–26.

40. This conclusion was strengthened by Ulbricht's reaction to the modified *Ostpolitik* of the Brandt–Scheel government in 1969–70.

41. See next chapter.

42. Ulbricht had outlined this strategy on 25 September 1965 (see note 2 above).

IV

Policy during the Initial Phase of the
Grand Coalition, 1966–1967

Background

Even though the Soviet leaders had convinced themselves that the
establishment of contacts with the Social Democrat opposition in the
West German Parliament would not lead to any significant change
in the foreign policy of the country, they did not give up all hopes
of effecting changes in West Germany's political orientation. Their
hopes were probably rekindled by the increasing problems facing the
Atlantic-oriented government of Erhard and Mende since the spring
of 1966. Throwing a bait to the West Germans, the central press
organs of the USSR were once again asking whether Bonn might not
wish to reconsider its policy of close cooperation with the USA and
cultivate better relations with the USSR.[1] Meanwhile the GDR leaders
were maintaining that the dialogue with the SPD must be conducted
'from below', in other words with the rank and file members and
supporters in confrontation with the SPD party leadership. It was the
declared aim to help those forces in the party which opposed the SPD
executive gradually to put themselves in a position where they could
'offer a genuine Social Democratic alternative' to the ruling CDU/
CSU.[2] At the same time the SED was whipping up polemics against
'revanchism' in the Federal Republic. This also served as a warning
to the GDR's East European allies not to be lured into accepting offers
made by Bonn.[3]

Course of Events

On 27 October 1966 open conflict developed between the coalition
partners in Bonn, the CDU/CSU and the Free Democrats (FDP),
over the budget. On 2 November Chancellor Erhard offered to
resign should this prove necessary. Having engineered a defeat in
Parliament for the Chancellor on 8 November, the CDU/CSU
parliamentary party nominated Kurt-Georg Kiesinger as its candidate
for Chancellor. Discussions followed between the parties on the

formation of a new government. It came down to a choice between two alternatives – either a coalition between the SPD and FDP (which would have had only a precariously weak majority) or a coalition between CDU/CSU and SPD. During the course of the month the idea of a government alliance between the two big parties clearly gained currency. On 1 December 1966 the new cabinet of Kiesinger and Brandt formally took office.

On 7 November, with an eye to the situation then developing in West Germany, Ulbricht used the occasion of a reception held at the Soviet Embassy in East Berlin to express his conviction that the 'great cause of peace, anti-fascism and democracy will triumph even in West Germany as a result of the efforts of the peace-loving and democratic forces in the West German population'. In his reply P. Abrasimov made no reference to these remarks.[4] The USSR very soon made it clear that its hopes rested less on a change in the internal correlation of forces within the Federal Republic in favour of pro-communist groups, than on fundamental changes occurring in the foreign policy of the Federal Republic. The reaction of the central organ of the CPSU to the CDU/CSU's choice of Kiesinger as candidate for Chancellor was extraordinarily positive. The new man was said to be a 'man of compromise'; concerning the East European countries he had spoken 'of the inevitability of a rapprochment, a reconciliation in the international arena'. It was as if it had already been decided that Kiesinger was to be the next head of government. It was noted with approval that neither the 'anti-communist' Franz-Josef Strauss nor the 'pro-American' Georg Schröder was in the running. Yet the article concluded by wondering whether Kiesinger, as an alleged exponent of national forces moving away from the USA, was really strong enough to put forward a new foreign policy programme against counter-forces represented by Strauss and Schröder.[5]

In East Berlin reaction to the possibility of a coalition government of the CDU/CSU and the SPD, with Kiesinger at its head, was decidedly negative. While there remained even a possibility of a coalition between Social Democrats and Free Democrats, SED officials refrained from commenting on the situation in Bonn and merely stressed the need for a fundamental change in the Federal Republic's attitude towards the GDR.[6] However, from 22 November 1966 onwards they mounted a campaign to discredit the CDU/CSU candidate and prospective West German head of government, using every tool of political defamation. On 29 November Ulbricht joined in personally. In an interview he condemned the emerging CDU/CSU–SPD coalition in Bonn as a government alliance uniting the 'revanchist politicians in the Social Democratic Party' with 'Adenauer [sic] and Strauss' in a chauvinistic, revanchist alliance against the GDR and the other East European states. By joining this 'reactionary front' the SPD would be set a on right-wing course in both domestic and foreign policy.[8] Probably this extreme attitude was meant primarily to influence the Soviet leaders. Ulbricht cannot have failed to notice the Soviet inclination to look favourably on a Federal government led by Kiesinger and to sound out the possibilities for an improved Soviet–West German relationship based on a modified foreign policy in Bonn. Thus, his contention that the SPD was simply adapting to the CDU/CSU course and that the Warsaw Pact states would be the target of attack for the new West German government was clearly meant to serve as a signal to East Germany's allies – of which the USSR was by far the most important. The speed with which Ulbricht registered his opinion, even before the formation of the Bonn government had been completed, clearly suggests that he did not have full confidence in his Soviet comrades.

The fears of the SED leaders were not without foundation. Once the new Kiesinger–Brandt cabinet had been formed the USSR began to suspend, or at least tone down, its polemics against the Federal Republic and to adopt a posture of watchful waiting. Soviet central press organs began publishing detailed reports on political developments in Bonn, the underlying question being whether, after the recent promising signs, there would really be a fundamental change of course in foreign policy. Previous allegations that the Federal Republic and its leading circles were tainted with Nazism and were plotting a Hitler-like expansion to the East disappeared from the Soviet mass media – to be replaced by well-intentioned exhortations to the Federal government not to underestimate the dangers of increasing neo-Nazi tendencies and to counter the success of the NPD by a reorientation of foreign policy. Comments in Soviet newspapers and journals seemed to imply a policy of 'wait-and-see' mixed with cautious optimism. At the same time Soviet commentators refrained from the usual exuberant praise of the GDR.[9] Should the West German government be considering the possibility of a change of course in foreign policy, then Soviet behaviour was designed to encourage it.

The inaugural statement of 13 December 1966 made it clear that the Federal government: (i) was prepared to relinquish any claim to atomic weapons in a national, though not a supranational framework; (ii) regarded relations with the USSR as being still hampered by the problem of German reunification; (iii) continued to uphold the right of the German people to national self-determination; (iv) maintained that the question of Germany's borders could only be settled in a peace treaty with a future united Germany, and (v) upheld the Federal Republic's claim to sole representation of the German people and refused to recognize the GDR, though conceding that intra-German

35

problems should be included in a renunciation of force agreement.[10] The Federal Chancellor may have advocated with particular emphasis a policy of reconciliation with the East European states, and above all the USSR, but he had refused to meet the most important demands made by the Warsaw Pact states on the Federal Republic.[11]

This provoked swift reaction from the Soviet mass media. Radio Moscow broadcast a commentary on the same day, and for the next two weeks the Federal government's inaugural declaration remained a major theme in numerous Soviet commentaries and analyses devoted to Bonn's political orientation. Up to 15 December the overall tone was positive, despite criticism of the new Federal government's 'half-measures' – such as its insistence on keeping the border question open and on non-recognition of the GDR.[12] But from 16 December onwards the Soviet mass media made statements by Foreign Minister Brandt and Defence Minister Schröder at NATO and WEU meetings the starting-point for sharpening their tone.[13] The bone of contention was that the declarations made by the two West German cabinet members, and the NATO resolutions concerning consultation mechanisms in questions of nuclear defence, had reawakened the danger of the Federal Republic gaining access to nuclear weapons. This would belie the professions of peaceful intent in the government declaration of 13 December.[14] The polemics escalated and remained at a high level for some time to come.[15]

For its part the GDR left not the slightest doubt at any time about its negative attitude towards the CDU/CSU–SPD coalition government. Right from the start the basic thesis was upheld that absolutely nothing had changed in the 'revanchist' and 'hostile' orientation of West German policy. The sole concern of the new Federal government was to adapt its methods to changed conditions. 'West German revanchism', it was asserted, merely threatened to become even more dangerous by adopting more effective means and attempting to deceive the people as to its true intentions.[16] On 15 December 1966 Ulbricht outlined to the SED Central Committee the official line towards the Federal Republic. The outlook of the Kiesinger–Brandt cabinet, according to Ulbricht, resembled previous West German foreign policy 'just as one rotten egg resembles another'. Moreover, the country's development would still be determined exclusively 'by the reactionary forces of armaments capital and militarism'.[17] After 20 December SED leaders even increased their hostility towards the Federal Republic by making personal attacks on the SPD Chairman and Foreign Minister, Willy Brandt.[18]

From 27 December 1966 onwards a common posture was restored once more in the anti-West German attitudes of the Soviet Union and the GDR. Both sides were now agreed that the Federal Republic would have to consent to an unconditional recognition of the GDR and unqualified rejection of access in any form to nuclear weapons if it wanted its readiness for a relaxation of tensions to be taken seriously. In addition West Germany would have to give up its designs on West Berlin so that the city would enjoy unmolested independent development.[19]

On 25 January 1967 the SED leadership launched a new campaign against the CDU/CSU–SPD coalition government. A spokesman for the East German Foreign Ministry declared, following the successful conclusion of negotiations between West Germany and Romania on the establishment of diplomatic relations,[20] that the Federal government was attempting to induce the 'socialist states' to accept and give legal sanction to its 'aggressive and expansionist programme, starting with its pretension to sole representation, continuing with territorial demands and the failure to reject the Munich Agreement *ex ante*, right up to the illegal incorporation of West Berlin into the Federal Republic'. This kind of behaviour harked back 'clearly to the practices of Nazi diplomacy' which 'demanded the toleration and fulfilment of its aggressive conditions as a prerequisite "for the preservation of peace" '.[21] The central organ of the SED further sharpened the polemics by depicting Bonn's demand as a 'blackmail threat' to the Warsaw Pact states.[22]

The East German argument was not taken up straight away by the Soviet mass media. However, the Soviet government did formulate its own version of the anti-West German polemics in a statement on 28 January 1967. According to this statement the Federal Republic had 'not thrown off the criminal past of Hitlerism'. Neo-Nazism was flourishing in West Germany, whereas 'democratic and progressive organizations' were subject to persecution. Given these conditions, the statement continued, no one could 'guarantee that a new Hitler might not spring up in the Federal Republic – and with nuclear weapons in his grasp'. The statement asserted that this would be the 'desired result' of official Bonn policy, and concluded that the Federal government could only counter national–socialist tendencies by a fundamental *volte face* in accordance with East European demands, especially those for recognition of the division of Germany and existing borders.[23]

The Foreign Ministers of the Warsaw Pact states met in Warsaw from 8 to 10 February 1967. According to the final communiqué they discussed problems arising from East–West relations in Europe – and above all developments since the Bucharest Conference of July 1966.[24] Doubtless, the formal establishment of diplomatic relations between the Federal Republic and Romania on 31 January 1967 played an important, perhaps even central role. The Romanian action had deeply disturbed the GDR leadership. In its view the anti-West German stipulations of 'European security', as formulated in the Warsaw Pact's Bucharest Declaration of 6 July 1966,[25] represented agreed objectives which were to be strictly implemented by all signatories. Thus, according to this interpretation, the GDR's East European allies had assumed the obligation, utilizing all means of political pressure, to make West Germany recognize the GDR as a second German state and sanction the borders on the Elbe, Werra, Oder and Neisse rivers.[26] That the Romanian leaders should exclude these controversial questions from their relationship with the Federal Republic implied not only a total disregard for their East German allies, but also the breaking of a solemnly sworn pledge.[27] Romania's action was even harder for the GDR leaders to accept, for it appeared that other Warsaw Pact states – notably Hungary, Czechoslovakia and Bulgaria – were preparing to follow its example.

In the preparations for, and during the course of, the Warsaw Conference the GDR representatives argued that, in offering the East European countries the prospect of normalizing and improving relations, the 'West German revanchists' were in reality pursuing aims hostile to the cause of peace and détente. The strategy of the Bonn government, the argument went on, was to create a split in the 'socialist community'. As the West German–Romanian agreement showed, 'West German imperialism', just like Hitler's 'German imperialism', was attempting to realize its aggressive and expansionist intentions step by step, professing peaceful intent and isolating the selected victim from other countries. Then it would be the turn of the next victim. The East German delegates declared that the Warsaw Pact states must draw the appropriate lessons from past history. 'West German imperialism' was now playing up to the East European countries in order first of all to isolate the GDR and soften it up. In this way the first stage of the West German programme of conquest would be completed, namely the incorporation of West Berlin and the GDR. Bonn would then turn its revanchist ambitions towards the Western territories of Poland, the Kaliningrad region of the USSR and territories in Czechoslovakia. In the final stage 'West German imperialism' would eventually turn against its neighbours in Western Europe.

The conclusion of this line of reasoning was that the allies must show unconditional solidarity with the GDR if they wanted to safeguard their own existence in the face of dangerous West German advances. It followed too that it was imperative for 'European security' that the East European states refrain from entering into a political and diplomatic relationship with the Federal Republic until it had satisfied all GDR demands and thereby unequivocally abandoned

38

its revanchist programme. In practical terms this would put the GDR in a position of determining how far its allies (with the exception of the USSR, which has had diplomatic relations with the Federal Republic since 1955) could go in establishing relations with West Germany.[28]

It would appear that, with the exception of Romania,[29] East Germany's arguments did not fail to impress the other Warsaw Pact countries. Also, the USSR apparently supported the GDR thesis in its major points.[30] Following the Warsaw Conference of Foreign Ministers, Ulbricht went public with an inflated report on the success realized. He declared himself 'very satisfied' with the result, and emphasized that the policies of 'West German imperialism' had been confounded because the Warsaw Pact states were consistently pursuing a policy of 'struggle against West German revanchism' and Bonn's 'arrogant claim to sole representation'.[31] Comments from other East European countries, including the Soviet Union, confirmed that the GDR's demands and been accepted,[32] although possibly the SED's reasoning did not yet meet with general unqualified approval in the USSR.[33]

The Warsaw Foreign Ministers' Conference seems to have given the impetus for the full integration of the GDR into the bilateral East European pact system.[34] Finally, at the Karlovy Vary Conference of European Communist Parties from 24 to 26 April 1967, Ulbricht succeeded with Soviet backing to make his line the obligatory guideline for the behaviour of all the Warsaw Pact states with the exception of Romania. The SED's arguments now found general acceptance: the establishment of relations with the Federal Republic was made dependent on West German acceptance of East German demands.[35]

Process of Decision-making

The differing evaluations evident in official statements and press comments in the USSR on the one hand and the GDR on the other during November and December 1966 expressed an apparent lack of coordination. Even the anti-West German attitudes subsequently expressed until the second half of January were not synchronized. Since the leaderships of the USSR and the GDR obviously had not coordinated or even discussed the line to be adopted towards the new CDU/CSU–SPD government in Bonn, the interview given by Ulbricht on 29 November 1966 almost leaves the impression that at this juncture he saw in making the whole affair public his only chance of alerting the Kremlin to his fears. To all appearances the first political dialogue between Moscow and East Berlin on the subject of their respective policies towards West Germany did not take place until the evening before the Warsaw Foreign Ministers' Conference, which quite possibly was called at the initiative of the GDR leaders. At the end of January 1967, when Ulbricht made representations to his Soviet allies, he could not only count on a change of attitude towards West Germany in the USSR, but he could also point to the clear dangers for bloc discipline which had become manifest since the formation of the Grand Coalition.

It may seem surprising at first that the Soviet leaders, who would normally take every opportunity to stress the need for close coordination among Warsaw Pact states, should for so long show no inclination for political coordination with the GDR. However, once it is realized that in the given situation Moscow had no need to cooperate with East Berlin, Soviet behaviour is more easily understood. The Soviet leaders were waiting to see if the Kiesinger–Brandt government would create opportunities for political cooperation. At this stage the GDR had no part to play; thus, to the Soviet leaders it may have seemed unnecessary to enter into consultations with GDR representatives. At the same time it may be assumed there were other important reasons for not entering into such discussions. To make policy on West Germany the subject of discussions with the GDR would have meant exposing the Soviet Union to the danger of East German objections and interference. Soviet policy-makers could well avoid such problems by signalling their readiness to negotiate with the Federal government without any prior consultations with the SED leaders. Discordant notes from East Berlin, from which Moscow could dissociate itself by adopting a cooler tone towards the GDR, were more likely to enhance rather than reduce the effect of Soviet advances towards Bonn.

Not until the Soviet policy-makers, of their own accord, arrived at an evaluation of the Federal Republic similar to that of their East German ally did they see fit to consult the SED leaders. Even then the USSR continued to display a reserved attitude for some time. Presumably this was partly due to the endeavour – clearly expressed by Brezhnev on 13 January 1967 – not to block a possible change of mind in Bonn despite all the anti-West German polemics. But in the end the establishment of diplomatic relations between West Germany and Romania seems to have given Ulbricht and his supporters the oppotunity to make the demands for a common policy on West Germany heard in Soviet circles. Evidently the argument that the Romanian action was in direct contravention of the need for solidarity between Warsaw Pact states, threatening to disrupt the unity of the Soviet camp, had some effect in Moscow. Accordingly it seemed imperative for the Communist countries of Eastern Europe to agree on a common policy to meet the West German challenge. In the process the SED leaders succeeded in making their claims the basis of a consensus directed against West Germany. This arrangement suited the USSR: as long as it served the purposes of Soviet foreign policy to use the Federal Republic as a bogeyman in Eastern Europe the USSR could use the commitment of the Warsaw Pact states to the GDR's demands as a suitable means of imposing discipline on its hegemonial sphere.

Motivation

Reports in the Soviet mass media concerning the situation in Bonn, as published in November–December 1966, suggest a clear interest in the prospect of change in West German foreign policy. But what kind of change was it to be? Some indication as to the answer to this question can perhaps be derived from the Soviet reaction to the Bonn government declaration of 13 December 1966. It was noticeable that Soviet reports at first maintained an expectant and favourable undertone, although Chancellor Kiesinger had clearly not acknowledged any of the demands made on to the Federal Republic by the USSR and its allies in the name of 'European security'. If this behaviour is taken as deliberate, then the conclusion must be that the Soviet leaders were prepared, at least for the time being, to waive the demand for recognition of the GDR and the borders. In that case the USSR must have had its sights set on other more important political objectives in its policy towards West Germany. The alternative hypothesis is that Soviet commentators had not yet received any new directives from above and therefore, for a short time, kept to the previous ruling. In this case, the relatively friendly comments during the first few days could be ascribed to the functional inertia of the Soviet press apparatus, and would offer no insights into the policies of the Soviet leaders.

However, as for the second hypothesis, it must be remembered that, unlike the Western press, the mass media in the USSR are under no pressure to report events immediately. For this reason, it would have been easy for radio, television and press in the USSR to delay comment on the Bonn government declaration pending the arrival of the necessary instructions from the top. In fact, the Soviet press in similar circumstances often delayed comment for many days, sometimes even for several weeks, waiting for the official line to be determined by the leadership. If, consequently, the Soviet mass media reacted swiftly to the Bonn government declaration it may be assumed that they did so with the approval of all superior authorities. However, Soviet commentators and the organs at the intermediate level directly controlling them might have followed outdated directives in good faith without being aware that attitudes at the top had changed as a result of the Bonn government declaration.

Thus one cannot say with absolute certainty that the Soviet leaders in December 1966 might not have allowed the contact with the Federal Republic to lapse due to the latter's unwillingness to recognize the GDR. However, it would seem that West German reluctance over another matter contributed a good deal to the negative reaction in the Soviet Union. This becomes apparent particularly from retrospective explanations given by Soviet commentators and experts in 1967. They saw the Federal Republic as playing a decisive role within the Atlantic alliance, whereas the USSR was precisely trying to bring about the dissolution of that alliance. Whether or not the Western alliance would be able to survive on the European continent would, it was thought, depend very much on West Germany.[37] Seen from this angle Soviet policy towards the Federal Republic had a clear function to fulfil within the framework of the anti-NATO strategy: the idea was to prevent West Germany from continuing to play her role within the Atlantic alliance, either by concerted pressure (struggle against 'West German revanchism') or by the offer of enticements (prospects of a more relaxed cooperative relationship). Apparently in December 1966 Moscow saw the possibility of bringing about an estrangement of the Federal Republic from NATO.[38] The subsequent allegation that talk of détente in Bonn was shown to be false by West Germany's continued allegiance to the Atlantic alliance,[39] is a clear reflection of dashed hopes.

Quite different considerations were uppermost in the minds of the GDR leaders. Just as in the case of the SED–SPD dialogue, they were less concerned with changing the foreign policy of West Germany than with increasing their influence over its internal affairs. Proceeding from this it is easy to see why Ulbricht and his followers would be most unhappy at the prospect of a CDU/CSU–SPD government in Bonn. A coalition between the two largest parties seemed to destroy any hope of a heightened internal struggle within the Federal Republic. The polarizing effects of such a struggle were what leading SED functionaries were counting on to forge a united action front with the SPD and so gain considerable influence over West German affairs. It is not coincidental that Ulbricht repeatedly appealed to the Social Democrats to react to the crisis in the CDU/CSU by building a political counter alliance.[40] The possibility of acceptable course corrections in foreign policy, though not discounted in East Berlin, meant nothing to the GDR leaders if the SPD in the process did not assume the desired posture of confrontation towards the CDU/CSU. Since the East German thesis – that Bonn's foreign policy had not and would not change significantly – was used by the SED leaders as justification for preventing their East European allies from establishing relations with the new Federal government, they had to deny every change of attitude in West Germany.[41]

As long as the USSR seemed in favour of improved relations with the new leaders in Bonn, it was difficult for the SED to adopt a demonstrative anti-West German line. This became possible only after the USSR itself had turned against the Federal Republic. It seemed logical to East Berlin that the policy pursued by the SPD – namely, joining forces with the CDU/CSU and thereby removing any basis for Communist hopes of an all-German, anti-CDU/CSU alliance – had to be met by a further deepening of the rift between the GDR and the Federal Republic.[42] Specifically, (i) From now on the official watchword was to be social antagonism between the two German states, and not national community. The concept of unity of the German people, the existence of state borders notwithstanding, was challenged by legislative measures, such as the proclamation of separate GDR citizenship. (ii) The Federal Republic was confronted with increasing demands, which had to be met if Bonn's protestations of peaceful intent were to be believed. The SED leaders began to emphasize claims which, if implemented, would involve the separation of West Berlin from West Germany and its orientation towards East Germany.

East German activity was apparently designed to sever previous ties with West Germany and, by advancing unacceptable demands, to block a possible reconciliation of interests between West Germany and Eastern Europe.[43] The concerted policy of the USSR and the GDR towards the Federal Republic from the second half of January 1967 onwards certainly gave the impression to the outside world that complete unanimity had been restored between Moscow and East Berlin. In reality, however, the motives of the respective parties still differed. Whereas the Kremlin turned against West Germany because it had not carried out the desired change in foreign policy, Ulbricht and his followers were disappointed because the exact opposite of the hoped-for left-right polarization in the Federal Republic had emerged – a rapprochement between the SPD and CDU/CSU. But provided the Federal government agreed to a change of course along the lines desired by the USSR, Moscow would consider the broadest possible base for this government desirable – for example, even the inclusion of groups from the opposite (right) end of the political spectrum.[44] This made for a potentially explosive situation in GDR–Soviet relations. As soon as Moscow and Bonn could arrive at a mutually acceptable political arrangement, the latent differences between the USSR and the GDR over this question were bound to surface. Consequently, over the next few years the GDR leaders

43

strove to prevent at any cost such a Soviet–West German rapprochement.

References

1. E. Pral'nikov in *Izvestiya*, 16 July 1966; P. Naumov in *Pravda*, 21 September 1966; (V. Michailov); L. Zamyatin and V. Falin, 'Vazhny garantiya mira', *Mirovaya ekonomika i mezhdunarodnye otnosheniya*, No. 9 (1966), pp. 10 ff.

2. W. Lamberz, 'Der Dialog geht weiter', *Deutsche Aussenpolitik*, No. 8 (1966), pp. 899–909, esp. 908.

3. Speech by Foreign Minister O. Winzer in September 1966: O. Winzer, *Deutsche Aussenpolitik des Friedens und des Sozialismus*, (East) Berlin, 1969, pp. 305–9.

4. *Neues Deutschland*, 8 November 1966.

5. V. Michailov in *Pravda*, 12 November 1966.

6. G. Eisler and H. Axen in a discussion on East German Radio, 20 November 1966, as reported in *Neues Deutschland*, 21 November 1966.

7. The starting point was an international press conference on 22 November 1966, where A. Norden, basing his case on 'authenticated documents', accused Kiesinger of having been 'chief of Hitler's fifth column on the air'. In the Federal Republic he had 'whipped up support for West German aggression and the emergency laws'; now he was acting as 'a lackey of Strauss' and the 'darling of the neo-Nazi NPD' (see: *Aussenpolitische Korrespondenz*, No. 48 (1966), pp. 393 and 396). There were further anti-Kiesinger articles in *Neues Deutschland*, especially on 26 November 1966 (by G. Kegel) and on 27 November 1966.

8. Ibid., 30 November 1966.

9. See, for example, the articles by E. Pral'nikov in *Izvestiya*, 1 and 2 December 1966; *Pravda*, 2 December 1966.

10. Text: *Texte zur Deutschlandpolitik*, Vol. I, Bundesministerium für gesamtdeutsche Fragen, ed., Bonn and (West) Berlin, 1968, pp. 7–27; B. Meissner, *Die deutsche Ostpolitik, 1961–1970*, Cologne, 1970, pp. 161–3 (exctracts).

11. As set out in the Bucharest Declaration of 6 July 1966, *Pravda*, 9 July 1966, *Europa Archiv*, No. 16 (1966), pp. D414–24; *SBZ-Archiv*, No. 14 (1966), pp. 219–24.

12. *Pravda*, 14 and 15 December 1966; E. Pral'nikov and A. Tyupaev in *Izvestiya*, 15 December 1966.

13. Extracts of Brandt's remarks to the WEU of 14 December 1966, in: *Die deutsche Ostpolitik, 1961–1970*, op. cit., p. 163.

14. See, among others, N. Polyanov in *Izvestiya*, 16 December 1966; S. Beglov in *Pravda*, 19 December 1966; Yu. Goloshubov in *Izvestiya*, 20 December 1966.

15. Leading article in *Izvestiya*, 27 December 1966. Simultaneously renewed emphasis of support for GDR demands on the Federal Republic: *Pravda*, 27 December 1966 (V. Kutzsnetsov).

16. See especially the speech by H. Kröger at an international conference of scientists in Warsaw from 8 to 10 December 1966, in: *Dokumentation der Zeit*,

No. 374 (1967), pp. 1-15; Commentary on East German Radio on the Bonn Government Declaration as quoted by L. Gorgey, *Bonn's Eastern Policy, 1964-1971*, Hamden, Conn., 1972, p. 96; *Neues Deutschland*, 14 December 1966.

17. Text: *Dokumentation der Zeit*, No. 373 (1967), pp. 24-9; *Aussenpolitische Korrespondenz*, No. 51 (1966), pp. 417-21.

18. *Neues Deutschland*, 20 December 1966.

19. See Ulbricht's New Year Address of 31 December 1966, in: *Dokumentation der Zeit*, No. 374 (1967), pp. 30-3; *Aussenpolitische Korrespondenz*, No. 1 (1967), pp. 1 ff. Speech by L. Brezhnev in Gorky on 13 January 1967, *Pravda*, 14 January 1967; Declaration by the GDR Foreign Ministry on West Berlin of 6 January 1967, *Aussenpolitische Korrespondenz*, No. 2 (1967), p. 12.

20. The talks had taken place from 7 to 16 January 1967 in Bucharest. This was announced on 19 January 1967 by West Germany. The Romanian government had not, as the SED leaders had demanded, insisted that the Federal Republic relinquish its legal stand on Berlin, the GDR and the Eastern borders.

21. Text: *Neues Deutschland*, 26 January 1967.

22. *Neues Deutschland*, 27 January 1967 and 2 February 1967.

23. Text: *Pravda*, 29 January 1967.

24. Text: *Aussenpolitische Korrespondenz*, No. 7 (1967), p. 49.

25. Text: *Pravda*, 9 July 1966; *Europa Archiv*, No. 16 (1966), pp. D414-24; *SBZ-Archiv*, No. 14 (1966), pp. 219-24.

26. This does not exactly follow from the text of the Declaration, which merely states that the signatories were of the 'opinion' that 'measures for establishing European security' would have to proceed in a corresponding 'general direction'. There was no mention at all of a specific sequence according to which certain demands would be made preconditions for other steps.

27. The GDR point of view can be ascertained from Ulbricht's statement on 13 February 1967 concerning the results of the Warsaw Foreign Ministers' Conference, extracts of which appeared in *Aussenpolitische Korrespondenz*, No. 8 (1967), pp. 59-63.

28. The argument and the consequences to be drawn from it are reflected in subsequent GDR statements, see the speech by Ulbricht on 13 February 1967 (*Aussenpolitische Korrespondenz*, No. 8 (1967), pp. 59-63) and the resolution of the GDR Staatsrat of 16 February 1967 (*Aussenpolitische Korrespondenz*, No. 8 (1967), p. 57). They also appear in part in earlier East German statements and in more detail later on.

29. Romania claimed that she had induced the Federal Republic to abandon the Hallstein Doctrine when she established diplomatic relations and thus had aided East Germany in her efforts to gain recognition of the existence of two states in Germany. The refusal by her allies to accept this interpretation probably played an important part in Romania's decision not to attend the Karlovy Vary Conference. That the USSR rejected this view was made clear when Prime Minister Kosygin, on 10 February 1967 in London, avoided expressing approval sought in a question by the correspondent of the *Frankfurter Rundschau* (*Izvestiya*, 11 February 1967).

30. The Soviet foreign policy journal closely associated with the Foreign Ministry published an article in its February issue – which went to press on about 25 January 1967 – containing among other things the idea of a multi-phase

West German revanchist programme: P. Kryukov, 'Germanski vopros i sovremennost', *Mezhdunarodnaya zhizn*, No. 2 (1967), pp. 18–21.

31. Text: *Aussenpolitische Korrespondenz*, No. 8 (1967), pp. 59–63, esp. pp. 59 and 63.

32. See the statements made by Gomulka and Hendrych – extracts in: *Aussenpolitische Korrespondenz*, No. 7 (1967), p. 50; *Pravda*, 24 February 1967 (Report on the Warsaw Conference by B. Pyadishev/R. Sergeev); Yu. Kotov, 'GDR-vazhny faktor mira v Evrope', *Mezhdunarodnaya zhizn*, No. 3 (1967), pp. 71 and 73 ff.

33. Brezhnev, for instance, in his Moscow election address of 10 March 1967 attacked the policy of the Federal Republic at length without, however, mentioning either the multi-phase programme of revanchism or the strategy of dividing the countries of the Soviet bloc. Text: *Pravda*, 11 March 1967.

34. Until then the GDR had a bilateral Treaty of Friendship and Mutual Assistance of the type customary between Warsaw Pact states only with the Soviet Union. On 15 March 1967 the GDR concluded a corresponding treaty with Poland, followed two days later by a similar agreement with Czechoslovakia. Treaties of Friendship and Mutual Assistance were concluded with Hungary and Bulgaria on 18 May and 7 September respectively.

35. See the text of the Karlovy Vary Declaration of 26 April 1967, *Pravda*, 27 April 1967; *Europa-Archiv*, No. 11 (1967), pp. D259–66; *Dokumentation der Zeit*, No. 383 (1967), pp. 37–40. For an evaluation: W. Berner, 'Das Karlsbader Aktionsprogramm', *Europa-Archiv*, No. 11 (1967), pp. 393–400; W. Berner, 'Die Karlsbader Konferenz der kommunistischen Parteien Europas', *Berichte des Bundesinstituts für ostwissenschaftliche und internationale Studien*, Cologne, No. 30 (1967). The Soviet Union's unqualified agreement with the GDR viewpoint is evident from Brezhnev's remarks on 18 and 24 April 1967 (*Pravda*, 19 and 25 April 1967) and from the fact that the USSR published in full Ulbricht's speeches of 17 and 25 April 1967 (*Pravda*, 18 and 29 April 1967).

36. See R. A. Remington, *The Warsaw Pact: Case Studies in Communist Conflict Resolution*, Cambridge, Mass. and London, 1971; G. Wettig, 'Die europäische Sicherheit in der Politik des Ostblocks 1966', *Osteuropa*, No. 2–3 (1967), pp. 95 ff.

37. *Novoe vremya*, No. 6 (1967), p. 4; P. Kryukov, 'Germanskii vopros i sovremennost', in *Mezhdunarodnaya zhizn*, No. 2 (1967), p. 19; *Pravda*, 5 March 1967 (V. Maevsky); 'V interesakh prochnogo mira v Evrope' (leading article), *Mezhdunarodnaya zhizn*, No. 6 (1967), pp. 5 ff.

38. These hopes were cautiously but repeatedly reflected in Soviet commentaries. Judging from the same sources they were based on the fact that in Bonn, apart from the Social Democrats, who had opposed the Atlantic orientation of the Erhard–Mende government previously, new men had come to power from the ranks of the CDU/CSU, who appeared to display tendencies which were more nationally-minded (i.e., not so pro-American) and quasi-Gaullist (i.e., not so closely allied to NATO).

39. Yu. Goloshubov in *Izvestiya*, 18 February 1967; R. Pyadyshev and R. Sergeev in *Pravda*, 24 February 1967; E. Grigor'ev in *Pravda*, 12 August 1967; E. Pral'nikov in *Izvestiya*, 23 August 1967.

40. On 29 November 1966, for instance (*Neues Deutschland*, 30 November

1966) and on 15 December 1966 (*Dokumentation der Zeit*, No. 373 (1967), pp. 24–9).

41. If the GDR had really been convinced that nothing was going to change in Bonn they would have been content to sit back and wait until the position had become clear to everyone. Instead, even before there was any concrete basis, they tried their best to persuade their allies that by its nature 'West German revanchism' could not change in the slightest. In other words the GDR leaders certainly did count on the possibility of course corrections in Bonn's foreign policy and were therefore trying, right from the start, to make all indications of such changes appear as mere propaganda.

42. This course was introduced by Ulbricht's New Year Address of 31 December 1966, *Aussenpolitische Korrespondenz*, No. 1 (1967), pp. 1 and 3. Further declarations and measures taken are to be found in *Aussenpolitische Korrespondenz*, No. 2 (1967), p. 11; No. 5 (1967), p. 35; No. 6 (1967), pp. 41 and 43; No. 9 (1967), pp. 65 and 67. See also J. Hacker, 'Furcht vor der Entspannung', and E. Albrecht, 'Nationaler Dialog völlig neuen Typs', *SBZ-Archiv*, No. 5 (1967), pp. 65–70 and Ulbricht's concluding remarks in *Dokumentation der Zeit*, No. 383 (1967), pp. 15–18; *Aussenpolitische Korrespondenz*, No. 17 (1967), pp. 129–36.

43. This impression derives from the fact, among other things, that in 1967 and 1968 the GDR leaders, each time the Federal government took a step towards them, reacted by increasing their demands.

44. It is in accordance with basic Soviet interests that at the end of 1971, the Soviet leaders tried to win the approval of the leader of the CDU/CSU opposition, R. Barzel, for the Moscow Treaty. It would have been more in accord with GDR interests if the treaty had been used to kindle the struggle against the CDU/CSU, which opposed the treaty and was (supposedly) a threat to peace.

V

The Conflict over Attitudes towards the Federal Republic, 1969

Development of the relationship between Moscow and Bonn over the winter of 1968-9.

Since February 1967 talks had been going on between the Soviet Union and the Federal Republic concerning an agreement on the mutual renunciation of force. As the talks continued the USSR's uncompromising attitude became increasingly clear. At the beginning of July the Soviet leaders finally broke off the dialogue.[1] However, by the autumn of 1968 they began to show an interest in improving their relations with the Federal government. On 7 October 1968 the Soviet Foreign Minister, Andrei Gromyko, and the Foreign Minister of the Federal Republic, Willy Brandt, used the opportunity of their both being in New York for the opening session of the UN General Assembly to meet for discussions. They agreed to put an end to the polemics over the question of the Soviet claim to intervention rights in the Federal Republic and to examine possible areas of mutual interest.[2] Two months later, during an interview with the West German Ambassador, the Soviet Foreign Minister expressed his country's readiness to engage in talks aimed at settling those questions which could be resolved at that time.[3] In January 1969 the Soviet Ambassador in Bonn dropped similar hints.[4] These preliminary approaches coincided with cautious Soviet overtures to the United States.[5]

Opposing views and approaches over Berlin were the main obstacle to an improvement in West German-Soviet relations. In the autumn of 1968 the Soviet leaders, after their anti-West German polemics over intervention rights had proved ineffective,[6] switched to attacks on Bonn's alleged interference in West Berlin.[7] During his talk with Ambassador Allardt in December 1968, Foreign Minister Gromyko left no doubt that, despite its interest in improved relations, the USSR would not tolerate any sovereign acts on the part of West Germany in West Berlin.[8]

The warning applied to the impending session of the *Bundesver-*

48

sammlung which, except in 1949, had always met in the city. This corresponded with basic Soviet strategy. Certainly it implied a more extreme attitude on the part of the Soviet Union inasmuch as in 1964 the USSR and the GDR had been content to issue protests only. This time the GDR, presumably, had pressed for more effective measures to be taken. It is also likely that the Soviet leaders were encouraged by the fact that the choice of meeting-place had long been the subject of discussion in the Federal Republic, and that West Germany's allies had apparently adopted a reserved attitude towards the matter.[9] In these circumstances a threat of counter-measures scarcely seemed to carry any risks.

Presumably Moscow did not consider it likely that the new President of the *Bundestag*, Kai-Uwe von Hassel, who had succeeded Eugen Gerstenmaier in January 1969, would press on with his predecessor's intention of convening the *Bundesversammlung* in West Berlin. When this in fact did happen, the USSR and the GDR on 5 February 1969 announced a series of measures which would be taken if the planned West German 'provocation' should take place.[10] Thereupon, the GDR government on 6 and 7 February sent threatening protests to the Federal government, the Mayor of West Berlin and the three Western powers. On 8 February the GDR Ministry of the Interior issued a decree restricting traffic between the Federal Republic and West Berlin, thereby demonstrating East Germany's sovereign jurisdiction over access routes. The restrictions had little practical significance, but they were presented as an initial step only and thus could be taken as harbingers of more severe measures to come.[11] At the same time not only the East German but also the Soviet mass media adopted a threatening tone. Several Soviet statements hinted at the possibility that Moscow might not be willing to tolerate much longer the inconveniences involved in the Western presence in Berlin – for example civilian transit via the GDR.[12]

If the Soviet leaders had counted on only half-hearted support from the Western powers for the covening of the *Bundesversammlung* in West Berlin, they were sadly mistaken. The three Western governments backed the West German venture in an unusually prompt, emphatic and demonstrative manner.[13] American diplomats let it be known to their Soviet counterparts that potential cooperation in questions of arms control would be jeopardized should tensions arise in Berlin. The Soviet leaders rapidly drew their own conclusions from the new situation. Beginning on 12 February, the Soviet campaign de-escalated noticeably and there was no more mention of further measures by the GDR. Bitter Soviet polemics against West Germany's Berlin policy did continue right up to the meeting of the *Bundesversammlung* at the beginning of March, but this was just a diversionary tactic aimed at concealing the fact that the previously announced threats and repressive measures had been abandoned.[14] Apparently Soviet policy-makers were not prepared to jeopardize their relations with the Western governments for the sake of gaining some small advantage in Berlin.[15] This came as a bitter surprise to the SED leaders: the preference for maintaining tolerable relations with the West induced the Soviet leaders to prevent the GDR from taking measures which seemed to have been agreed upon earlier.[16]

From the beginning Soviet policy-makers appear to have had more in store than mere threats in their endeavour to prevent the convocation of the *Bundesversammlung* in West Berlin. This, at least, should be the reading of remarks made by Ambassador P. Abrasimov as early as 31 January in a conversation with the Mayor of West Berlin, Klaus Schütz, when he spoke of the possibility of renewing border passes to West Berliners, provided the Federal Presidential elections took place somewhere else. In mid-February, when Bonn seemed unable to work out exactly what Soviet intentions were, and was consequently deeply concerned, Abrasimov's comments were received with interest in West Germany. On 19 February, encouraged by reports from Washington concerning indications of a more conciliatory Soviet attitude, Chancellor Kiesinger put out feelers to the Soviet Embassy in Rolandseck to determine whether the USSR was ready to grant border passes to the West Berliners in exchange for West Germany abandoning the idea of holding the *Bundesversammlung* in Berlin. The initiative apparently gave Soviet diplomats the impression that the Federal government might be prepared to hold the *Bundesversammlung* elsewhere in return for a single programme of visits.[17] Reaction therefore was swift: on 21 February the West Berlin Senate received a letter from Ulbricht, addressed to Brandt in his capacity as SPD Chairman, offering favourable East German consideration of an application by the Senate for the granting of border passes for the Easter holiday season, provided the Social Democrat ministers in Bonn succeeded in changing the proposed meeting-place of the *Bundesversammlung*.[18] The following day this proposal was made public in an interview with the Chairman of the Socialist Unity Party in West Berlin (SEW), G. Danelius, published in the central organ of the SED.[19] Soon afterwards the offer was repeated by the Chairman of the GDR Council of Ministers, Willy Stoph, in a letter to the Mayor of West Berlin.[20]

The lines connecting the West German feelers to the Soviet Embassy in Rolandseck and the GDR proposal cannot be traced with certainty. As the USSR had apparently been considering a political barter of this kind for some time, it could well have been Brezhnev who brought up the idea during his talks with Ulbricht on 17 February, i.e., before the latter returned home. The situation created by Kiesinger's soundings may have also been discussed during Prime Minister Kosygin's talks with the GDR Ambassador, Bittner, on 20 February. Events moved so quickly that on 22 February the Soviet Ambassador to the Federal Republic had not received any instructions on the matter.[21] It seems certain that the SED leaders were less than pleased by the Soviet proposal. Although they followed up the Moscow recommendation with their own proposals, their reluctance was apparent when it came to putting the barter idea into effect. The GDR authorities made no preparations for the suggested talks with West Berlin, even though time was short. When the talks on the issuing of border passes finally began on 26 February, the GDR representatives blocked all hopes of progress by making unacceptable demands and raising preconditions.[22] The GDR's behaviour came as no surprise. From the point of view of the SED officials it must have seemed hard to accept that the GDR, having already had to abandon its actions against West Berlin, should now also have to meet the political cost of a settlement.

For the USSR it must have been embarrassing to see the GDR sabotage the proposed arrangement.[23] As no agreement was reached and the USSR had no wish to provoke a serious conflict with the West over Berlin, the *Bundesversammlung* was able to meet on 5 March 1969 in West Berlin without having to suffer any real harassment.[24] Based on the experience at the beginning of February that pressures merely brought the Federal Republic and the Western powers closer together, Moscow may have been induced to ease its relations with Bonn. The Soviet leaders were confronted more clearly than ever with the realization that their actions in Czechoslovakia in August 1968 had heightened Western sensitivity to threats from the East, and that therefore their previous policy of selective détente aimed against West Germany no longer had any prospects of success. Moreover, since the military intervention in Czechoslovakia, the USSR's relations with China had reached a new low level. Immediately before the convocation of the *Bundesversammlung* in West Berlin, the first armed clashes between the two Communist superpowers had taken place and were given much publicity. Certainly from that date onwards it was in the USSR's interests to achieve some kind of political arrangement in Europe.[25] Finally, it also is possible that in the winter of 1968–9 the Soviet leaders' desire – articulated some nine months later – to solve their country's economic problems with Western, and not least West German, assistance played a role in determining Soviet policy.[26]

The Budapest Appeal and the Question of Relations with the Federal Republic

On 17 March 1969 the Party leaders of the Warsaw Pact member-countries, meeting in Budapest, issued a public appeal.[27] This document differed in several respects from previous declarations. The usual 'anti-revanchist' and 'anti-militaristic' polemics were absent, and the Federal Republic was no longer singled out for special treatment. Instead, the appeal spoke of cooperation and trust between the peoples of Europe. Those demands which were addressed to the Federal Republic were mild in comparison with the substantial catalogue presented at Karlovy Vary;[28] and they were reduced more or less to the dimensions of the Bucharest declaration of 6 July 1966.[29] The demands included the 'inviolability of Europe's borders, including the borders along the Oder and Neisse rivers and the border between the GDR and the Federal Republic'; 'recognition of the existence of the GDR and the Federal Republic as a fact'; West German renunciation of the claim to sole representation of all Germany and of control over nuclear weapons 'in any form'; and acceptance of a special status for West Berlin, separate from the West German state. These were held to be the 'basic prerequisites of European security'. However, it was conspicuous that, unlike previously, there was no requirement that the Federal Republic meet all these demands before negotiations could even begin. Some time later the Soviet Ambassador to Bonn again assured representatives of the Federal government that there were no preconditions attached to the opening of a diplomatic dialogue.[30] Thus if Bonn wanted to respond to the Eastern proposals, it would find itself with a certain amount of political room for manoeuvre. It would now be possible to begin talks with Moscow on how the Eastern demands could be satisfied and on what West Germany could expect in return. However, for the most part the programme outlined in the Budapest Appeal did not so much emphasize the desirability of a bilateral Soviet–West German bargaining process as the holding of a multi-lateral European Conference. If the Federal Republic were to agree to such a procedure, without corresponding guarantees, it could turn out that the slogans of European security and cooperation, in essence, would mean acceptance by West Germany of demands made by the Warsaw Pact countries.

According to information passed on to a West German correspondent in Budapest, the phrasing of the appeal was not arrived at without controversy. The delegations from the GDR and Poland had supposedly pressed for the adoption of a harsh, anti-West German line but were opposed by the Romanians in particular and, in a more cautious manner, by the Hungarians. When the East Germans sought support from the USSR, this was refused.[31] Even if the exact source of this report is not known, the mere fact that it was leaked by one of the East European allies has important implications. The partners of the GDR were obviously concerned to make clear to the West German public that extreme interpretations of the appeal, which might reach the Federal Republic from East Berlin in particular, would not correspond to the intentions of its major sponsors. It is highly unlikely that such a signal would have been given contrary to Soviet wishes. This is corroborated further by the subsequent covert conflict between the USSR and the GDR concerning the correct course to be followed over the Federal Republic. It is therefore fairly certain that the SED leaders pressed for clearly anti-West German phraseology in Budapest and that it was due to Soviet support that a more conciliatory line prevailed.

From then onwards there were increasing indications that the Soviet leaders wanted to improve relations with the Federal Republic. Although the anti-West German polemics in the Soviet press were not toned down to the same degree as in the Budapest Appeal, they were certainly more reserved than usual – with the sole exception of the army newspaper.[32] During a visit to Moscow a West German journalist with good connections in leading circles of the CDU received assurances from several influential Soviet discussion partners that the USSR was greatly interested in cultivating good relations with the Federal Republic.[33] Brezhnev and Kosygin demonstrated their interest in the Federal Republic during an international exhibition in Moscow. Instead of their normal practice of avoiding the West German stand, they made a point of visiting it and stopping for a chat. Demonstrations in front of the Soviet Embassy in Rolandseck, which had got out of hand, were given noticeably low-key treatment.[34]

On 25 March 1969, at a conference marking the fiftieth anniversary of the founding of the Comintern, the Soviet speakers, M. Suslov and B. Ponomarov, criticized the Stalinist thesis of the 1920s and 1930s, according to which Social Democracy was the main danger and should be treated as the main enemy. The Communist party, in attempting to appeal to the masses behind the backs of the Social Democrats, had isolated itself to a certain extent and brought about a sectarian situation.[35] Since, during the period in question, Soviet attention had been directed towards relations with the SPD, it was clear that this was an indirect reference to relations with the West German Social Democrats.[36] Furthermore, the Soviet hosts are said to have encouraged their foreign guests to lend the SPD as much support as possible.[37] However, this was unacceptable to the SED leaders. In his speech Ulbricht stressed the continued need for a 'principled struggle' against the Social Democrats, whom he attacked as being 'bourgeois agents

53

operating among the working class', opponents of the class struggle and responsible for the Nazi seizure of power. As for the SPD, he continued, the Communists must close their ranks, increase their vigilance and rely on their own efforts.[38] He is said to have openly protested against the Soviet appeal for a change of policy.[39] The GDR leaders further made clear that they would continue their hostility to the SPD and try to persuade their East European partners of the perfidiousness of the Social Democrats.[40]

At the same time Ulbricht and his supporters took pains to prevent any aspect of West German foreign policy appearing in a positive light. Wherever such a danger arose they denounced it as a mere change of tactics, leaving the essential basis of policy totally unaffected. What is more, Bonn's apparent change of attitude was declared to be nothing more than a deceitful diversionary manoeuvre, incomparably more evil and dangerous than the previously open aggression. By seeking to obfuscate its real aims, and drawing new strength from its adaptation to changed realities, 'West German revanchism' threatened to penetrate the 'socialist community' and undermine it from the inside. The struggle of the Warsaw Pact states to 'promote European security' was essentially a 'struggle against West German revanchism' – which implied the need not only for a struggle against 'revanchist forces' within the Federal Republic, but also against the whole West German state.[41] The GDR portrayed itself as the guarantor of European security, holding the West German danger in check and therefore being entitled to ask other states for support in its demands on the Federal Republic.[42]

In particular the SED leaders demanded that their claim to recognition under international law be accepted unconditionally by the Federal Republic, if the talk of a change of mind on the part of the latter was to be believed.[43] In other words, Bonn would have to meet East German demands as a pre-condition of any dialogue.[44] This would have given the GDR leaders the right to decide at what point their sovereign rights had been achieved and, consequently, when their allies could be allowed to begin negotiations with the Federal government. However, the Soviet leaders were not prepared to leave the desired establishment of political contacts with Bonn to the discretion of their East German allies.[45]

The SED leadership was obliged to back down to a certain extent. For instance, the SED virtually ceased to mention directly the idea of political preconditions attached to political discussions with the Federal Republic. Instead, the leaders of the Party suggested more cautiously that the fulfilment of East European demands presented a 'decisive objective precondition' or a 'central problem' of 'European security'.

54

Final agreements, rather than negotiations were now said to depend on the satisfaction of GDR demands. Even so, SED spokesmen did their best to hinder preparations for a dialogue with the Federal government. As long as Bonn failed to renounce its previous attitudes on the German problem, they claimed, it was imposing 'unreasonable preconditions' on political discussion, in essence demanding acceptance of its terms by the East Europeans. For all practical purposes, this kind of reasoning adopted by the SED was the same as the one used previously, namely that it would not be worthwhile to talk to the Federal government until it had renounced its views.[46] Soviet spokesmen replied by pointing out that the increasing international standing of the GDR was an irreversible trend[47] – the implication being that there was no need to enforce GDR claims prematurely. Accordingly the joint declaration by the USSR and the GDR of 14 July 1969 states that West German attempts at international discrimination were destined to fail, and that it would be in West Germany's own interests to revise its political stance. Relations between the USSR and GDR and the Federal Republic could 'only develop on the basis of generally accepted norms of international law governing relations between sovereign states'.[48]

Despite clearly manifest Soviet interest in a rapprochement with the Federal Republic, there were no diplomatic moves in that direction during the spring and summer of 1969. The demands put forward by Moscow were not meant to be a starting point but the final objective of future negotiations. However, they met with only limited sympathy in West Germany. Soviet policy-makers were accordingly waiting to see what the situation would be in Bonn after the Federal elections. Apparently contrary to initial Soviet intentions, the preparatory political dialogue shifted from the level of inter-governmental exchange to exploratory contacts with the SPD. The visit of a Social Democrat delegation to Moscow in mid-August 1969 represented an important stage in this development. Thus, as the summer drew to a close, it became increasingly evident that the Soviet Union would welcome an SPD electoral victory and the formation of an SPD-led government. Meanwhile the GDR continued to attack the Federal Republic in general and the SPD in particular.[49] Thus the result in the elections and the decision to form a coalition government of SPD and FDP met with a positive response from Moscow.[50] Speaking of East Berlin on 6 October 1969, Brezhnev praised this development as an 'undoubted victory for the democratic forces in the Federal Republic' and declared that the USSR would welcome 'a change towards realism in the policies of the Federal Republic' and would be ready to respond accordingly.[51] Ulbricht, on the other hand, issued a further warning against West German policy, which he still classified as being nothing but aggressive and hostile, even under Social Democratic leadership;[52] however, he stopped short of an unambiguous and irrevocable condemnation of the Soviet desire for improved relations.

The Decision to begin Negotiations with Bonn, December 1969

The Soviet leaders wanted to take advantage of the favourable situation which had arisen in Bonn. On 31 October 1969, in their Prague Declaration, the Warsaw Pact states renewed their suggestion of a European conference. They put forward proposals for an agenda and for two resolutions. The demands directed at the Federal Republic hardly figured in these documents – all that was mentioned was the need to recognize and respect the 'territorial integrity of all European states within their present borders'.[53] The GDR delegation tried in vain to gain acceptance of an anti-West German line. The SED leaders were particularly worried at the prospect of bilateral discussions between their allies – particularly the USSR – and the Federal Republic.[54] The new Federal government had by this time made it known that it wanted to discuss problems of special interest on a bilateral basis with the states in the Soviet sphere of influence and would only consider the idea of a European conference after bilateral negotiations had been successfully concluded. In these circumstances the fact that the Prague declaration failed to reiterate familiar demands on the Federal Republic could be taken to imply East European readiness to go along with the procedure as suggested by Bonn. However, the East German leaders regarded this as most dangerous. If the Federal government were able to make Soviet-bloc demands a matter of negotiation, and even use its approval of a European conference as a bargaining counter, there would be no prospect of an automatic and speedy recognition of the GDR. But this is precisely what East Berlin hoped to gain from such a conference. What is more, there was a danger that West Germany would come to some kind of arrangement with the USSR and other states at the expense of the GDR.

The dissonance between Moscow and East Berlin reached such proportions that the difficulties which had arisen could only be overcome by a calling a further meeting of the member-countries of the Warsaw Pact. As the majority of the participants were interested in talks with the new leaders in Bonn, several attempts were made to encourage the SED to give up its opposition to a preliminary bilateral phase of negotiations. As a result, Ulbricht and his followers, who had arrived in Moscow on 1 December 1969, a full two days before the meeting was officially due to begin, found themselves entangled in numerous bilateral preparatory talks held informally.[55] The communiqué issued at the end of the two days of official discussions on 4 December 1969 expressed the determination of the participants 'to develop relations with those states in Europe' that were ready to engage in cooperation 'according to the principles of equality, non-interference in internal affairs, respect for sovereignty, territorial integrity and inviolability of existing borders'. At the same time it was stressed that 'all states [should] establish relations with the German Democratic Republic on the basis of equality and in accordance with the principles of international law, and recognize the existing borders in Europe, including the Oder–Neisse border, as final and inviolable' As for the evaluation of West German policy, the tone fell somewhere. between hopeful expectation and continued concern.[56]

Implied in the phrasing of the declaration was the consent to bilateral talks with the Federal Republic – though subject to the condition that West Germany accept in particular the basic principle of the inviolability of existing borders. This was in the interests of the GDR as well as the USSR. The idea that all countries – and the Federal Republic in particular should establish relations with the GDR on a basis of equality and according to the principles of international law, if they wanted to receive favourable responses from the Warsaw Pact states, was designed to meet East Germany's particular needs. For the SED leaders this represented an important step forward from the Budapest appeal, which had merely called for 'recognition of the existence of the GDR'. Finally, in order to ensure concerted action, the communiqué contained an undertaking to engage in mutual consultations on future talks. The East German party officials could now hope that they would not be excluded from any arrangement with the Federal Republic. At the same time the Soviet leaders could be sure of retaining the right to supervise the bilateral contacts established by the smaller Warsaw Pact states with the West.[57]

In November 1969, the USSR had already made diplomatic contact with the new leaders in Bonn. These discussions were now intensified.[58] Following the Moscow meeting, several other of the GDR's allies began to put out feelers towards Bonn.[59] In these circumstances Ulbricht and his supporters considered it advisable to create the impression of at least going along with this new development. On 26 December 1969 they presented the Federal Republic with the draft of a treaty between the two German states on full mutual recognition under international law. The proposed terms were so extreme that the SED leaders could be sure that the Federal Republic would reject the draft even as a basis for discussion,[60] thereby providing evidence to the GDR's allies of the 'revanchist' obduracy of the 'new' regime in Bonn. On the other hand, the draft, correspondingly modified, could serve as a starting point for GDR participation in the

57

process of negotiations with the Federal Republic should this become necessary at some future point. In the course of the next nine months, however, the SED did not show the slightest inclination to realize such a prospect. By the time they made the first hesitant steps in that direction, the political constellation had already changed radically.

References

1. See C.-W. Sanne, 'Zur Vorgeschichte des Vertrages', *Der Vertrag vom 12 August 1970 zwischen der Bundesrepublik Deutschland und der Union des Sozialistischen Sowjetrepubliken*, Bonn: Federal Press and Information Office, September 1970, pp. 75-9; H. U. Behn, 'Chronik zur Vorgeschichte des Vertrags', ibid., pp. 115-32. Documents: *Die Auswartige Politik der Bundesrepublik Deutschland*, published by the Foreign Ministry in collaboration with a scientific advisory board, Cologne 1972, pp. 593, 611-14 and 624-9; *Izvestiya*, 13 and 14 July 1968; *Europa-Archiv*, No. 16 (1968), pp. D362-86.

2. L. Whetten, 'The Role of East Germany in West German–Soviet Relations', *The World Today*, No. 12 (1969), p. 508.

3. H. Allardt, *Moskauer Tagebuch*, Düsseldorf, 1973, pp. 128-30.

4. L. Whetten, op. cit., p. 508; H. Allardt, op. cit., p. 160.

5. 'Soviet–U.S. Relations Under the Nixon Administration – A Search for Dialogue and Detente, Nov. 1968–March 1969, Part I: 6 November–20 January', Radio Liberty: *Research Bulletin*, CRD 109/69, 24 March 1969.

6. Since the beginning of 1967 the USSR had emphasized its right, if not duty, to intervene in the Federal Republic to avert dangers to peace resulting from 'revanchism' and 'neo-Nazism'. Following the military intervention in Czechoslovakia this doctrine rebounded back on the Soviet Union. The prospect of USSR intervening in West Germany was now seen as evidence of the Soviet Union's dangerous expansionist intentions.

7. G. Wettig, 'Die Berlin-Krise 1969', *Osteuropa*, No. 9 (1969), pp. 686 ff.

8. H. Allardt, op. cit., p. 154.

9. Reports in the West German press, for example, claimed that 'a friendly power' had strongly advised the Federal President against it. The three Western Ambassadors in Bonn responded immediately to a protest from Ambassador Abrasimov in January with a verbal rejection. See also the commentary in the section 'Erläuterungen' in *Das Viermächte-Abkommen über Berlin vom 3 September 1971*, Bonn: Federal Press and Information Office, September 1971, p. 157.

10. Communiqué of 5 February 1969 of the Joint GDR–Soviet Commission set up pursuant to the Treaty of 20 September 1955: *Aussenpolitische Korrespondenz*, No. 7 (1969), p. 53. As Ulbricht was in Moscow at this time, the decision was probably taken there.

11. For documents see: *Aussenpolitische Korrespondenz*, No. 7 (1969), pp. 49-53; *Deutschland-Archiv*, No. 3 (1969), pp. 299-303.

12. G. Wettig, 'Die Berlin Krise', op. cit., pp. 687 ff.

13. The working group on Berlin, in which the three Western powers are represented along with the Federal Republic, protested loudly and clearly just two days later. The British Prime Minister repeated his country's commitment

to defend the security of West Berlin. The American President announced that he was to visit the city.

14. G. Wettig, 'Die Berlin Krise', op. cit., pp. 688, 690 and 692. The fact that thoughts of serious reprisals had been abandoned was disguised by statements of a potentially threatening nature – but nothing concrete ever came of them; so, for instance, the announcement of joint USSR–GDR manoeuvres on 20 February 1969 (Deutschland-Archiv, No. 3 (1969), p. 305); a note from the government of the USSR to the government of the GDR of 28 January 1969 (Pravda, 1 March 1969; Aussenpolitische Korrespondenz, No. 10 (1969), p. 73; Deutschland-Archiv, No. 3 (1969), pp. 311 f.); and the declaration of the Soviet representative at the Berlin Air Security Control at the beginning of March 1969 (Deutschland-Archiv, No. 3 (1969), p. 313).

15. This was also the impression of the Federal Republic's Ambassador to Moscow, who incidentally still thinks that the Soviet leaders had no intention of straining their relations with Bonn. In his view the Soviet Union, from the beginning, was doing nothing more than 'fulfilling its duty' towards the GDR: H. Allardt, Moskauer Tagebuch, op. cit., p. 156.

16. On 22 March 1969 Ulbricht gave vent to his displeasure at Soviet behaviour with the bitter remark that 'the West German imperialist press' was 'most satisfied with the situation which has arisen' in West Berlin (Aussenpolitische Korrespondenz, No. 13 (1969), p. 98). The Soviet Ambassador to East Berlin made it clear that the final responsibility for events in connection with the Federal Presidential elections lay with his own government – and not with the government of the GDR (H. Allardt, Moskauer Tagebuch, op. cit., p. 154).

17. Chancellor Kiesinger's assurances in a later conversation with Ambassador Tsarapkin that he was thinking only of a lasting agreement on visits was not accepted. For coverage of the events see the reports in Die Welt, 22 March 1969 and Der Spiegel, 24 March 1969, p. 29 (presumably based to a large extent on Soviet information) and the declaration by the Press Secretary of the Soviet Embassy of 14 March 1969.

18. Text: Deutschland-Archiv, No. 3 (1969), p. 307.

19. Text: ibid.

20. See the corresponding bulletin of the GDR Presseamt of 25 February 1969, in Deutschland-Archiv, No. 3 (1969), p. 308.

21. The Soviet Ambassador consequently was unable to furnish additional information during his talk that day with the Chancellor. See reports in Frankfurter Allgemeine Zeitung, 24 February 1969; K. R. Dreher in Süddeutsche Zeitung, 25 February 1969; Der Spiegel, 3 March 1969, p. 25.

22. They not only refused point blank to discuss the request of their opposite numbers for a border pass agreement beyond the Easter period. They also demanded that the West Berlin Senate definitely call off the holding of the Bundesversammlung in the city before any talks could take place concerning an agreement for Easter (no concessions were offered by East Berlin). Moreover, this was to be done in a form demonstrating Senate jurisdiction over West German federal bodies, thereby practically declaring Federal presence in West Berlin to be an illegal interference in the affairs of a foreign state. See official bulletins on the meetings in Deutschland-Archiv, No. 3 (1969), pp. 310 ff. and 314–16.

23. Western correspondents in Moscow at the time were of the impression that the Soviet leaders wanted to achieve some kind of settlement. They were told by Soviet sources that the USSR had again put pressure on the GDR to adopt a less negative attitude. West German insistence on a long-term border pass agreement created considerable problems for Moscow. But if genuine negotiations had got under way a compromise would have been possible.

24. See G. Wettig, 'Die Berlin Krise', op. cit., p. 693.

25. The Soviet Union responded to the SED leaders' objections to Gromyko's conciliatory remarks directed at the Federal Republic and the Western powers on 10 July 1969 by reference to the strained relations with China. Leslie Colitt in *The Observer*, 17 August 1969.

26. See Brezhnev's remarks to the Central Committee of the CPSU on 15 December 1969, excerpts in *Pravda*, 13 January 1970 (leading article); commentary and evaluation by G. Gwertzmann in *International Herald Tribune*, 17 January 1970 and in C. Duevel, 'Brezhnev's Secret Report', Radio Liberty: *Research Bulletin*, CRD 29/70, 29 January 1970. On the subject of Soviet economic problems see K. Bush, 'The Implementation of the Soviet Economic Reform, Timetable and Results', Radio Liberty: *Research Bulletin*, CRD 288/69, 30 June 1969; 'The Soviet Economic Dilemma', ibid., CRD 148/70, 28 April 1970; R. W. Judy, 'The Case of Computer Technology', in S. Wasowski, ed., *East–West Trade and the Technology Gap*, New York, Washington and London, 1970, pp. 43–72; J. Nötzold, *Untersuchungen zur Durchsetzung des technischen Fortschritts in der sowjetischen Wirtschaft*, Stiftung Wissenschaft und Politik, Ebenhausen, 1972, p. 207, and the case-studies by H.-J. Wagener, J. Slama, H. Vogel and G. Fink in ibid. (supplementary volume), p. 207A.

27. Text: *Pravda*, 18 March 1969 (in Russian); *Aussenpolitische Korrespondenz*, No. 12 (1969), pp. 89 ff.; *Europa-Archiv*, No. 7 (1969), pp. D151–3 (in German). The German version occasionally uses slightly different phraseology; for instance, it speaks of 'recognition of the existence of the GDR and the West German Federal Republic', whereas the Russian reads 'recognition of the fact of the existence of the GDR and the Federal Republic'. Quotes are taken from the Russian text.

28. See the Karlovy Vary Declaration of European Communist Parties of 26 April 1967, *Pravda*, 27 April 1967 (in Russian); *Dokumentation der Zeit*, No. 383 (1967), pp. 37–40; *Europa-Archiv*, No. 11 (1967), pp. D259–66 (in German).

29. Text: *Pravda*, 9 July 1966 (in Russian); *Europa-Archiv*, No. 16 (1966), pp. D414–24 (in German).

30. *Frankfurter Allgemeine Zeitung*, 8 May 1969; *Frankfurter Rundschau*, 8 May 1969; *Neue Zürcher Zeitung*, 9 May 1969; report by the German press agency (dpa), 21 May 1969. See also the toast given by Ambassador P. Abrasimov on 12 June 1969, *Neues Deutschland*, 13 June 1969.

31. H.-U. Kempski in *Süddeutsche Zeitung*, 19 March 1969.

32. R. A. Remington, *The Warsaw Pact: Case Studies in Communist Conflict Resolution*, Cambridge, Mass., and London, 1971, p. 116.

33. See the travel report by R. Heizler, *Bonner Rundschau*, 26 March 1969.

34. H. Allardt, op. cit., pp. 180–3.

35. *Kommunist*, No. 5 (1969), pp. 9 and 24. See also B. Ponomarov in *Probleme des Friedens und des Sozialismus*, No. 2 (1969), p. 153.

36. It is normal practice in the 'esoteric' way of conducting inter-communist differences of opinion for an ideologically charged political controversy, such as the correct attitude towards the SPD, to be discussed in disguised form, for example, by reference to the past.

37. L. Whetten, op. cit. (see note 2), p. 509, relying on records by the *Washington Post*, 27 March 1969; *International Herald Tribune*, 28 March 1969; *Zycie Warszawy*, 1 April 1969; and on an analysis by Radio Free Europe of 1 March 1969. According to the Italian Communist Party the first half of 1968 saw a first agreement between SPD and CPSU concerning, among other things, a relaxation of relations between the USSR and the Federal Republic and assurances concerning opportunities for political action on the part of West German communists. See H. Timmermann, 'Im Vorfeld der neuen Ostpolitik. Der Dialog zwischen italienischen Kommunisten und deutschen Sozialdemokraten', *Osteuropa*, No. 6 (1971), pp. 388–99.

38. Text: *Neues Deutschland*, 26 March 1969.

39. L. Whetten, op. cit., p. 509. Ulbricht left Moscow without having met Brezhnev. He was seen off at the airport by Central Committee Secretaries Pelshe and Katushev and not by Brezhnev or Podgorny.

40. See Ulbricht's speech to the National Front on 22 March 1969, *Aussenpolitische Korrespondenz*, No. 13 (1969), pp. 99–102; H. Barth, 'Europäische Sicherheit – ein dringendes Gebot der Gegenwart', *Einheit*, No. 6 (1969), p. 690; R. Graf, 'Bonner Alleinvertretungsanmassung: Haupthindernis für friedliches Sicherheitssystem', ibid., No. 8 (1969), p. 925; report by Ulbricht at the XI session of the Central Committee on 31 July 1969, *Neues Deutschland*, 1 August 1969.

41. See the *Izvestiya* interview with Foreign Minister O. Winzer on 16 April 1969, *Aussenpolitische Korrespondenz*, No. 17 (1969), p. 129 and Winzer's remarks at an international conference in East Berlin 21 May 1969, ibid., No. 22 (1969), p. 171; H. Barth, op. cit., p. 690; R. Graf, op. cit., pp. 923 and 925; the toast by W. Stoph at an athletics meeting in Leipzig on 27 July 1969, *Neues Deutschland*, 28 July 1969; the report by H. Axen to the 11th session of the Central Committee on 29 July 1969, ibid., 30 July 1969; the report by W. Stoph to the 11th session of the Central Committee on 30 July 1969, ibid., 31 July 1969; and the report by W. Ulbricht to the 11th session of the Central Committee on 31 July 1969, ibid., 1 August 1969.

42. O. Winzer on 16 April 1969, *Aussenpolitische Korrespondenz*, No. 17 (1969), p. 130; R. Graf, op. cit., pp. 924 and 927 f.

43. See W. Ulbricht on 22 March 1969, *Aussenpolitische Korrespondenz*, No. 13 (1969), pp. 97–102; speech by O. Winzer to the GDR Staatsrat on 30 March 1969, *Neues Deutschland*, 1 April 1969; report by E. Honecker to the X session of the Central Committee on 28 April 1969, ibid., 29 April 1969; and the report by W. Ulbricht to the X session of the Central Committee on 29 April 1969, *Aussenpolitische Korrespondenz*, No. 21 (1969), p. 164 and No. 22 (1969), p. 175.

44. See W. Ulbricht on 22 March 1969, ibid., No. 13 (1969), pp. 97–102;

O. Winzer on 16 April 1969, ibid., No. 17 (1969), pp. 129–31; interview with the Deputy Foreign Minister O. Fischer on Radio GDR, 14 May 1969, ibid., No. 21 (1969), p. 167; R. Graf, op. cit., pp. 924 ff., 928, 930 933, and 935.

45. The summary of Ulbricht's speech of 22 March 1969 in *Izvestiya*, 23 and 24 March 1969, does not refer to these remarks. The interview with O. Winzer, which was to appear in the same paper, was not published. The GDR's claim of protecting other states was only recognized by the Soviet Union in a general and non-committal form. See V. Khvostov, 'Politicheskoe znachenie GDR', *Mezhdunarodnaya zhizn*, No. 7 (1969), pp. 62–6.

46. See O. Winzer on 21 May 1969, *Aussenpolitische Korrespondenz*, No. 22 (1969), pp. 172–4; W. Ulbricht, *in Pravda*, 12 June 1969; H. Barth, op. cit., p. 690; R. Graf, op. cit., pp. 924, 928 and 935; W. Ulbricht on 31 July 1969, *Neues Deutschland*, 1 August 1969; 'Bonn behindert europäische Sicherheitskonferenz', *Aussenpolitische Korrespondenz*, No. 3 (1969), pp. 257 ff.

47. Speech by A. Gromyko to the Supreme Soviet on 10 July 1969, *Pravda*, 11 July 1969; Brezhnev's welcoming speech to the Party and Government delegation from the GDR on 7 July 1969, ibid., 8 July 1969; message from the Soviet leadership to the SED on 6 October 1969, ibid., 7 October 1969; and the speech by L. Brezhnev in East Berlin on 6 October 1969, ibid., 7 October 1969.

48. Text: ibid., 15 July 1969 (in Russian); *Aussenpolitische Korrespondenz*, No. 30 (1969), pp. 233–8 (in German). Significantly only the development of, not the preparation for, relations with the Federal Republic were made dependent on a sovereign relationship between the two states based on international law.

49. See H. Allardt, op. cit. (note 3), pp. 145, 151–3, 160–5 and 205–7; G. Zalitach, 'Die Regierung Brandt aus der Sicht der Moskauer Presse', *Osteuropa*, No. 7 (1970), pp. 467–71; H.-U. Behn, op. cit. (note 1), pp. 132–5; R. A. Remington, op. cit. (note 32), p. 121.

50. H. Allardt, op. cit., p. 214; *Frankfurter Allgemeine Zeitung*, 4 April 1972 (see also the report by H. Pörzgen on the same subject); G. Zalitach, op. cit., pp. 471–3.

51. Text: *Pravda*, 7 October 1969.

52. Text: *Neues Deutschland*, 7 October 1969. Only excerpts of the speech appeared in *Pravda*, 7 October 1969, and then only in milder form. Similarly, Brezhnev's speech appeared in the GDR press in mutilated form. See also R. W. Herrick, 'Brezhnev, Ulbricht Leave Door Open for Detente Talks with Bonn', Radio Liberty: *Research Bulletin*, CRD 351/69, 23 October 1969.

53. Texts: *Pravda*, 1 November 1969 (in Russian); *Europa-Archiv*, No. 23 (1969), pp. D551–3 (in German); *Europa-Archiv*, No. 4 (1970), pp. D89–90.

54. R. A. Remington, op. cit. (note 32), pp. 122 ff.

55. A. Jacob in *Le Monde*, 4 December 1969; *Frankfurter Allgemeine Zeitung*, 4 December 1969.

56. *Pravda*, 5 December 1969 (in Russian); *Europa-Archiv*, No. 4 (1970), pp. D76 ff. (in German).

57. See R. W. Herrick, 'Moscow Summit Sanctions Controlled Steps toward Bilateral Detente with Bonn', Radio Liberty: *Research Bulletin*, CRD 417/69, 15 December 1969.

58. C.-W. Sanne, op. cit. (note 1), p. 80; H.-U. Behn, op. cit. (note 1), p. 137; H. Allardt, op. cit. (note 3), p. 260.

59. See *Rudé Pravo*, 10 December 1969; *Le Monde*, 13 December 1969.

60. Text: *Aussenpolitische Korrespondenz*, No. 52 (1969), p. 402.

VI

Negotiations with the Federal Republic, January–August 1970

The political Dialogue between the Soviet Union and the Federal Republic, January–March 1970

The talks between Foreign Minister Gromyko and Ambassador Allardt, begun on 8 December 1969 in Moscow with a view to improving Soviet–West German relations, revealed that the two sides held opposing views on many points. The Soviet Minister tried to test West German resolve by pressing maximum demands. His opposite number tried to determine whether Moscow had any serious interest in a political settlement with the Federal Republic, rejecting at the same time the idea of a unilateral recognition of the Soviet sphere.[1] The point at issue was whether Bonn would recognize the political *status quo* in Eastern and Central Europe in exchange for Soviet acceptance of the political *status quo* in West Berlin. From the course of the talks the Federal government concluded that it must give some visible sign of a fresh start in Soviet–West German relations. State Secretary Bahr, a personal adviser and close friend of Chancellor Brandt, assumed responsibility for the dialogue and received new instructions.[2] In taking this decision, the Federal government took as its target the conclusion of a treaty with the USSR.

From 30 January to 8 February 1970 Bahr discussed the question of a renunciation of force agreement with Foreign Minister Gromyko in Moscow. Initially Bonn saw such a treaty exclusively in terms of a mutual renunciation of the use and threat of force. The USSR, on the other hand, felt that agreement on renunciation of force could only be meaningful if a simultaneous attempt were made to settle the conflicts which threatened to involve the use of force. Above all, the Federal Republic's refusal to recognize the existing borders in Europe was said to be a dangerous source of tension. And for this reason, in conjunction with the principle of renunciation of force, there was to be recognition of the principle of the irrevocability of the borders.[3]

During the first round of talks it appears that State Secretary Bahr was prepared to accept in principle the Soviet idea of a direct link between renunciation of force and a settlement of border issues.[4] Gromyko's demand for the sanctioning of existing borders in Europe meant first of all that the Federal Republic should recognize the *status quo* as absolutely unalterable, renounce all future claims to the reunification of Germany and to national self-determination for the German people, and no longer tolerate the expression of such claims within the country or abroad.[5] But it also meant that the USSR wanted the Federal Republic to accept its role as trustee of the other Warsaw Pact states and thereby recognize indirectly the USSR's hegemony in Eastern Europe[6] in accordance with the so-called 'Brezhnev Doctrine'.[7] The Federal Republic should undertake to respect the 'irrevocability of the borders', the 'territorial integrity of all states in Europe' and especially the inviolability of the Oder–Neisse border and the border between the two German states. In its relations with the GDR it should meet certain requirements and regard the agreements to be reached with the countries in the Soviet sphere of influence as 'an integral whole'.[8]

During the course of the discussions, the international status of the GDR and the nature of the relationship between the two German states played an important part. In his government declaration of 28 October 1969 Chancellor Brandt had met the East Europeans half way: for the first time in an official West German statement the existence of two German states had been recognized, thereby accepting the GDR unconditionally as a political counterpart to the Federal Republic. However, at the same time Brandt had excluded the possibility of 'recognition of the GDR by the Federal government under international law', and he declared that the two German states were 'not foreign countries to each other', their mutual relations being 'of a special nature'.[9] For its part Moscow backed the claim of the SED leaders to unconditional legal recognition of the GDR, and acquiesced in the East German rejection of any kind of all-German community with the Federal Republic.[10]

From Bonn's point of view 'foreign' relations between the two German states were out of the question inasmuch as German capacity to act independently was limited by authority still vested in the former occupying powers. The three Western states, suspicious of Soviet intentions, had deliberately and *expressis verbis* retained responsibilities concerning Berlin and Germany as a whole. In their view the Four Powers were competent to act in all 'German' affairs extending beyond the borders of any one of the two separate states. This seemed necessary, since the division had been a consequence of Four-Power occupation and therefore could only be overcome on this basis. As far as the Federal government was concerned Germany, after it had ceased to exist as a state, still remained an international legal entity under Four-Power jurisdiction. The victorious powers had an inalienable and supreme responsibility for the situation in West Berlin. The right of access, which belied GDR jurisdiction and arbitrary actions on the transit routes, could only be maintained and justified if the two German states did not enjoy unconditional competence to act under international law, but were obliged to respect superior norms codified in inter-Allied agreements.

Taking this as his starting point, State Secretary Bahr pointed out to Foreign Minister Gromyko that there was no possibility of the Federal Republic unconditionally recognizing the GDR under international law until such time as a Peace Treaty was concluded. And until that time the rights of the four former occupying powers had continued validity for Berlin and Germany as a whole. The Federal Republic could not exercise power over the rights of other states by recognizing the GDR under international law, and deciding unilaterally to settle the question of Germany's division and Germany's border, because this would imply presumption of sovereignty and negation of the competence of the three Western states and the USSR. The same applied to the GDR if it wanted to give formal recognition to the Federal Republic under international law.[11] The argument that recognition along the lines demanded by the SED would necessarily invalidate Soviet rights did not fail to impress the Soviet side.[12]

Gromyko and Bahr agreed that the two German states could not alter their status under international law. In their mutual relations, too, they must take into account the fact of limited room for political and legal manoeuvre, and not assume false status as fully sovereign states by establishing full diplomatic relations. Accordingly the phrase West German 'relations with the GDR based on the principles of full equality, non-discrimination and non-interference in internal affairs' was used.[13] In the Soviet–West German declaration of intent of 22 May 1970, respect for mutual 'independence and autonomy', which was supposed to obtain in relations between the two German states, was expressly applied only to areas of 'domestic legal competence'.[14] Although the Soviet leaders did emphasize their responsibilities in all-German affairs, and consequently gave only limited support to GDR claims, they came no closer to accepting Bonn's concept of a national community of all Germans and a special political relationship between the two German states.[15]

For the GDR the Soviet change of attitude signified not only the loss of crucial political backing in its attempt to gain unconditional recognition from the Federal Republic. The SED leaders also suffered a severe setback in their efforts to free themselves from the state of servitude which had characterized post-war history as a result of the occupation regime. In their view, by fulfilling the terms of the Potsdam Agreement (which they claimed the Federal Republic had not), they had met all the terms laid down by the victorious powers, and had consequently regained complete freedom of action. And for this reason the Western powers could not validly assert access rights to West Berlin either for military or civilian traffic.[16] Likewise, the USSR should no longer be in a position to invoke its rights resulting from the victory of 1945 in its relations with the GDR.

This did not mean that the GDR wanted to emancipate itself from ties with the USSR. As far as the SED leaders were concerned this was ruled out by their unstable internal position and the GDR's rivalry with the larger and more prosperous Federal Republic. This was shown, for example, by the fact that they tried to press the political and economic integration of their country with the USSR as far as possible and that, with the exception of the USSR itself, they were the most enthusiastic proponents of the so-called 'Brezhnev Doctrine'. The GDR leaders' close contacts with Soviet hegemonial power are meant to guarantee their existence, but not to lead to total dependence. Whenever Moscow attacked deviationist tendencies in the 'socialist community' and cultivated particularly close relations with the GDR, SED functionaries could persuade themselves that their mighty ally would never abandon them. But there were no assurances of continued existence implied when the USSR stressed its rights derived from the occupation regime. Quite the contrary: as Ulbricht and his followers learned at the beginning of the 1950s, these rights could be used to force them to accept a policy on Germany which was in direct contradiction to their own ideas on the subject.[17]

The degree to which influential circles in East Berlin opposed the idea of the continued validity of occupation rights is evident from Ulbricht's elaborations at an international press conference on 19 January 1970. In answer to a question concerning Four-Power responsibilities, Ulbricht insisted that the Allied Control Commission, which had previously embodied these responsibilities, was no longer in existence, and that therefore the former occupying powers no longer had such authority with respect to the GDR. 'In none of our negotiations – either in 1955 or since – has the USSR said anything to us about a Four-Power responsibility. We only know the date on which the Control Commission ceased to exist. We know nothing more. We are completely unaware of a Four-Power responsibility for the GDR.' Ulbricht also denied that the Four Powers had any rights with respect to Berlin. He concluded: 'Well, we can really say we have nothing to do with the matter at all. We are a sovereign state and the capital of our sovereign state, our GDR, is Berlin. That is what it says in the [GDR] Constitution and that is how the matter stands.'[18] In a previous statement the SED chief had also referred to a treaty with the USSR as proof of GDR sovereignty, and challenged the Federal Republic to claim equal rights of autonomy (a suggestion which, if West Germany had accepted it in this form, would have represented nothing short of withdrawal from the Western alliance).[19]

On 24 February 1970 Foreign Minister Gromyko visited East Berlin in order to gain East German acceptance of the stage reached so far in talks with State Secretary Bahr. As was to be expected, his mission met with considerable difficulties. The consultations lasted a full four days. In the final communiqué both sides criticized all attempts to prejudice the 'international position and sovereign rights' of the GDR. This served the GDR's need for a demonstration of Soviet support and the USSR's interest in an outward appearance of unqualified solidarity with its East German ally. The formula used was at the same time quite loose, because the USSR since 1955 had always expressed support for the principle of GDR sovereignty, but in practice had asserted certain reservations. What was politically more illuminating, therefore, was the phrasing used with regard to the question of recognition. The GDR, it ran, must participate 'without restriction and on a basis of full equality' in international cooperation. The 'principles of sovereign equality, respect for territorial integrity', 'inviolability of state borders and internal system' were to be the guidelines for inter-state relations. The GDR declared its readiness to regulate its relations with the Federal Republic and other states 'on this basis as generally recognized in international practice'. There was no mention of full diplomatic recognition by Bonn of the GDR under international law. The East German Foreign Minister, in his address to mark the occasion of the Soviet visit, limited himself to demanding recognition of the 'sovereign equality of the GDR and the Federal Republic'.[20] Furthermore, Gromyko apparently persuaded the SED leaders to tone down their polemics against the Federal Republics: the GDR mass media became less abusive. However, the Federal government was still being portrayed as an unworthy negotiation partner.[21]

After the conflict between Moscow and East Berlin had been resolved in the USSR's favour, nothing more stood in the way of discussions on the text of a treaty between Foreign Minister Gromyko and State Secretary Bahr. On 6 March 1970 the Soviet delegation presented a draft, the contents of which had been accepted by the SED leaders.[22] Subsequent discussions concentrated on the form in which existing borders were to be accepted. Soviet negotiators wanted them to be 'irrevocable', meaning that the borders would not be revised under any circumstances. This demand was designed to cement the division of Germany and exclude the possibility of the two German states coming to some kind of agreement on their own. A stipulation of this sort had aroused increasing interest among leading SED officials ever since the Federal Republic had begun to play a role in the process of détente and take up earlier GDR offers of reconciliation.[23] However, State Secretary Bahr rejected the formula of the irrevocability (*nezyblemost'*) of the borders, which would have turned the proposed treaty into a border settlement and therefore given it the air of a sort of peace treaty. In such a case ratification would have required a two-thirds majority, which the ruling SPD/FDP coalition government had no hope of achieving. Foreign Minister Gromyko compromised in that he accepted the formula of the 'indestructibility' (*nerushimost'*) or 'inviolability' (*Unverletzlichkeit* in the German draft) of the borders. He also agreed to the stipulation that the borders be inviolable in conjunction with a preface pointing out the need to preserve peace. This modification also served to prevent the treaty from taking on the appearance of a border settlement.[24] However, the Soviet side continued to lay great stress on the *status quo* being taken as the actual basis of the proposed agreement.[25]

Any attempt by State Secretary Bahr to discuss the Berlin question with the Soviet Foreign Minister also impinged on GDR interests. However, Gromyko refused to discuss Berlin with a representative of the Federal Republic. In so doing he could point to the irrefutable logic of international law: West Germany, the Western powers and the USSR all agreed that the problems concerning Berlin were the responsibility of the four major victorious powers of 1945, who moreover had been conducting negotiations on this very subject since 26 March 1970. However, Soviet objections tended to overlook the political fact that the fate of West Berlin was hardly a matter of indifference to the Federal Republic and that good relations between Moscow and Bonn were inconceivable without a settlement of the Berlin issue along lines acceptable to Bonn.

As the talks between Gromyko and Bahr continued, the Federal Republic was being made the subject of a good deal of press comment. There were clear differences of interpretation between the USSR and the GDR. The tenor of Soviet statements was designed to encourage the Federal government to be even more bold in its new policies. Thus, criticism of the continuation of earlier modes of behaviour was intermingled with approval of decisions advocating change. Where it was necessary to indulge in sharp polemics, blame was laid on the domestic opponents of the Federal government. East Germany, on the other hand, following the meeting of Warsaw Pact member countries in Moscow on 3–4 December 1969, had at first toned down its remarks on West Germany, but had reverted once again to sharp anti-West German attacks at the beginning of 1970. The GDR statements emphasized that a fundamental antagonism existed in relations between the two German states. They tarred both the ruling coalition and the opposition in Bonn with the same brush; progress in détente, they asserted, could only be achieved by putting considerable pressure on leading circles in West Germany. Warnings were given against the 'Trojan horse' tactics of the Social Democrats in their appeals for détente. All the SPD wanted, it was claimed, was to promote the 'export of counter-revolution' into the 'socialist countries'.[26]

In the USSR too there was concern that the Federal Republic might try to 'break off individual countries from the world system of socialism' and 'under the guise of "bridge-building" and "selective coexistence" ' to penetrate into Eastern Europe. However, unlike the GDR, the USSR combined this with an appeal to Bonn 'decisively and unconditionally to put an end to all manifestations of revanchism'.[27] After 22 May 1970, when the talks between Gromyko and Bahr had produced concrete results, Soviet comments concerning the Federal Republic became a shade more positive. At the same time the GDR was obliged to be considerably more guarded in its polemics.[28]

The Meetings Between Chancellor Brandt and Prime Minister Stoph in the Spring of 1970

On 22 January 1970 Chancellor Brandt wrote to the Chairman of the GDR Council of Ministers, Willy Stoph, with the aim of opening a dialogue on the future of relations between the two German states. As the Federal government had made clear on previous occasions, the Chancellor wanted to persuade the representatives of the GDR to agree to a kind of 'orderly co-existence' on the basis of political equality and national community. In so doing he hoped to increase the possibilities for contacts on a private level between Germans in the two parts of the country, which had hitherto been blocked by the SED. The leading party officials in East Berlin were not interested in promoting such a discussion. Prime Minister Stoph replied on 13 February 1970 suggesting joint meetings to discuss the draft treaty presented by the GDR on 17 December 1969, which had dealt exclusively with mutual recognition under international law. At the same time, the East German head of government was not sparing in the reproaches he levelled at the Federal government.[29]

In his reply five days later, Chancellor Brandt set aside all controversial questions and accepted the offer to talk, provided there were no restrictions on the subject-matter. He suggested that representatives of the two sides should meet sometime between 23 and 27 February to prepare the ground for the proposed meeting. His suggestion was accepted by the GDR Prime Minister after some delay, and the first in a series of preparatory talks opened on 2 March.[30] It became apparent that the GDR government had taken up the West German suggestion only with hesitation. Presumably it had felt itself unable simply to reject the Chancellor's conciliatory offer. Judging from subsequent Soviet behaviour, it may be assumed that during his visit to East Berlin from 23 to 27 February, Foreign Minister Gromyko had pressed hard for GDR acceptance. One West German press report – probably based on leaks in the USSR[31] – sounds plausible: Gromyko is said to have come to an understanding with the SED leaders that Stoph would continue to pursue adamantly the GDR claim to full recognition under international law, but would not allow the talks to break down.[32]

It may seem surprising that in the final communiqué of 27 February, 1970 the Soviet Foreign Minister should deny East Germany her claim to recognition under international law[33] and then allow her to use it in the forthcoming talks with the West Germans. But in view of the continuation of the Bahr–Gromyko dialogue, it made a difference whether the Soviet leaders themselves would advocate GDR claims to unconditional recognition or simply allow Ulbricht and his supporters to try their luck over the issue. In any case the Soviet leaders could be sure that the East Germans would have little success. What is more, the inflexibility displayed towards the Federal government at the time by leading SED functionaries had the effect of blocking the GDR's policy on Germany, thus in theory creating room for the Soviet Foreign Minister to conduct talks with State Secretary Bahr without GDR interference. But in practice this required that Chancellor Brandt should not consider himself snubbed over his offer to open a dialogue with Prime Minister Stoph, and that after the meeting there would be no open break betweeen the two heads of government. Also, the increased prestige which the GDR could hope to gain from the meeting would suit Soviet purposes. It would be in Moscow's own interests if, after the meeting,[34] the Soviet mass media could express their unqualified approval of the GDR.[35]

As the SED leaders were reluctant to agree to the Brandt–Stoph meeting, they tried also to avoid coordination with Foreign Minister Gromyko. During the preparatory talks on 2 March 1970, the GDR representatives demanded that Chancellor Brandt should not pass through West Berlin on his way to the first meeting with Prime Minister Stoph, which was scheduled to take place in East Berlin. A 'demonstrative' visit by the Chancellor to the city would 'underline the alleged adherence of West Berlin to the West German Federal

Republic' and would, therefore, be an act 'in contravention of international agreements', which would also affect the forthcoming round of Four-Power negotiations. The GDR could not allow that to happen.[36]

It hardly seems likely that the East German leaders could have expected the Federal government to submit to their conditions. Since, in the past, Brandt and his colleagues had not submitted to much greater pressure over much less fundamental issues of Federal presence in the city, it was not to be expected that they would give way this time, thereby significantly compromising West Germany's position in West Berlin. Moreover, it is hard to imagine how Brandt as Chancellor of the Federal Republic and former Mayor of West Berlin could, from a purely political point of view, have allowed the GDR to forbid him to enter the city. For this reason, the only logical explanation of the actions of the SED leaders is that they wanted to provoke a rejection from West Germany in the hope of thwarting the plans for a Brandt–Stoph meeting.

The Soviet leaders were not in a position to contest East Germany's right to demand a reduction of the Federal presence in West Berlin, because they had supported it in principle in the past. However, the Soviet leaders were not prepared to allow Ulbricht and his supporters to use this excuse for getting around the agreement they had made. Thus, a report claiming that Foreign Minister Gromyko presented State Secretary Bahr with a way out of the deadlock seems entirely plausible.[37] The solution involved setting aside the point of controversy by chosing a meeting place which did not involve stopping over in West Berlin. On 9 March West Germany's representatives at the preparatory talks handed their East German counterparts a letter to this effect from Chancellor Brandt to Prime Minister Stoph.[38]

The East German leaders were at first hesitant to accept this suggestion. On 10 March the central organ of the SED published a declaration, issued by the Council of Ministers the previous day, reiterating the GDR's readiness to hold the meeting in East Berlin and blaming Bonn for not having accepted the proposal.[39] On the same day the GDR's State Secretary for West German Affairs, J. Herrman, sharply criticized the Federal government's 'unreasonable precondition' and the policy of 'revanchist claims' which was behind it. Bonn must first un-ambiguously renounce such ideas before it could be considered a worthy negotiating partner.[40] Presumably it was due to Soviet influence that the GDR finally decided to end its opposition to the Brandt–Stoph meeting. The representatives of the two German states agreed on Erfurt as the meeting place. On 19 March 1970 Chancellor Brandt and Prime Minister Stoph met there. The tone of Prime Minister Stoph's statements was so harsh and his demands so wide-ranging that any discussion seemed hopeless.[41] Chancellor Brandt, on the other hand, tried to avoid any hostile polemics.[42]

During the Erfurt meeting it was agreed to hold a second meeting in Kassel (West Germany). A few days before the second meeting took place, Foreign Minister Gromyko on 15 May 1970 received a GDR delegation, headed by Ulbricht, in Moscow. According to subsequent official statements, the talks produced 'full agreement of views and interpretations in all questions discussed'.[43] However, news leaked out that the two parties had agreed to adopt delaying tactics over the Kassel meeting. Stoph was to be intransigent but, instead of working for the complete breakdown of the intra-German dialogue, as the SED leaders wanted, he was to strive only for a suspension of talks for an indefinite period.[44] The Soviet leaders, apparently, did not want to give their West German partners the impression that their GDR policy had finally collapsed. Consequently, in Kassel the Chairman of the GDR *Ministerrat* adopted a harsh line, and then declared that a 'pause for thought' was needed before further talks could be held; but at the same time he did not use an incident involving the burning of the East German flag as an excuse to break off the talks.[45] East German behaviour was noted with approval by the Soviet mass media – a clear indication that the GDR had kept within the bounds set by Moscow.[46]

The Moscow Treaty of 12 August 1970

After Foreign Minister Gomyko and State Secretary Bahr agreed, on 22 May 1970, on a detailed draft to serve as the basis for subsequent official treaty negotiations, Bonn was beset by unforeseen difficulties regarding further progress. Influential coalition members, as well as experts on international law in the Foreign Ministry, criticized the text of the draft, which was only made available to them in its final version. Moreover, it seems that the Chancellor and his colleagues were not really sure how best to gain acceptance at home for their *Ostpolitik*, the first results of which had now materialized. They therefore hesitated at this point, and as a result Soviet–West German talks were not, as had been intended, continued immediately in the form of official negotiations.

This provoked confusion and annoyance on the Soviet side. However, Foreign Minister Gromyko was quick to see the opportunity which this situation presented to the USSR. In July, he declared that the talks broken off on 22 May constituted the final result of negotiations as no modifications had been proposed in the meantime. In the Soviet view there were to be no more discussions as the text merely awaited formal confirmation.[47]

All this made it very difficult for Foreign Minister Walter Scheel to effect those changes which he was instructed to negotiate when, on 27 July, he began discussions with his Soviet colleague Gromyko concerning the final form of the treaty. At first his opposite numbers were not prepared to deviate in the slightest from the test agreed on 22 May. Only after a great deal of argument did the Soviet representatives agree to discuss modifications and amendments. Most significant of these was the agreement to link article 3, which described the borders as 'indestructible' (in the Russian text) or 'inviolable' (in the German) to article 2 containing a clause on renunciation of force. Accordingly, the territorial *status quo* was only fixed to the extent that it was a consequence of renunciation of force.[48] As a result, changes in borders were clearly only in contravention of the treaty if they were demanded and/or carried out unilaterally and consequently involved an element of force. Foreign Minister Gromyko confirmed this interpretation with the legally binding statement that the 'concept of recognition' had been dropped, and that 'if two states of their own free will agreed to unite or modify their borders', this still remained one of their 'inalienable rights'. What is more, the reunification of Germany remained a 'possibility for the future'; thus, to maintain this as an aim did not contradict the provisions of the treaty.[49] This clarification of the situation, which Foreign Minister Scheel obtained, ran counter to East German policy, which stressed more and more strongly the irrevocability of the division of Germany and pressed for all-round delimitation (*Abgrenzung*) from the Federal Republic.

The treaty was initialled by the two Foreign Ministers on 7 August. Only five days later Chancellor Brandt went to Moscow in order to sign it. During the course of a long discussion which took place after the ceremony, the Chancellor outlined among other things his views on the Berlin situation to the Soviet party leader, Brezhnev. He explained that an extension of détente to Berlin was indispensable if good relations were to be achieved between West Germany and the USSR and if peaceful relations were to prevail in Europe. He appealed to Brezhnev to help bring about a mutually acceptable settlement of the Berlin problem. In addition, Brandt is said to have pointed out that without a satisfactory settlement on Berlin it would not be possible to secure a majority in the West German Parliament for ratification of the treaty just signed. Brezhnev is reported to have answered that he was not going to be forced into making concessions, but that he would consider presenting new proposals at the Four-Power negotiations on Berlin which had just been opened. The Chancellor felt that Brezhnev realized the full implications of the problem.[50] From the time of the arrival of Foreign Minister Scheel in Moscow, the Soviet mass media had adopted an objective and favourable tone towards the Federal government – although adding the reservation that Bonn's declared intentions must now be reinforced by deeds.[51] Following the visit of the Chancellor, West German policy was treated almost in a friendly manner.[52] Where it was felt necessary to criticize, the blame was usually laid on the 'reactionary CDU/CSU'.

The SED leaders were not pleased with the Moscow Treaty. The fact that their Soviet ally had formally accepted West German assurances on the renunciation of force and respect for borders, and thereby publicly acknowledged to the world its confidence in positive changes in Bonn's policies, robbed Ulbricht and his supporters of the possibility of projecting a plausible image of West Germany being enemy number one. At the same time the provisions of the treaty did not correspond to East Germany's maximum demands: recognition of the GDR under international law by the Federal Republic was not made a precondition for the settlement, and the USSR had expressly allowed for the possibility of agreement between the two German states on unification. Finally, Chancellor Brandt had made it clear to the Soviet party leader that the treaty would only come into force on condition that the East made concessions on Berlin. By its very nature such an agreement could only be achieved at the expense of East German claims. But the East German leaders could not openly oppose the Moscow Treaty. So the central organ of the SED made brief mention of the 'good news' and then, in the name of peace, repeated the usual (but neglected) East German demands on the Federal Republic. This represented tacit but unambiguous criticism of the Soviet Union.[53]

On 14 August 1970 the GDR Council of Ministers commented officially on the Moscow Treaty. Ritual approval was accompanied by interpretations depicting the event in a very different light. It was said that the Federal government had simply responded to pressing necessities in concluding the treaty, and that consequently it could claim no political credit for it. Finally it was asserted in East Berlin that the West German ruling circles, even after the conclusion of the treaty, were attempting to pursue the same devious course as previously. As evidence of this it was maintained, on the basis of its treaty with the USSR, that the Federal Republic was in duty bound to establish full diplomatic relations with the GDR immediately – a prospect which the Council of Ministers, without acknowledging it, did not expect to materialize. At the same time the assertion was made that there was no longer any excuse for third parties to avoid establishing diplomatic relations with the East German state.[54] The USSR immediately expressed disapproval of these interpretations. Reports in the Soviet press omitted those paragraphs in East Berlin's statements questioning the West German readiness to act and portraying the establishment of full diplomatic relations as the logical consequence of the treaty.[55]

In view of the disagreement with the GDR, the Soviet leaders deemed it advisable to discuss the meaning and significance of the Moscow Treaty within the framework of the Warsaw Pact and press for formal approval of the document. The SED party leaders, it was apparently thought, would not be able to defy such a request, and would therefore be prevented from pursuing an obstructionist policy. The meeting took place on 20 August 1970 in Moscow. In the final communiqué the preparation and signing of the Soviet–West German treaty was described as 'an important step along the path to détente and a normalization of the situation in Europe'. It corresponded to 'the interests of all peoples', and created the 'foundation for the development of active inter-state relations between all European countries on the basis of the principles of peaceful coexistence'.[56] This implied that the interests of the East Germans had also been taken into consideration and that the way was open for normal East–West relations in Europe without prior recognition of the GDR under international law. The SED was obliged to adopt a positive attitude towards the Moscow Treaty. However, at the same time, it thought up new arguments to be used against the Federal government, and presented its demand for recognition as a requirement of 'European security'.[57] The Soviet Union attempted to counteract the implied East German criticism that the USSR had not shown sufficient solidarity by demonstrative professions of friendship.[58]

The discussions which took place at the Moscow Conference of Warsaw Pact states have never been made public. However, pausible inferences can be drawn from Soviet statements made in other contexts illuminating the arguments which the hosts might have used to refute the East German allegation that GDR interests had been neglected. Certainly the Soviet representatives attempted to persuade the other delegations that the clause on respecting the borders also held vital guarantees for the East German state; also that the Federal government had declared its readiness to establish relations on a basis of 'full equality, non-discrimination and respect for independence and autonomy'[59] with the GDR, and its readiness to propose that both German states be accepted as members of the UN. However, wider issues may have been brought up. The Soviet Union may have elaborated that the Federal government's renunciation of previously held positions had removed a decisive element of Western unity and Western opposition to the USSR.[60] This may have given rise to hopes that the Federal Republic would assert itself in the face of the Western powers and thus cast doubt on the viability of the Western alliance.[61] Seen in this light, the Moscow Treaty could appear as a decisive breakthrough on the path to 'European security'.[62] References suggesting that the adversaries had lost ground implied hopes for the gradual emergence of a zone of West European states free from United States and NATO influence.[63] At the same time, Moscow was attempting to improve its position in the conflict with China by establishing peace on the Western front.[64] With such important problems on its mind, the USSR could afford to disregard as being of secondary importance GDR demands for unqualified recognition under international law.

References

1. C.-W. Sanne, 'Zur Vorgeschichte des Vertrages', in *Der Vertrag vom 12 August 1970 zwischen der Bundesrepublik Deutschland und der Union der Sozialistischen Sowjetrepubliken*, published by the Federal Press and Information Office, Bonn, September 1970, p. 80; H. Allardt, *Moskauer Tagebuch*, Düsseldorf, 1973, pp. 260–3.

2. C.-W. Sanne, 'Der Vertrag', op. cit., p. 80; H. Allardt, *Moskauer Tagebuch*, op. cit., pp. 264–6.

3. This argument is repeated countless times in Soviet official statements and the media.

4. This can be inferred from the relevant passages in the Gromyko draft of 6 March 1970, drawn up by the Soviet Union on the basis of impressions gained during the first round of talks. The draft served to determine the Soviet position for the subsequent discussions (see *Die Welt*, 23 July 1970).

5. See the report by Ambassador Allardt to the Foreign Office concerning a conversation with a Soviet official acting as an informal go-between at the end of February 1970, *Die Welt*, 10 April 1972.

6. The Soviet tendency to elevate the so-called 'Brezhnev Doctrine' (known as 'proletarian' or 'socialist internationalism' in Eastern Europe) by means of treaties to a norm of international law is expressed particularly in the Treaty of Friendship and Mutual Assistance between the USSR and Czechoslovakia of 6 May 1970. See D. Frenzke, 'Der neue Bündnisvertrag CSSR–UdSSR', *Aussenpolitik*, No. 7 (1970), pp. 406–15.

7. B. Meissner, 'Die "Brezhnev-Doktrin": Dokumentation', Cologne 1969; *Osteuropa*, No. 9 (1969), pp. A189–97.

8. Gromyko's draft of 6 March 1970, *Die Welt*, 23 July 1970. In this German translation the term *Unveränderlichkeit*, is used, meaning that the borders cannot be changed, instead of *Unverbrüchlichkeit* or *Unerschütterlichkeit* (both 'irrevocability'). Although the former is not wrong, the two latter come closer to the Russian *nezyblemost'*.

9. Bundesministerium für innerdeutsche Beziehungen, ed., *Texte zur Deutschlandpolitik*, Vol. 4, Bonn, 1970, p. 12.

10. See Ulbricht's statements at the international press conference as reported in *Pravda*, 20 January 1970.

11. G. F. Duckwitz, 'Die Wende im Osten', *Aussenpolitik*, No. 11 (1970), pp. 649 ff.

12. From February 1970 onwards the Soviet Union began to display increasing consciousness of its responsibilities for Germany ensuing from the occupation regime. Accordingly the phrase Soviet troops 'temporarily stationed in the GDR' (which implied that the GDR could withdraw its consent on the basis of the treaty of 1957) was replaced by the term 'Soviet troops in Germany' (which conveyed the idea of a Soviet right to such a presence).

13. Gromyko draft of 6 March 1970 as published in *Die Welt*, 23 July 1970. See also D. Cramer in *Frankfurter Allgemeine Zeitung*, 5 October 1972; *Neue Zürcher Zeitung*, 25 October 1972.

14. C.-W. Sanne, 'Der Vertrag', op. cit., pp. 17–29 (numbers 5–10), esp. 17 (in German); *Mezhdunarodnaya zhizn*, No. 2 (1973), pp. 156 ff., esp. p. 156 (in Russian).

15. The Soviet Union continued to attack the West German thesis of 'internal' relations between the Federal Republic and the GDR. See, for example, the assessment of Brandt's declaration at the Kassel meeting, E. Grigor'ev in *Pravda*, 22 May 1970.

16. G. Görner, *DDR gewährleistet friedlichen Westberlin-Transit*, (East) Berlin, 1969, pp. 32, 33, 66 and 106; G. Kegel, *Ein Vierteljahrhundert danach*, (East) Berlin, 1970, pp. 165–8. See GDR measures on the access routes in spring 1968 and the justification given for them mentioned in G. Wettig, 'Aktionsmuster der sowjetischen Berlin-Politik', *Aussenpolitik*, No. 6 (1968), pp. 330–8.

17. For brief account, see G. Wettig, 'Die sowjetische Deutschlandpolitik 1942–1955', *Politische Bildung*, No. 2 (1971), pp. 25 ff.

18. According to an exact transcription of the press conference. In the official GDR version of the question and answer game, which also included answers given in writing (*Aussenpolitische Korrespondenz*, No. 5 (1970), pp. 29–30), these remarks have been deleted. This could be taken to indicate that the Soviet Union did not want them published particularly since the questioner (editor-in-chief of the East German newspaper *Berliner Zeitung*) must have been aware of the meaning the SED leaders intended to convey by the statement.

19. Text: ibid., No. 4 (1970), p. 23. The comparison Ulbricht made between the sovereignty of the two states was designed on the one hand to denigrate the Federal Republic (as a state of inferior status and being responsible for its own dependency on the West) and on the other to publicize the principle of sovereignty (as a weapon against the unity of the Western alliance).

20. Texts: *Pravda*, 28 February 1970 (in Russian); *Aussenpolitische Korrespondenz*, No. 10 (1970), pp. 69–71 (in German). Soon after his arrival the Soviet Foreign Minister made it clear that East German demands for recognition went too far. When the GDR Foreign Minister in a toast spoke of the 'inalienable recognition' of the GDR's 'sovereign rights', his guest replied simply that the GDR was an 'inseparable part of the great family of socialist states' (ibid., p. 70).

21. A. D. Mallinckrodt, *Wer macht die Aussenpolitik der DDR?*, Düsseldorf, 1972, pp. 274–83 and pp. 285 ff.

22. Text: *Die Welt*, 23 July 1970.

23. When the Federal government first began trying to establish limited political contacts with the GDR regime, the SED began to cast doubt on the idea of national community which it had been proclaiming for so long and

dropped its suggestion of a German confederation. See Ulbricht's speech to the 7th Party Congress of the SED on 17 April 1967 (*Dokumentation der Zeit*, No. 383, pp. 7–18) and E. Albrecht, 'Nationaler Dialog völlig neuen Typs', *SBZ-Archiv*, No. 3 (1967), pp. 68–70. The GDR constitution of 6 April 1968 (*Aussenpolitische Korrespondenz*, No. 15 (1968), pp. 123–34) dropped the rhetoric on reunification contained in its predecessor of 1949, but the GDR was still described as a 'socialist state of the German nation' – which presupposed the existence of a nation despite the division into separate states. However, the East German draft treaty on relations between the Federal Republic and the GDR, which the SED leadership published on 17 December 1969 in response to the growing readiness of the new SPD–FDP coalition government to enter negotiations and come to an understanding, made no mention of a German nation (ibid., No. 52 (1969), pp. 401 f.). At his press conference of 17 January 1970 Ulbricht still made allowance for the existence of national ties, but not to the so-called bourgeoisie (which included the SPD); only the so-called workers (in other words Communist supporters and sympathizers) in the Federal Republic were to be included (ibid., No. 4 (1970), p. 23). Other leading functionaries went even further. On 4 February 1970 Winzer declared that the idea of the unity of the nation was just an instrument to be used by West German imperialism to infiltrate the GDR and overthrow socialism (ibid., No. 8 (1970), p. 55). Ulbricht stuck by his ideas up to his fall (see Central Committee report of 29 January 1971, *Neues Deutschland*, 31 January 1971), but met with increasing opposition from leading party circles (F. Oldenburg, 'Das 6. ZK-Plenum', *Deutschland Archiv*, No. 8 (1972), p. 789; F. Oldenburg, 'Konflikt und Konfliktregelung in der Parteiführung der SED 1945/46 – 1972', Berichte des Bundesinstituts für ostwissenschaftliche und internationale Studien, No. 48 (1972), p. 81; A. D. Mallinckrodt, *Wer macht die Aussenpolitik der DDR?* op. cit., pp. 269 f.

24. The changes can be seen when the Gromyko draft of 6 March 1970 (*Die Welt*, 23 July 1970) is compared with the so-called 'Bahr Paper' of 22 May 1970 (C.-W. Sanne, *Der Vertrag*, op. cit., pp. 15–19).

25. H. Allardt, *Moskauer Tagebuch*, pp. 306–8. Text of 22 March 1970: C.-W. Sanne, *Der Vertrag*, op. cit., p. 143.

26. Partial survey in G. Wettig, 'Die Interessen der Sowjetunion und der DDR in der Anerkennungsfrage', in *Deutschland Archiv*, No. 7 (1970), pp. 706 f. and R. A. Remington, *The Warsaw Pact*, Cambridge, Mass. and London, 1971, pp. 135–7. See also the speech by A. Norden in Prague on 7 May 1970, *Neues Deutschland*, 8 May 1970.

27. According to P. Abrasimov, *Neues Deutschland*, 1 April 1970.

28. Referred to in a report in *Neue Zürcher Zeitung*, 4 April 1971. See also R. A. Remington, *The Warsaw Pact*, op. cit., p. 146.

29. Texts: *Deutschland Archiv*, No. 2 (1970), p. 196.

30. Texts: ibid., No. 4 (1970), pp. 402–4.

31. During this period the Soviet Union was clearly trying to persuade the Federal government that it could count on cooperation from the Eastern side if it agreed to accept Moscow's ideas. The GDR, on the other hand, did its best to discourage the advocates of the new West German *Ostpolitik*.

32. Annamarie Doherr in *Frankfurter Rundschau*, 28 February 1970. The

Erfurt meeting followed exactly this pattern. The GDR described the West German refusal to give unconditional recognition to the East German state under international law as tantamount to 'declaration of war' on the Soviet camp (P. Steiniger in *Aussenpolitische Korrespondenz*, No. 11 (1970), p. 79); a continuation of the CDU/CSU policy of revanchism (G. Kohrt, on 8 May 1970, in ibid., No. 18 (1970), pp. 133 ff.; or an attempt at blackmail (ibid., No. 5 (1970), p. 33); W. Stoph in *Pravda*, 8 May 1970; O. Winzer in *Mezhdunarodnaya zhizn*, No. 6 (1970), p. 104.

33. Text: *Pravda*, 28 February 1970 (in Russian); *Aussenpolitische Korrespondenz*, No. 10 (1970), pp. 69–70 (in German).

34. Texts: *Deutschland Archiv*, No. 5 (1970), pp. 505–25.

35. See TASS report in Russian, 19 March 1970; *Novosti* report by J. Nikolaev in English, 19 March 1970; *Pravda*, 22 March 1970; and *Pravda*, 30 March 1970.

36. The East German argument is contained in a major article in *Neues Deutschland*, 6 March 1970, reproduced in *Deutschland Archiv*, No. 4 (1970), pp. 403 ff.

37. B. Conrad in *Die Welt*, 14 March 1970.

38. Text: *Deutschland Archiv*, No. 4 (1970), p. 404.

39. Text: ibid., No. 4 (1970), pp. 405 ff.

40. Text: ibid., No. 4 (1970), pp. 406–8.

41. Text: ibid., No. 5 (1970), pp. 505–16.

42. Text: ibid., No. 5 (1970), pp. 516–24.

43. *Pravda*, 16 May 1970.

44. *Die Welt*, 25 May 1970.

45. Documents on the agreement in *Deutschland Archiv*, No. 6 (1970), pp. 620–55. Brief survey in H. Ludwig, 'Rache für Erfurt?', in ibid., No. 6 (1970), pp. 656–8.

46. See E. Grigor'ev in *Pravda*, 22 May 1970; Y. Borisov, V. Serov and S. Tosunyan in *Izvestiya*, 22 May 1970; E. Grigor'ev in *Pravda*, 27 May 1970; Y. Sibirtsev, 'Posle Kasselya (GDR–FRG)', *Mezhdunarodnaya zhizn*, No. 7 (1970), pp. 115 ff.

47. H. Allardt, *Moskauer Tagebuch*, op. cit., pp. 51 and 336–52; E. Bölte in *Kölner Stadt-Anzeiger*, 1/2 August 1970. Text of the 'Bahr-Papier' of 22 May 1970: C.-W. Sanne, *Der Vertrag*, op. cit., pp. 15–19. Only points 5–10 of the Russian version were published, representing a declaration of intent to accompany the draft treaty (numbers 1–4): *Mezhdunarodnaya zhizn*, No. 2 (1973), pp. 156 ff.

48. The changes can be seen by comparing numbers 1–4 of the *Bahr-Papier* of 22 May 1970 in C.-W. Sanne, *Der Vertrag*, op. cit., pp. 15–17 with the final text of the treaty, ibid., pp. 7–9, *Europa-Archiv*, No. 17 (1970), pp. D397–8; *Deutschland Archiv*, No. 12 (1970), pp. 821–2; *Die Auswärtige Politik der Bundesrepublik Deutschland*, published by the Foreign Office in collaboration with an advisory board, Cologne, 1972, pp. 761–5; *Osteuropa*, No. 12 (1970), p. 821 (in German); *Mezhdunarodnaya zhizn*, No. 2 (1973), pp. 155 ff. and *Osteuropa*, No. 12 (1970), p. 822 (in Russian).

49. Quoted from the text of the West German press agency, dpa, 14 December 1971. It was an integral part of the treaty. For purely domestic reasons the Federal government delayed publication until 14 December 1971

(the dpa text was the official version released to the Press at this time); the declaration by the Soviet Foreign Minister was to be used as a trump card at the right moment before ratification to persuade the public that the treaty was acceptable.

50. E. Bölte and H.-W. Kettenbach in *Kölner Stadt-Anzeiger*, 14 August 1970; *Der Spiegel*, 17 August 1970, pp. 17-26.

51. See the review of international affairs by Yu. Zhukov in *Pravda*, 26 July 1970. Both *Pravda* and *Izvestiya* published photos of Scheel next to Gromyko – a clear indication of a positive attitude towards the West German government in the Soviet Union.

52. H. R. Löser, 'Moskau über Nacht konziliant und sachlich', Monitor-Dienst, Deutsche Welle (Cologne), 22 September 1970, p. 154. Chancellor Brandt was given a favourable reception in the press. It published his picture together with a short biography and photos showing him in conversation with leading Soviet officials.

53. G. Hagen, 'Die DDR und der Moskauer Vertrag', *Aussenpolitik*, No. 11 (1970), pp. 661 ff.

54. Text: *Neues Deutschland*, 15 August 1970.

55. *Pravda*, 15 August 1970.

56. Ibid., 21 August 1970 (in Russian); *Dokumentation der Zeit*, No. 20 (1970), p. 43 and *Europa-Archiv*, No. 1 (1971), p. D4 (in German).

57. G. Hagen, 'Die DDR und der Moskauer Vertrag', op. cit., pp. 663-6; see also H. R. Löser, 'Moskau über Nacht konziliant und sachlich', op. cit., pp. 4-7.

58. See the article by I. Sivcev, 'Unser Freund – die DDR' in *Izvestiya*, 20 September 1970.

59. See the declarations of intent of 22 June 1970, in C.-W. Sanne, *Der Vertrag*, op. cit., pp. 17 ff. (in German); *Mezhdunarodnaya zhizn*, No. 2 (1973), pp. 156 ff. (in Russian).

60. *Izvestiya*, 13 August 1970; see also the contribution by L. Vidyasova to a discussion among experts in August 1970, *Mezhdunarodnaya zhizn*, No. 9 (1970), p. 31; A. Gorokhov, 'Bor'ba SSSR za obespechenie evropeiskoi bezopasnosti, ibid., No. 12 (1970), pp. 19-11.

61. Y. Rzhevsky in *Pravda*, 18 August 1970. And Radio Moscow, in Russian, on 27 August 1970.

62. A. Gorokhov, 'Bor'ba SSSR', op. cit., p. 10, described the Moscow Treaty as a 'catalyst' for 'European security'.

63. Radio Moscow in Russian, 27 August 1970.

64. The Soviet leaders had used this argument *vis-à-vis* their East German ally in the summer of 1969 in defence of their policy of détente in Europe, see Leslie Colitt in *The Observer*, 17 August 1969.

VII

Berlin as the Pivotal Issue in Soviet Policy towards the West, 1970–1971

Prospects of a Berlin Settlement in the Autumn of 1970

It was a Western initiative, accepted in principle three months later by the USSR, which led to the opening on 26 March 1970 of the Four-Power negotiations concerning Berlin.[1] During the first round of talks, in the spring and summer of 1970, the USSR adopted a posture so totally opposed to that of the Western governments that there seemed to be no prospects of achieving agreement. As far as the USSR was concerned, only West Berlin came within the jurisdiction of the Four Powers. East Berlin was to be considered an integral part of the GDR.[2] From this it followed that the USSR asserted exclusive rights to participate in decisions on West Berlin.[3] The object of negotiations, from the Soviet point of view, amounted in essence to the strict separation of the city from the Federal Republic, confirmed by international law.[4] This involved not only turning the city into an isolated state. The aim was also to attack the vital links between West Berlin and the Federal Republic. Political ties should be eliminated and economic and social ties loosened. In contrast to this, the aim of negotiations from the Western point of view was to induce the USSR to respect the essential elements of West Berlin's allegiance to the West German state. But the Soviet representatives refused to discuss the question of access rights, which the West considered vital. They argued that, since the GDR exercised sovereignty over its territory and over its lines of communication,[5] application for the granting of any transit rights must be made through these channels.

The SED leaders were in basic agreement with the Soviet position. However, there were hidden differences on individual points. Concerning the idea that East Berlin was an integral part of the GDR, Moscow failed to draw the practical conclusions from this and eliminate all remaining vestiges of Four-Power status in the city. Thus, in the autumn of 1969 the East Germans failed in their attempt to revoke the special status of East Berlin representatives in the *Volkskammer* by modifying the voting procedure.[6] Apparently the

Soviet leaders wanted to avoid the conflict with the Western powers which would inevitably result from such an action. Moreover, the Western occupation authorities could have reacted to an open breach of East Berlin's Four-Power status by taking action against the remaining Soviet presence in West Berlin (the Soviet war memorial in the Tiergarten district and administrative rights in the Spandau military prison). What is more, it was doubtful whether the USSR would want to relinquish its occupation rights over the GDR. As for rights to participate in decisions affecting West Berlin, Soviet demands were accompanied by similar GDR demands, partly for assurances of good conduct, and partly for changes in the social and political system in reference to the Potsdam Agreement.[7] Views also differed over the question of access rights. While the GDR claimed unrestricted control in principle over all West Berlin traffic, the USSR insisted on retaining for itself supervision of Western military traffic.[8]

The talks held between Chancellor Brandt and Foreign Minister Scheel on the one hand and Brezhnev and other Soviet leaders on the other during the signing of the Moscow Treaty had aroused hopes in West Germany that the Soviet Union would be prepared to make concessions on Berlin. Soviet diplomats and commentators did their best to scotch such expectations by displaying inflexibility and casting doubt on any prospect of compromise.[9] The Western powers, on the other hand, gave effective support to West German policy by making Soviet concessions on Berlin the test case for the USSR's readiness for détente. In fact, not only ratification of the Moscow Treaty but also the convening of a European Security Conference now depended officially on an acceptable settlement in Berlin. In other words, from then on the success of the whole of Soviet policy towards the West would hinge on this issue. In September 1970 negotiations between the Four Powers were resumed after a summer recess. The Soviet delegation now began to adopt a more flexible attitude. On 23 September, the four Ambassadors exchanged the first position papers, though there was still little sign of progress. From 7 October onwards, there were regular meetings of experts to prepare the ground for agreement. An informal inventory was drawn up of all points which the two sides wanted to include in a settlement.[10]

However, Soviet ideas were still completely unacceptable to the West. According to a reliable report, Ambassador Abrasimov demanded on 9 October a formal Four-Power declaration to the effect that West Berlin did not belong to the Federal Republic. This was to be phrased in such a way as to imply Soviet co-responsibility for West Berlin's affairs. The Soviet Ambassador further demanded that the USSR be allowed to set up consular and trade missions in the city and that Federal German bodies cease their activity there. The Federal

83

Republic should relinquish its rights to represent the interests of West Berlin abroad. In exchange, the USSR would be prepared to accept continued financial, economic, cultural and legal links between the city and West Germany. The relationship between Liechtenstein and Switzerland was put forward as a model, although modifications were not excluded. If agreement could be reached along these lines, the GDR government would be prepared to negotiate with its German partners concerning civilian transit traffic.[11]

To the West this offered no basis for realistic discussions. The United States government consequently began trying to persuade the USSR to modify its extreme positions. The first success came in mid-October, when Secretary of State Rodgers succeeded in extracting the concession from his Soviet colleagues that talks concerning traffic through the GDR should no longer be made dependent on Western acceptance of Soviet demands concerning the status of West Berlin.[12] The same theme was brought up again shortly afterwards in a discussion between President Nixon and Foreign Minister Gromyko. Apparently the Soviet Foreign Minister no longer raised any objections to the problem of transit traffic being discussed by the Ambassadors.[13] A week later the Federal Government entered the fray. On 31 October Foreign Minister Scheel succeeded in persuading Gromyko at a meeting in Kronberg not to oppose detailed discussion of the Berlin question with a representative of West Germany.[14]

At the next meeting of the four Ambassadors, on 4 November, the Soviet representatives were not only prepared to discuss the question of traffic between the Federal Republic and West Berlin, but they also withdrew their demand that the USSR be given veto rights in the Western Sectors. Changed attitudes towards an agreement were reflected in a new interim report. Opposing views on legal problems and status were to be set aside so that agreement could be reached on practical matters.

West Berlin was accorded a status outside the Federal Republic, but this would in no way impair financial, economic, cultural and legal links. But the Federal presence in the city was to be considerably reduced. Certain concessions were also envisaged concerning West German representation of the city abroad. The Soviet paper proposed that West Berlin be required to give assurances of good conduct inasmuch as it would undertake to cease disseminating 'hostile propaganda' directed at the GDR and other Communist countries. There should be free and unimpeded transit via the GDR. The Four-Powers would have the task of formulating basic principles, to serve as a framework for negotiations on a settlement between German authorities. Mention was also made of an arbitration authority in which the GDR was to be represented. East German participation would have the effect of formally demonstrating GDR sovereignty over its transit routes.[15]

Negative Reactions in the GDR

Even before the Soviet Union presented its interim paper, the GDR had begun to draw its own conclusions from the changed situation. On 29 October two emissaries from the GDR Council of Ministers called at the Chancellery and, on behalf of its Chairman, proposed that negotiations should begin in the near future on the conclusion of a transit agreement.[16] Judging from circumstantial evidence, the decision was taken in a hurry by East Berlin and without any preparation.[17] It coincided with a visit by the Soviet Foreign Minister to the East German capital,[18] and the initiative may well have been taken at his instigation.

The GDR's offer of negotiations was designed to draw the Federal Government into talks on transit arrangements before the four Ambassadors had had a chance to formulate a basic agreement and directives.[19] This would have negated the Western thesis that questions of transit were based on Western access rights, and consequently were an exclusive responsibility of the Four Powers. It may be presumed that this GDR counter-proposal fitted in with Soviet interests. For if the procedure of its East German ally had been successful, the Soviet Union could have avoided having to face up to the implications of Four-Power jurisdiction over the access routes, although it had already partly conceded to the Western powers that such a claim was valid. The Federal Government accepted the proposals of the GDR Council of Ministers in principle, but it was neither prepared nor in a position to conduct negotiations on the question of transit until the Four Powers had issued a mandate to that effect.[20]

On 8 November 1970 Ulbricht thought it necessary to announce unequivocally that any restrictions on the sovereign rights of the GDR over its communication routes were out of the question. 'On condition that all activity by other states in West Berlin, which is in contravention of the international legal status of the city and detrimental to the interests of the GDR and other socialist states, ceases', his government would be prepared 'to enter into negotiations with the government of the Federal Republic on the question of civilian and commercial transit traffic'. By saying that in this formulation 'every word was chosen deliberately', he may have had in mind the GDR concept whereby transit rights were granted voluntarily and could in principle be revoked. Arrangements were to be agreed separately with the Federal Government and the West Berlin Senate.[21] This would clearly establish the special political status of West Berlin.[22]

These statements were basically in harmony with the Soviet view-point.[23] However, despite this, it seems doubtful whether Ulbricht's words could have been welcomed by the Soviet leaders. In effect Ulbricht had made a transit arrangement dependent on prior acceptance of a special political status for Berlin – a precondition which the Soviet Union had dropped. This could only have the effect of restricting Soviet room for manoeuvre in the negotiating process. Moreover, the assertion that 'all activity by other states' in West Berlin must cease was also directed at the presence of the Western powers in the city. All this ran counter to the USSR's interest in not allowing the problems of Berlin to block a more satisfactory relationship with the Western powers and the Federal Republic. However, it was this very Soviet interest which Ulbricht perceived as a direct challenge. His words clearly implied concern that his Soviet ally, once on the road towards concessions to the West, would sacrifice vital positions. In order to prevent this, notice was unmistakably served that the GDR stood resolutely by its rights. The Soviet leaders were to be made conscious of the fact that East German interests were not to be over-looked.[24]

On 13 November Ulbricht brought out this point even more clearly. He warned that 'greater use should be made' of the opportunities for 'joint discussions or at least consultations between the fraternal parties'. In accordance with traditional Communist practice, the real significance of his remarks was disguised as far as possible. Consequently Ulbricht addressed himself to 'theoretical problems'. However, there was a broad hint contained in his phrase that, 'for example, new manifestations of imperialism' had arisen, and 'consultations' should be held as to 'how under these conditions the struggle [can] effectively be continued'.[25] The argument that 'imperialism', particularly in the shape of West Germany, was appearing in new guises and that basic theoretical analysis was required to determine how to master this phenomenon, had been used by the SED leaders for some time in their attempts to persuade their allies to support the East German line on the Federal Republic.

The rift between Moscow and East Berlin was spelled out to the rest of the world when, at the end of November, the Soviet leaders tried to use the occasion of the Hungarian Party Congress for an informal summit meeting to iron out all differences of opinion. Ulbricht refused to attend, and sent a third-ranking party official (F. Ebert) to head the delegation to Budapest.[26] Obviously he could not be considered a suitable partner for talks with the other East European party leaders, who had all appeared for the meeting. Consequently Foreign Minister Gromyko was forced to visit the recalcitrant Ulbricht on 25 November while the Congress was still in progress. Apparently the talks produced no agreement.[27] The GDR did not tone down its harsh line concerning the Federal Republic and the Berlin question; on 29 November Brezhnev appealed publicly for a 'mutually acceptable agreement' on Berlin, in accordance with the 'wishes of the population of West Berlin' but also the 'legitimate interests' and the 'sovereign rights' of the GDR.[28] The uncertainty which had arisen in relations between the Soviet Union and its East German allies led to a stagnation in the Four-Power negotiations.[29]

During their talks, Gromyko and Ulbricht had agreed to settle the differences which had arisen at a conference of Warsaw Pact member-states to take place on 2 December in East Berlin. Apparently the SED leader had also told the Soviet Foreign Minister that the proposed meeting of the CDU/CSU parliamentary group, due to take place at the same time in West Berlin, should be considered a serious 'provocation' – a suggestion endorsed by Gromyko. (It may have been important to the Soviet Union that the reproach was not directed against the coalition in office but exclusively against the 'reactionary CDU/CSU'.)[30] The protest issued by the GDR Foreign Ministry on 27 November was taken up immediately and without reservation by the Soviet mass media.[31] On the same day Ambassador Abrasimov sent a letter to the three Western Ambassadors accredited in the Federal Republic protesting against the meeting.[32] At the beginning of December the Western reply, rejecting all accusations, was described as unsatisfactory, and a campaign was launched against 'organized provocations' in West Berlin.[33]

It is not clear whether Gromyko had also promised Ulbricht that the USSR would tacitly support certain measures should the CDU/CSU parliamentary group hold its meeting in West Berlin. But Ulbricht rightly assumed that the Soviet leaders would not want to exacerbate the existing crisis in their mutual relations by opposing limited steps designed to uphold an East German right which in principle had Soviet support. Thus, for one week starting from 29 November, the GDR authorities decreed that traffic between West Berlin and the Federal Republic would be subject to serious delays. This was the SED leaders' way of demonstrating to the West that control over the access routes was in their hands. At the same time, however, they demonstrated to the USSR their potential for disruption in the event of an unsatisfactory Berlin settlement. Moreover, they jeopardized the credibility of the USSR's readiness to compromise, which the Soviet delegation had built up during the Four-Power negotiations on Berlin.

According to an apparently reliable report, Brezhnev travelled to the conference in East Berlin with the intention of convincing Ulbricht of the need for major concessions on Berlin.[34] What is certain is that the leaders of the USSR and the GDR clashed sharply with one another at the conference.[35] Ulbricht is said to have accused the Soviet leadership of sacrificing vital East German rights; in doing so he probably also pointed out that the Soviet Union's policy on Berlin gave the impression of confirming Chinese accusations of a Soviet 'betrayal' of the GDR.[36] Once the conference was over the participants proclaimed officially their 'unanimous solidarity with the policy of peace pursued by the German Democratic Republic' and declared that in their view 'lasting peace' in Europe could not be achieved without the participation of the GDR. Thus it was imperative that 'relations be established between the GDR and the Federal Republic on the basis of generally accepted norms of international law'. The conference participants then reiterated Brezhnev's formula of 29 November – though in a modified form: whereas Brezhnev had promised to take into account the 'wishes' of the population of West Berlin, the conference participants pledged themselves only to pay attention to the 'needs' of the West Berliners.[37]

The official formulations of the meeting are open to broad interpretation. Undoubtedly the East Germans had managed to uphold their claim to recognition even if this was not made a precondition for further negotiations, as the SED had wanted. However, in the relations between Warsaw Pact states, the most difficult problems to be resolved were whether the GDR would be able to set the criteria by which to measure progress in the policies of the Warsaw Pact member-states towards the West and, more important, whether the GDR could claim veto rights concerning the policy on Berlin. Did the declaration of solidarity with the GDR represent more than just lip-service? Did the switch from subjective 'wishes' to objective 'needs' of the West Berliners imply that the East Europeans intended to decide for themselves what was in the best interests of the city? If the answer to both questions was in the affirmative, then it must be assumed that Ulbricht and his supporters had gained acceptance for their hard line. One of the participants at the conference, the Hungarian Foreign Minister Janos Peter, disputed this hypothesis in a conversation in mid-December with the Foreign Minister of Austria. He explained that, on the contrary a successful attempt was made at overcoming the existing difficulties standing in the way of a Berlin settlement.[38] An American political scientist, who has analysed the events, comes to a similar conclusion: she believes that it was unrest in Poland, occurring shortly after the meeting in East Berlin and seeming for a time to pose a threat to Soviet supremacy (it resulted in the dismissal of Party leader Gomulka),[39] that induced the Soviet leaders to seek closer understanding with the more stable GDR, thus presenting Ulbricht with greater room for manoeuvre.[40]

A number of important facts contradict this assumption. On 10 December at the first meeting of the four Ambassadors after the conference in East Berlin – i.e., before the events in Poland could have influenced the political decisions – Abrasimov reverted to the position taken in October that the dismantling of the Federal presence in West Berlin was a precondition for discussions on all other questions.[41] In setting this precondition the Soviet delegation blocked all further progress in the negotiations. Shortly after the consultations in East Berlin between the East European leaders had ended, Soviet and East German party officials both assured Western journalists that the SED's position had essentially been endorsed. According to these assurances, the USSR in the future was to safeguard the GDR's interests in having the treaty confirm the status of West Berlin as an 'independent political entity'; ensure participation of the GDR on an equal basis in the Four-Power settlements affecting its interests; and insist that the GDR gain exclusive rights in matters concerning transit.[42] Eleven days after the East Berlin conference Radio Moscow, in a 'round table' broadcast in Russian, accused the West of wanting 'permanent links between West Berlin and the Federal Republic', thereby 'ignoring the rights and sovereignty of the GDR' and only serving 'anti-European ends'. These unusually harsh comments reflected a more general serious hardening of views.

Quite possibly, though, the Soviet leaders, prior to the events in Poland, had not wanted to go as far in their support of the GDR as they ultimately did. If this is true, it may be that a compromise was reached between the USSR and the GDR involving some hardening of attitudes without excluding all possibility of an understanding. This hypothesis is borne out by the Hungarian Foreign Minister's optimism and a shortened TASS version of Ulbricht's report to the Warsaw Pact meeting (leaving out the issue of sovereignty over transit arrangements).[43] No firm conclusions can be drawn from the facts that reports of Soviet intransigence over Berlin only began to filter through shortly before the turn of the year[44] and that renewed disruptions on the transit routes only began from 19 December onwards, this time directed at the SPD.[45] The time-lag before the course of confrontation set in could well have been attributable to a further hardening of attitudes in the second half of December, an information lag or lack of suitable pretext.

Whatever the answer, it is certain that by 18 December at the latest Ulbricht's policy had prevailed. Reports by journalists also agreed that the USSR had now granted the GDR exclusive responsibility for all questions concerning traffic to Berlin, and that Soviet negotiators were refusing to discuss the question of access. According to one report, the SED leaders were now in a position to demand assurances of good conduct from West Berlin. With this the talks with Western representatives reverted to the situation which had existed in the spring and summer – a verbal confrontation without any apparent signs of progress. At the same time the USSR used diplomacy and the press to back up the GDR's actions – though on occasion with scarcely concealed displeasure.[46] Surprisingly, the Soviet press backed the GDR claims over West Berlin without expressly sanctioning the accompanying interferences.[47] However, it is doubtful whether this can be considered an indication of Soviet displeasure, because for a while the Soviet authorities also indulged in harassments of their own, directed against military transit traffic of the Western powers.[48]

The Stagnation of the Soviet Union's Policy towards the West and the Reasons behind it

Up to the beginning of February 1971 the Soviet delegation at the Four-Power negotiations on Berlin showed no inclination to discuss any of the controversial issues.[49] Soviet spokesmen and commentators turned their attention to attacking the idea that ratification of the Moscow Treaty, the convening of a Conference on European Security and further progress in détente should depend on an agreement being reached on Berlin. Such an attitude, they stated, was harmful to détente and understanding, and was designed to counteract efforts to improve the situation in Europe.[50] This line of argument fitted in quite neatly with the ideas of the SED[51] and negated the possibility of Soviet acquiescence in Western views on links between Berlin and détente, hinted at by Brezhnev on 29 November 1970 when he said that the West Berlin problems under negotiation were of 'major significance for the normalization of the situation in Europe'.[52] In contrast to that, the Soviet leaders were now attempting to shake Western confidence by stressing that there was no prospect of any concessions from Eastern Europe. This was also the aim behind reports put about by Soviet diplomats in Washington and Stockholm that Moscow had already achieved its main objective with the signing of the Treaty on 12 August 1970, and was particularly disillusioned by the attitude of West Germany. It would therefore be wrong to assume, the argument continued, that the USSR was still interested in the ratification of the Moscow Treaty or that it hoped to achieve further results from its Western policy.[53] It is fair to assume that these comments were disseminated with approval from Moscow.[54]

The central political organs may have continued to avoid polemics, but the Soviet mass media gave full expression to their reservations regarding West Germany.[55] Possibly this policy was intended not only to demonstrate dissatisfaction with Bonn, but also to appease critics within the Soviet Communist Party *Apparat* of the Soviet Union's policies towards the West. Western Ambassadors in Moscow and Western experts on Soviet affairs discovered numerous indications that a group of prominent party officials existed which opposed in particular the abandonment of the image of West Germany as the Bogeyman of Europe.[56] The indications were that the opposition came above all from military circles and the party organization in the western Union Republics.[57] The First Secretary of the Ukranian Communist Pary, P. Shelest, had been critical of such policies since 1969–70; in November 1971 he reiterated his criticisms. Apparently the main fear was that the GDR's internal order would not be able to survive a rapprochement between Eastern Europe and the Federal Republic.[58] But these oppositionist tendencies were reflected only marginally in Soviet newspapers and journals. The army paper *Krasnaya zvezda* and the Party press of Lithuania and the Ukraine put more emphasis on the theme of neonazism than *Pravda* and *Izvestiya*, but all painted an essentially similar picture of West Germany. Only very rarely did mild criticism of the West German leaders filter through. There is no evidence to suggest even the beginnings of polemics against the ruling SPD–FDP coalition.[60] In other words, there were only indications of an attitude of greater reserve towards Bonn.

The GDR, on the other hand, was in the throes of a campaign directed openly against the Federal Government. The main theme was that the official objectives of the Federal Republic had not changed in the slightest, that the politicians in Bonn did nothing to prevent the 'revanchist' attacks on the Moscow Treaty and that the SPD and FDP were the sworn enemies of the Soviet camp.[61] It was the duty of the Federal Republic to meet the GDR's demands for recognition unconditionally and without delay – the implication being that refusal to comply was evidence of the Federal Government's evil intentions.[62] The USSR clearly wanted no part in the accusations which its East German ally was hurling at the socialist–liberal coalition.[63] Also the SED leaders can hardly have been pleased with the fact that Soviet diplomats were telling West German discussion partners that the GDR would respect a negotiated settlement on Berlin, and even hinting that such an arrangement might restrict the East Germans' room for manoeuvre.[64]

The joint opposition of anti-West German circles in the USSR and party officials in East Berlin to the official Soviet policy of détente with the coalition government in Bonn raises the question not only of the extent to which both groups were pursuing parallel interests, but also of the degree to which they actually coordinated their actions. There is certainly some evidence to suggest that the SED leaders cooperated politically with Brezhnev's critics in the Soviet Party apparatus. The theoretical organ of the Latvian Communist Party repeated, in its January issue, evaluations and arguments concerning the Moscow Treaty that Ulbricht had used in *Neues Deutschland*. The conclusion to be drawn by the reader was that ratification of the treaty was unnecessary.[65] This amounted to support for a policy which involved no compromise on Berlin or any other problem. The Soviet army newspaper published attacks by the GDR Defence Minister, H. Hoffman, on the NATO resolution of 4 December 1970 which had officially made Berlin the test case of détente, and then a commentary claiming that the Federal Government was the most reliable and, in the eyes of the Warsaw Pact countries, the most dangerous ally of the USA, their main enemy.[66] According to reports reaching the Federal Republic, certain members of the SED Central Committee had established contact with circles within the Soviet Party apparatus advocating rapprochement with China in place of an East–West settlement in Europe.[67] It could be interpreted as one indication of the accuracy of these reports[68] that Ulbricht, unlike the party leaders of Poland, Bulgaria and Czechoslovakia, avoided all anti-Chinese polemics at the XXIV Congress of the CPSU.

Signs of Relaxation in the Soviet Union's Hard Line on Berlin

At the end of January 1971 the American President appealed to the USSR to adopt a more cooperative attitude towards the Berlin question.[69] On 5 February the three Western Ambassadors presented a draft agreement, hoping to provoke some tangible reaction from the USSR.[70] At the next meeting, on 8 February, Western representatives noticed a slightly increased readiness to negotiate on the part of the USSR. Ambassador Abrasimov was now presenting a more rosy picture to the public.[71] This was followed by gestures on the part of the USSR indicating their desire for détente. On 12 February the journal published by the Soviet Embassy in the Federal Republic brought to an end a series of articles which had been stressing maximalist positions on Berlin.[72] On 15 February the SPD executive met in West Berlin without provoking retaliation against the access routes.[73] Presumably Ulbricht had been persuaded during his talks with Soviet leaders in Moscow to suspend all harassment.[74]

Although there were still no real prospects of agreement in the Four-Power negotiations, the SED leaders reacted in just the same way as they had done at the end of October 1970 (when they had received the first hint of a changed attitude on the part of the USSR) by re-activating their own Berlin policy. East Berlin party officials sharply attacked a report in the *Stuttgarter Zeitung* concerning declining Soviet interest in the ratification of the Moscow Treaty,[75] and on the next day, 5 February, Prime Minister Stoph met the Chairman of the West Berlin branch of the SED and proposed that transit negotiations begin between the West Berlin Senate and the GDR government.[76] The party official in question then made the proposal public, as directed. Evidently the offer was designed to demonstrate East German readiness to negotiate, in view of the forthcoming elections to the West Berlin parliament on 14 February. But there was more to it than this, since the campaign was kept up afterwards – and even heightened.[77] The aim was to create a broader basis for attacks on the Western position that the four Ambassadors were competent to negotiate civilian transit arrangements between West Berlin and the Federal Republic. Furthermore, if the GDR had in fact conducted separate negotiations with the Federal Government and the Senate on this matter, it would have had a prejudicial effect on the controversial question of the relationship between West Berlin and the Federal Republic. Such a development would also have been in the Soviet interest. The USSR, therefore, backed up the GDR initiative.[78]

During February and March the USSR displayed greater flexibility on individual points during the Ambassadorial talks than it had done over past months, but retained its uncompromising attitude over matters of principle. Its main objective was to formulate some kind of interim arrangement for West Berlin which would not stand in the way of what was seen as an inevitable process of incorporation of the city into the GDR.[79] Thus the Soviet leaders insisted that the West had no *prima facie* rights to a presence in the city, that the Federal Republic too had no claims to competence in the internal or external affairs of West Berlin, and that it was an anomaly that Berlin did not belong to the GDR.[80] On 26 March Ambassador Abrasimov presented his colleagues with a draft agreement which in essence, although based on the previous Western proposal, repeated all the major Soviet demands.[81]

At the XXIV Congress of the CPSU both Brezhnev and Gromyko, on 30 March[82] and 3 April[83] respectively, called for a settlement of the problems connected with West Berlin. The Soviet Foreign Minister came part of the way towards accepting the Western idea of Berlin as a test case of détente by referring to a parallel – though by no means interdependent – procedure for the realization of the Treaties with West Germany, the European Security Conference and a Four-Power agreement on Berlin. However, this did not imply acceptance of substantive Western demands on Berlin.[84] There was no prospect of achieving agreement acceptable to the West. Thus, at the end of April, the American President, acting on advice from Ambassador Rush, made a fresh attempt at inducing a more cooperative attitude from the USSR.[85] Moscow had apparently decided that the success of the rest of its policy towards the West depended on the adoption of a more conciliatory attitude on Berlin.[86] After Brezhnev's clear victory over the opponents of his foreign policy strategy, evident from the Party Congress, the Soviet leaders gained increased room for political manoeuvre. However, Ulbricht and persistent East German demands still represented a major obstacle.

The Fall of Ulbricht

Even within the leading circles of the SED, Ulbricht was increasingly felt to be in the way, for reasons of both personal rivalry and domestic expediency.[87] Quite probably the party officials in East Berlin and in Moscow, who had taken exception to the East German leader, decided to join forces. It is widely believed that the decision to dismiss Ulbricht had already been taken by the time of the XXIV Party Congress of the CPSU, which took place from the end of March to the beginning of April. The evidence in support of this assumption is either far from convincing or based on inaccurate reports. There was nothing to suggest, even after Ulbricht's remarks to the Congress, which certainly angered his Soviet hosts in parts,[88] that he would be treated as anything but top leader of the SED. It is true that on 3, 4 and 5 April Honecker led a SED delegation attending meetings of workers in the USSR. However, this was in no way unusual, as the Soviet press reveals: other party leaders had been known to delegate subordinates to attend such meetings. Ulbricht's state of health made it advisable for him to avoid special strain and extra trips, even more so than the much younger party leaders of the other Warsaw Pact states. Ulbricht appeared at all the many farewell ceremonies in Moscow after the XXIV Congress as number one man in the SED, followed by Honecker and Stoph. At the reception for the Parties invited he spoke on behalf of the SED.[89]

The assertion that Ulbricht's talks with Soviet party officials over the last few weeks or months of his rule were no longer accompanied by the usual professions of friendship and harmony is contradicted by the relevant reports in the Soviet press. The first evidence of Soviet displeasure was the congratulatory telegram sent by the CPSU to the SED on 21 April on the occasion of the 25th anniversary of its founding. Contrary to previous practice, the telegram was not sent to Ulbricht but to the Central Committee as a whole. In its review of past history it praised the achievements of Pieck and Grotewohl, but not Ulbricht.[90] During the next few weeks hints were dropped to Western diplomats in Eastern Europe that Ulbricht intended to give up the leadership of the Party at the VIII Congress of the SED in June. This was said to be due to 'gentle pressure from the Soviet Union', which had found his hard line in foreign policy tiresome.[91] Similar hints were also given to Western correspondents in Moscow. When Ulbricht's dismissal was eventually announced, these correspondents were convinced that the Soviet leaders had found the former SED chief more and more intractable, and that the change of leadership must have been decided following discussions in the Politburo of the CPSU.[92]

The subsequent behaviour of leading figures in the USSR is further indication that the USSR was directly involved in the SED leader's replacement. The general Secretary of the CPSU and the Supreme Commander of Soviet troops in Germany sent the usual congratulations to Ulbricht as well as to his successor, Honecker. Ambassador Abrasimov, however, only sent a message to Honecker. What is more, he praised Honecker's life and career in detail, but made no mention of Ulbricht's role in the Communist movement.[93] This is a measure of the deep resentment which, in substantive matters, was engendered by the problems of finding an acceptable Berlin settlement. In mid-June, immediately before the SED Congress was due to open, it was announced that Ulbricht would not attend because of a cold. Brezhnev saw no reason to pay the 'sick man' more than a brief duty call, and then only at the very end of his long stay in East Berlin.[94] Once Ulbricht had been dismissed, Soviet leaders ceased to oppose basic concessions to the Western Powers on Berlin.[95]

Aside from individual pieces of evidence that the Soviet leadership had decided to act against Ulbricht, it seems unlikely that such an important decision as a change of leadership in East Berlin could have been taken without prior Soviet approval. Considering the circumstances, it may seem puzzling that the Soviet leadership did not wait for the SED Party Congress to make the change. Ulbricht's dismissal would then have created less of a stir; and Ulbricht too, who had wanted to make the Congress the crowning event of his career, would then have been more ready to step down voluntarily. It would have come soon enough anyway, if only for reasons of ill-health. It appears, however, that SED party officials contending for power wanted him out of the way before he could use Congress resolutions to set the framework for future policy. The overriding concern of the Soviet leaders was for a speedy ratification of the Moscow Treaty and the convening of the European Security Conference. As this depended on a successful conclusion of the Berlin negotiations, Ulbricht's continuance in power would have meant a further delay in achieving the objectives of Soviet policy towards the West. Evidently the month and a half before the SED Congress was too long to wait. Moreover, as Honecker had recommended himself to the Soviet leaders by his demonstrative anti-Chinese attitude, it may have been that they were anxious to encourage Ulbricht's successor and to support him in his intended reorientation of domestic policy in the GDR.

References

1. For the historical background see *Das Viermächte-Abkommen über Berlin vom 3. September 1971*, Bonn: Federal Press and Information Office, September 1971, pp. 159 ff.; D. Mahncke, 'Um einen Modus vivendi in Berlin', *Europa Archiv*, No. 5 (1970), pp. 157 ff.; G. Wettig, 'Die Berlin-Politik der UdSSR und der DDR', *Aussenpolitik*, No. 5 (1970), pp. 285–7.

2. Foreign Minister Gromyko addressing the Supreme Soviet on 10 July 1969, *Pravda*, 11 July 1969; V. Boldyrev, 'Vopros kotoryi zhdet resheniya', *Novoe vremya*, No. 25 (1970), pp. 7 ff. 'V. Boldyrev' and 'V. N. Vysotsky' are pseudonyms for V. N. Beletsky who is responsible for West Berlin affairs at the Soviet Embassy in East Berlin: see G. Wettig, 'Die Rechstlage Berlins nach dem Viermächte-Abkommen aus sowjetischer Sicht', *Deutschland-Archiv*, No. 4 (1974), p. 378, footnote 2.

3. See the declaration issued by the Soviet Embassy in East Berlin on 31 January 1970, *Pravda*, 2 February 1970 and *Neues Deutschland*, 2 February 1970; V. N. Vysotsky, *Zapadny Berlin v sisteme sovremennykh mezhdunarodnykh otnoshenii*, Moscow, 1971, pp. 375 and 413 ff.

4. See the report by R. Heizler concerning conversations with prominent Soviet Party officials in Moscow, *Bonner Rundschau*, 26 March 1969; A. Gromyko on 10 July 1969, *Pravda*, 11 July 1969; V. Boldyrev, 'Vopros kotoryi zhdet resheniya', op. cit., pp. 6 f.; E. Grigor'ev in *Pravda*, 22 May 1970; V. N. Vysotsky, *Zapadny Berlin*, op. cit., pp. 291 ff., 357–65, 371 ff., 374 and 443; see also G. Wettig, 'Die Berlin-Politik der UdSSR und der DDR', op. cit., pp. 287–9.

5. V. N. Vysotsky, *Zapadny Berlin*, op. cit., pp. 381–6, 394 and 395 f.; I. Sivtsev in *Izvestiya*, 20 September 1970.

6. B. Conrad in *Die Welt*, 4 October 1969; D. Cramer in *Frankfurter Allgemeine Zeitung*, 4 October 1969; Annmarie Doherr in *Frankfurter Rundschau*, 7 October 1969; D. Cramer in *Frankfurter Allgemeine Zeitung*, 7 October 1969; ibid., 18 December 1969; *Telegraf*, 16 January 1970.

7. See the report by State Secretary M. Kohl, at an international conference of scientists held in East Berlin on 21–22 May 1969, *Aussenpolitische Korrespondenz*, No. 27 (1969), p. 214; Speech by Secretary of State, J. Herrmann, in East Berlin on 10 March 1970, *Deutschland-Archiv*, No. 4 (1970), p. 407. The different treatment of the Potsdam Agreement in this context is evident when comparing V. Boldyrev's article, 'Vopros kotoryi zhdet resheniya', op. cit., p. 8 and M. Kohl's report, *Aussenpolitische Korrespondenz*, No. 27 (1970), p. 213. On this matter see the elaboration by G. Wettig, 'Die Berlin-Politik der UdSSR und der DDR', op. cit., pp. 289 ff.

8. For the East German point of view see G. Görner, *DDR gewährleistet friedlichen Westberlin-Transit*, (East) Berlin, 1969, pp. 34–105 and 108; G. Kegel, *Ein Vierteljahrhundert danach*, (East) Berlin, 1970, pp. 168 ff., 176 ff.; J. Herrmann on 10 March 1970 in *Deutschland-Archiv*, No. 4 (1970), pp. 407 ff.; for the

Soviet point of view see S. Sivtsev in *Izvestiya*, 20 September 1970 (a reservation is made there by reference to the Agreement of 20 September 1955); V. N. Vysotsky, *Zapadny Berlin*, op. cit., pp. 382–5.

9. For more detail see G. Wettig, 'Das Entspannungsproblem Berlin', *Osteuropa*, No. 1 (1971), pp. 13 ff.

10. For the historical background see *Das Viermächte-Abkommen über Berlin*, op. cit., p. 163. In August 1970 the USSR had already indicated that in the future it would adopt a more conciliatory attitude. Whereas it had previously backed unconditionally all GDR protests over West Berlin, it toned down considerably the protest issued by the East German Foreign Ministry over the visit by the Federal President to West Berlin on 21 August 1970 and also dropped the term 'autonomous political entity' (compare the text in *Neues Deutschland*, 22 August 1970 with the TASS version on 24 August 1970).

11. *Der Spiegel*, 26 October 1970, pp. 44 ff. Some additional information is scattered in other press reports.

12. *Südwestfunk*, broadcast on 21 October 1970.

13. *Kölner Stadt-Anzeiger*, 31 August 1970. See the remarks made by K. Rush during an interview on 9 September 1971, *Texte zur Deutschlandpolitik*, Bonn: Bundesministerium für innerdeutsche Beziehungen, 1972, Vol. 9, pp. 71 ff.

14. C. Kaiser in *Die Zeit*, 3 September 1971; *International Herald Tribune*, 3 November 1970.

15. *Kölner Stadt-Anzeiger*, 31 August 1971; see also the report by dpa correspondent W. Marquardt, 4 November 1970; B. Conrad in *Die Welt*, 5 and 6 November 1970; *Der Spiegel*, 9 November 1970, pp. 29 ff. The proposals represented the first stage of the Soviet draft agreement of 26 March 1971, excerpts in *Quick*, 4 August 1971, pp. 8 ff.

16. W. Osten in *Stuttgarter Zeitung*, 7 November 1970; the proposal was mentioned in *Neues Deutschland*, 30 November 1970 and *Sovetskaya Rossiya*, 21 November 1970 (quoting the East German news agency, ADN).

17. Until then the SED leaders had given no indication that they were prepared to end the 'pause for thought' announced by Prime Minister Stoph in Kassel. It was even repeated several times that talks could only be resumed after the Federal Republic had first recognized the GDR. Remarks in this vein were also made at the time of the offer to the Federal Chancellor.

18. ADN report of 29 October 1970, published in *Neues Deutschland*, 30 October 1970.

19. Report by dpa correspondent, W. Marquardt, on 4 November 1970, *Frankfurter Allgemeine Zeitung*, 24 November 1970; see also *Kölner Stadt-Anzeiger*, 24 November 1970 and *Frankfurter Allgemeine Zeitung*, 16 January 1971.

20. In mid-November the Federal government and its three Western allies finally agreed on a common line on Berlin, including among other things adherence to the idea of delegated intra-German negotiations on transit to West Berlin; see Th. Sommer in *Die Zeit*, 8 January 1971.

21. Text, *Neues Deutschland*, 9 November 1970. Quoted from a transcript.

22. For the elaborations in question see ibid., 5 November 1970.

23. *Pravda*, 10 November 1970.

24. It probably came as a shock to Ulbricht to hear at a reception given by

the Soviet Ambassador on 6 November, that 'agreement on this question [of Berlin]' was 'possible and within reach' and that the USSR would not oppose such a development. Ulbricht avoided making any reference whatsoever to this in his reply (*Neues Deutschland*, 7 November 1970).

25. W. Ulbricht, on 13 November 1970, at a reception on the occasion of the international conference of scientists marking the 150th anniversary of the birth of F. Engels, ibid., 14 November 1970.

26. R. A. Remington, *The Warsaw Pact*, Cambridge, Mass., and London 1971, p. 160.

27. Also taking part in the talks between Gromyko and Ulbricht were, for the USSR, P. Abrasimov and V. Falin, and for East Germany, W. Stoph, E. Honecker, H. Axen and O. Winzer. That no agreement was reached is evident from the official declaration on the talks. Contrary to normal practice *Izvestiya* (27 November 1970) omitted all reference to the spirit in which the talks had been conducted (indicating that there were serious differences), whereas *Pravda* (26 November 1970) kept up appearances with the empty formula of a 'warm, friendly atmosphere' (but blatantly omitted any reference to any agreement having been reached); similarly *Neues Deutschland* (26 November 1970) spoke of a 'warm and friendly atmosphere'.

28. Text: *Pravda*, 30 November 1970. Bearing in mind that the Soviet-East German Treaty of 20 September 1955, despite the limitations it retained, also spoke of a GDR sovereignty, it would follow that the idea of the 'sovereign rights' of the GDR did not exclude all possibility of compromise over the question of access.

29. *Frankfurter Rundschau*, 27 November 1970; see also the report by dpa correspondent Schavoir from Brussels on 29 November 1970 and the dpa-report from London on 1 December 1970.

30. This is also evident from the fact that the CPSU, when it published the GDR protest on 28 November 1970, stressed that the act in question was 'part of the campaign of the rightist forces in the Federal Republic'.

31. *Pravda*, 28 November 1970. From the second half of August onwards press support was no longer automatic.

32. *Izvestiya*, 29 November 1970; *Neues Deutschland*, 29 November 1970; see also *Frankfurter Allgemeine Zeitung*, 30 November 1970.

33. *Pravda*, 1 December 1970; M. Ponomarev in *Krasnaya zvezda*, 1 December 1970; Yu. Yasnev and B. Kodakovsky in *Pravda*, 2 December 1970; and V. Kukushkin in *Izvestiya*, 3 December 1970.

34. In conversations with other Warsaw Pact members at the Hungarian Party Congress, for instance, as reported by Th. Sommer in *Die Zeit*, 4 December 1970. Immediately prior to the East Berlin conference Soviet Party officials pointed out to journalists that Brezhnev's formula of 29 November 1970, which among other things made the 'wishes of the West Berlin population' the guideline for a future agreement on Berlin, expressed the desire for a settlement even at the cost of making concessions (*Frankfurter Allgemeine Zeitung*, 3 December 1970).

35. H. Pörzgen in ibid., 8 December 1970; see also *Der Spiegel*, 20 September 1971, p. 108.

36. Towards the end of the Ulbricht era the SED usually abstained from

joining in the obligatory anti-China polemics as practised by the rest of the Soviet bloc and apparently made repeated attempts to exploit the political implications of the Chinese accusation that the USSR was not displaying sufficient solidarity with the GDR (H. Zöger, 'Die Beziehungen zwischen Ost-Berlin und Peking', *Dokumentation der Deutschen Welle*, Cologne, Part I, No. 98 (1972), 12 May 1972, p. 2). In September 1970, when the SED could no longer evade indulging in the polemics against China (H. Zöger, ibid., Pat II, No. 99 (1972), 12 May 1972, pp. 4 ff.), it chose to express itself in an unusual way in *Neues Deutschland* on 22 September 1970: (1) The statements in question were hidden in a wide collection of foreign press commentaries on the Moscow Treaty, instead of devoting a separate article and headline to China; (2) readers of *Neues Deutschland* were given a detailed account of the Chinese thesis of a 'betrayal of the sovereignty of the GDR' and the 'tacit toleration of West German militarism' on the part of the USSR (a matter close to the heart of East German Party officials), only to declare abruptly and without the usual explanatory remarks that such accusations were 'quite monstrous'. In this way they met Soviet demands for a rejection of the Chinese argument without actually taking issue with the Chinese claims.

37. Text: *Pravda*, 4 December 1970; *Aussenpolitische Korrespondenz*, No. 50 (1970), pp. 389 ff.

38. *Frankfurter Allgemeine Zeitung*, 15 December 1970.

39. G. Strobel, 'Die Dezemberkrise 1970 in Polen – Gründe und Aus-wirkungen', Bundesinstitut für ostwissenschaftliche und internationale Studien, Cologne, *Berichte*, No. 9 (1972).

40. R. A. Remington, *The Warsaw Pact*, op. cit., pp. 161–4.

41. Report by dpa correspondent, W. Marquardt, from West Berlin on 10 December 1972.

42. *Der Spiegel*, 7 December 1970, p. 29. When the Soviet mass media published the GDR protest against the visit of the Federal President to West Berlin on 21 August 1970, the status formula of an 'autonomous political entity' was dropped (see above, note 10), whereas it was used again in similar circumstances on 4 December 1970 (*Pravda*, 4 December 1970).

43. Compare the text of the report of 9 December 1970 (*Aussenpolitische Korrespondenz*, No. 51 (1970), pp. 397–402) with the TASS version (*Pravda*, 11 December 1970).

44. Report by J. Anderson in AFRTS (New York), 27 December 1970; report by dpa correspondent W. Nölter from Washington, 28 December 1970; *Politisch-Parlamentarischer Pressedienst*, 6 and 8 January 1971; AFP report from Paris 20 January 1971; and J. Schwelien in *Die Zeit*, 22 January 1971.

45. The disruptions of West Berlin traffic began on 19 December 1970.

46. For example, Ellen Lentz in *International Herald Tribune*, 21 December 1970.

47. See TASS report (foreign service) by Yu. Kornilov, 21 December 1970; TASS correspondents Yu. Voronov and B. Khodakovsky in *Pravda*, 22 December 1970; L. Bezymensky in *Sowjetunion heute*, No. 1 (1971), p. 24; B. Kodakovsky in *Pravda*, 27 January 1971; *Izvestiya*, 31 January 1971; V. Kukushkin in *Izvestiya*, 30 January 1971; P. Verin in *Izvestiya*, 31 January 1971; B. Kodakovsky in *Pravda*, 31 January 1971; B. Kodakovsky, *Pravda*,

8 February 1971. When the Soviet diplomats received the Western protests against GDR measures they defended their ally's actions.

48. On 12 January 1971 the West was asked to comply with formalities for military vehicles not previously in operation; as the West objected, passage was refused. But the Soviet authorities desisted following sharp Western protests. See B. Conrad in *Die Welt*, 15 January 1971.

49. Ibid.; AFP report from Paris on 20 January 1971; J. Schwelien in *Die Zeit*, 22 January 1971; and UPI report from West Berlin on 7 February 1971.

50. For example, L. Bezymenski, 'Eine Zeit der Verhandlungen', *Sowjetunion heute*, No. 1 (1971), p. 24 and Prime Minister Kosygin in an interview with the Japanese newspaper *Asahi*, published by the TASS German language service of 2 January 1971 (all references to Berlin were omitted from the version published by the Soviet press). For subsequent Soviet explanations to West German journalists see the dpa report from Moscow on 3 January 1971.

51. P. Florin, 'Initiativreiche Friedenspolitik', *Horizont*, No. 4 (December 1970), p. 2; see also the joint declaration of the commission of research institutes on questions of European security of 5 March 1971, *Aussenpolitische Korrespondenz*, No. 11 (1971), p. 80.

52. Text: *Pravda*, 30 November 1970.

53. dpa report from Washington, 3 February 1971; *Frankfurter Allgemeine Zeitung*, 5 February 1971; dpa report from Washington, 7 February 1971; *Kölner Stadt-Anzeiger*, 8 February 1971; *Frankfurter Allgemeine Zeitung*, 10 February 1971; USIS report from Washington, 11 February 1971; Th. Sommer in *Die Zeit*, 12 February 1971. The Soviet diplomat in Washington described himself as 'authorized' to make the statement and granted a second interview along the same lines to American journalists. Official Soviet denials followed: no member of the Embassy staff had held such a conversation. However, the American reporter insisted that his story was correct. Since the denials concern unofficial acts they need not be taken too seriously because it is not unusual for the USSR to try to cover its tracks in this way.

54. In view of the strict hierarchy in the Soviet diplomatic service it seems unlikely that opposition forces would press on with their actions, even if these forces were highly placed in Moscow.

55. From the end of December 1970 to 10 March 1971 *Pravda* and *Izvestiya* reported numerous instances of supposed or actual neo-Nazi activities in such a way that the reader must have gained the impression that such forces were the sole determinants of political life in the Federal Republic.

56. See the remarks by Secretary of State Rogers at a State Department press conference, on 11 February 1971, as reported by H. Barth in *Die Welt*, 12 February 1971; H. Allardt, *Moskauer Tagebuch*, Düsseldorf, 1973, p. 381; C. Duevel, 'Is there a Conservative Press Brain Trust in the USSR?' Radio Liberty, *Research Bulletin*, CRD 423/70, 3 December 1970.

57. Ibid.

58. H. Allardt, *Moskauer Tagebuch*, op. cit., p. 381.

59. In the Ukraine collaborators from the Second World War were put on trial again and sentenced (*Pravda Ukrainy*, 6 March 1971). The Lithuanian Party paper traced people living in the Federal Republic and announced that

the DKP wanted the Federal authorities to hand these people over to the USSR (*Sovetskaya Litva*, 8 January 1971); this, however, was never brought up by the USSR via diplomatic channels. On 6 February 1971 *Sovetskaya Litva* gave prominence to the opportunities for publicity enjoyed by the refugee organizations in the Federal Republic. On 3 March 1971, I. Maslov in *Pravda Ukrainy* criticized the 'remarkable' tolerance shown by the West German police towards known right-wing terrorists. Four days later, in the same paper, E. Logvin criticized the 'inconsistency of the ruling circles' in the Federal Republic for having renounced earlier 'revanchist' policies in general, but not their ideas on West Berlin in particular.

60. References to the 'refusal' of the Federal Government were too widely scattered and cautious to build up a really negative picture.

61. So, for example, S. Doernberg and H. Lange, 'Der Vertrag UdSSR–BRD und seine Gegner in der Bundesrepublik', *Einheit*, No. 12 (1970), pp. 1551 and 1557-9.

62. Ulbricht's New Year address of 31 December 1970 in *Aussenpolitische Korrespondenz*, No. 2 (1971), pp. 9-12.

63. The *Pravda* report of Ulbricht's speech of 17 December 1970 (*Neues Deutschland*, 14 January 1971; *Texte zur Deutschlandpolitik*, op. cit., Vol. 6, pp. 291-6) omitted all recriminations against 'right-wing Social Democratic leaders', including the accusation that they wanted to 'liquidate socialism step by step'.

64. This is what V. Falin said to D. Scheel the Consul General in Helsinki on 29 January 1971, as reported in *Die Welt*, 12 April 1972.

65. C. Duevel, 'The Soviet Conservative "Press Brain Trust" Changes its line on the Moscow–Bonn Treaty', Radio Liberty, *Research Bulletin*, CRD 27/71, 25 January 1971.

66. G. Gofman (as transliterated from Russian) in *Krasnaya zvezda*, 28 February 1971.

67. H. Zöger, 'Die Beziehungen zischen Ost-Berlin und Peking', Part III, *Dokumentation der Deutschen Welle*, Cologne, No. 100 (1972), 12 May 1972, p. 1.

68. Text of this speech in *Neues Deutschland* and *Pravda*, 1 April 1971. Texts of other speeches in *Pravda*, 2 and 3 April 1971.

69. L. Ruehl in *Die Welt*, 12 August 1972.

70. Text in *Quick*, 4 August 1971, pp. 10 ff.

71. *Kölner Stadt-Anzeiger*, 9 February 1971 and *Neue Zürcher Zeitung*, 12 February 1971.

72. These were only slightly edited versions of the book by Yu. Rshevsky, *Westberlin – ein Gebilde sui generis*, Moscow (1966-7), appearing in *Sowjetunion heute*, Nos. 4, 5 and 6 (1971). The final instalment was announced but never published.

73. *Frankfurter Allgemeine Zeitung*, 16 February 1971; and for accompanying polemics see A. Barysev in *Sovetskaya Rossiya*, 17 February 1971.

74. *Pravda*, 9 February 1971 and *Neue Zürcher Zeitung*, 14 February 1971.

75. *Der Spiegel*, 8 February 1971, p. 21.

76. ADN report from East Berlin, 4 February 1971; for a subsequent declaration by SEW Chairman see *Neues Deutschland*, 9 February 1971.

77. Ibid., 24 February 1971; for the letter from the Chiarman of the GDR

Council of Ministers to the Mayor of West Berlin of 24 February 1971 see *Texte zur Deutschlandpolitik*, op. cit., Vol. 8, pp. 80 ff.; for the statement of the press office at the GDR Council of Ministers see *Berliner Zeitung*, 3 April 1971.

78. *Izvestiya*, 6 February 1971; *Pravda*, 9 February 1971. The East German initiative corresponded exactly with the Soviet negotiating position: Ambassador Abrasimov had declared that the competency of the Four Powers for the situation in Berlin implied merely a Soviet guarantee for Western military traffic crossing the GDR (UPI report from London on 16 February 1971; *Südwestfunk* broadcast on 16 February 1971).

79. On 29 January 1971, the head of the department responsible for the Federal Republic in the Soviet Foreign Ministry, V. Falin, made quite clear to the Consul General, D. Scheel, his country's expectation with regard to the future of West Berlin and the idea of an interim arrangement (*Die Welt*, 12 April 1972).

80. This was mentioned by the Soviet Ambassador-designate to the Federal Republic, V. Falin, on 18 March 1971, in a conversation with a delegation of the *Junge Union* under the leadership of J. Echternach. For press reports on this see H. Pörzgen in *Frankfurter Allgemeine Zeitung*, 19 March 1971; E. Bölte in *General-Anzeiger*, 19 March 1971; and J. Riedmiller in *Süddeutsche Zeitung*, 19 March 1971.

81. Text (omitting several unimportant passages) in *Quick*, 4 August 1971, pp. 8 ff.

82. Text: *Pravda*, 31 March 1971; *Europa-Archiv*, No. 10 (1971), pp. D232–48 (excerpts).

83. Text: *Pravda*, 4 April 1971; *Europa-Archiv*, No. 10 (1971), p. D248 excerpts).

84. The harsh Soviet line was outlined again following the 24th Party Congress by Party official reponsible for German affairs at the Soviet Embassy in East Berlin V. N. Beletsky (using a pseudonym); see *Dokumentation der Zeit*, No. 12 (1971), pp. 7 ff. In April the USSR tried to mobilize popular support for its one-sided proposals with a tendentious attack on the draft agreement (*Zycie Warsawy*, 15 April 1971, repeated in translation by *Neues Deutschland*, 16 April 1971).

85. *Kölner Stadt-Anzeiger*, 31 August 1971; for remarks, made by K. Rush during an interview on 9 September 1971, see *Texte zur Deutschlandpolitik*, op. cit., Vol. 9, pp. 71 ff.

86. The USSR is said to have declared as early as April 1971 that it was prepared to discuss Four-Power responsibility for civilian traffic to West Berlin and a continued Federal presence in the city (report by UPI correspondent, M. R. Dederichs on 15 June 1971).

87. F. Oldenberg, 'Die personalpolitischen Entscheidungen des VIII. Parteitages der Sozialistischen Einheitspartei Deutschlands', Bundesinstitut für ostwissenschaftliche und internationale Studien, *Berichte*, No. 43 (1971), pp. 2–8 and 11–13; W. Schulz, 'Die SED nach dem VIII. Parteitag', *Deutschland-Archiv*, No. 7 (1971), p. 675; H.-D. Sander, 'Das Ende der Ära Ulbricht', *Deutschland-Archiv*, No. 12 (1971), pp. 1241–3.

88. The absence of obligatory anti-Chinese polemics, the pretentious reference to personal ties with Lenin and the reference to Lenin's statement

that 'Russian comrades must learn in their own way', can hardly have endeared Ulbricht to the Soviet Party leaders. Text of the speech in *Neues Deutschland* and *Pravda*, 1 April 1971. *Pravda* published the text in full (to have shortened it would have been a serious sign of disapproval which would have been noticed by all the 'fraternal parties').

89. *Pravda*, 4, 5, 6, 8, 10, 12, 13 and 14 April 1971. Honecker was not the only one to make a speech in Ulbricht's absence (*Neues Deutschland*, 4, 5 and 6 April 1974). According to official reports the talks between Ulbricht, Honecker and Brezhnev on 12 April 1971 were said to have produced 'complete harmony of views' and to have taken place in an atmosphere of 'fraternal friendship and cordiality' (*Pravda*, 13 April 1971).

90. *Neues Deutschland*, 21 April 1971 and *Pravda*, 21 April 1971.

91. *Frankfurter Neue Presse*, 29 April 1971 (according to a UPI report from London).

92. H. Lathe in *Handelsblatt*, 5 May 1971; *Stuttgarter Zeitung*, 5 May 1971.

93. *Neues Deutschland*, 5 May 1971. Brezhnev's telegrams were also published in *Pravda*, 4 May 1971.

94. F. Oldenburg, 'Die personalpolitischen Entscheidungen', op. cit., p. 6.

95. AFP report from Moscow, 5 May 1971; *Die Welt*, 8 May 1971; *Frankfurter Allgemeine Zeitung*, 10 May 1971; E. Weisenfeld in *Die Zeit*, 14 May 1971; and the report by UPI correspondent, M. R. Dederichs on 16 May 1971.

96. Unlike Ulbricht, Honecker and Stoph directed sharp polemics at China during their visit to the USSR for the XXIV Party Congress (see *Neues Deutschland*, 5 and 6 April 1971).

VIII

Negotiation of a Berlin Settlement in 1971

The Four-Power Agreement on Berlin

Following the session on 7 May 1971 the USSR began to show a more conciliatory attitude in the Ambassadorial talks on Berlin.[1] As a result, the following weeks brought the first signs of progress concerning the extent to which the Four Powers were to control and supervise civilian traffic to and from West Berlin. However, the relationship of the city to the Federal Republic remained in dispute.[2]

On 28 May the negotiators began work on a joint framework for a treaty, with controversial issues and alternative solutions noted in annotations and parentheses.[3] The two drafts submitted by the Western powers and the USSR on 5 February and 26 March 1971 respectively formed the basis of efforts to reach agreement.[4] The four Ambassadors had agreed to set aside the basic legal problems concerning the status of Berlin. When it became evident that no agreement could be achieved on this subject, efforts were concentrated on alleviating practical difficulties in Berlin. However this did not entirely prevent questions of principle intruding on the discussions. For example, when the Western powers refer to Berlin in their draft of 5 February 1971 they distinguish between the 'city' (as a whole) on the one hand and the 'Western sectors' and the 'remaining parts of the city' on the other. This suggested the interpretation that the whole of Berlin was to be covered by the agreement. For its part the USSR by its exclusive use of the term 'Berlin (West)', intended that the agreement should apply only to the Western part of the city.

However, by 26 March 1971 the USSR had withdrawn the demand that Four-Power status be expressly applied only to West Berlin and that the Western powers could only assert authority in the Western part. The 'responsibility' of the three Western powers for West Berlin was acknowledged. At the same time, however, the Soviet text claimed that the Western powers had certain responsibilities towards the USSR, thereby implying that the latter was in a position to claim a voice in West Berlin affairs. According to the Soviet proposal, the governments of the three Western powers were 'to ensure that the provisions concerning demilitarization are carried out in their sphere of responsibility'. Also, it reserved the right to take the 'necessary steps' to prevent 'neo-Nazi and similar activities [in West Berlin] which could disrupt public order or create tension in the area'. For a long time the USSR had used the idea that 'militarism' and 'neo-Nazism' must be stamped out in order to justify manifold and wide-ranging demands on West Germany and West Berlin. Moreover, the Soviet leaders could claim, when it suited them, that tension was created by any institution, circumstance or event of which they did not approve in the Western part of Berlin; thus the USSR was attempting to create a situation in which it would enjoy almost un-limited rights of intervention there. At the same time the Western powers were being asked to accept East Berlin as the capital of the GDR – and therefore outside the realm of Four-Power control.

Whereas the Western draft envisaged agreement between the Four Powers on the handling of civilian road traffic to and from West Berlin, and allocated to the Four Powers supervision rights with respect to such traffic, the USSR merely wanted to 'inform' their opposite numbers of the GDR government's readiness to conclude a transit agreement with the 'interested parties' (i.e., the Federal govern-ment and the Senate) on the basis of certain principles. This would have meant that, as regards civilian traffic to West Berlin, the West enjoyed no rights of access via East German territory. In fact, the GDR's unrestricted jurisdiction over the access routes would have been acknowledged, and any access via East German territory would have been subject to the approval of the East German authorities. This view was underlined by the statement that transit traffic would be regulated 'on the basis of hitherto existing norms of international law' (i.e., in particular, the norms of territorial jurisdiction). The demand for exclusive GDR competence was also expressed in the provisions of the draft agreement according to which persons using the transit routes would be subject to the 'civil order' and 'laws' of the GDR. Where disagreements arose, these were to be dealt with in consultations between the GDR and the other parties to the treaty.

Western proposals envisaged 'special ties' between the Western sectors of Berlin and the Federal Republic, although the Western part of the city would still not constitute a part of the Federation. In return for assurances that 'official constitutional acts' by West German bodies would not take place in the city, the USSR was asked to recognize the adherence of West Berlin to the Federal Republic in terms of both domestic and foreign policy. The USSR in its draft insisted that in principle West Berlin could not be a part of the Federal Republic and was 'not to be governed by it'. German constitutional law, which maintains the opposite view, should unconditionally be declared invalid. 'Relations between Berlin (West) and the Federal

Republic', the argument ran, 'should in no way conflict with this state of affairs.' This meant that basically everything inferring a special relationship between the city and the West German state should be considered unconstitutional. West Berlin would still be able to 'maintain and develop broad ties (*svyazi*) and contacts (*kontakty*)' in economic, scientific, technical, cultural and 'other peaceful' spheres. Such ties were to be of a social rather than a political nature, and relations with West Germany were to come under the general heading of 'foreign' relations.

More particularly the Soviet draft envisaged that West German federal organs in West Berlin should 'engage in no official acts or activities . . . which would represent an extension of their jurisdiction to Berlin (West)', that they should 'not interfere in its affairs' and that they should 'not use the territory of Berlin (West) for purposes harmful to the interests of other states'. The first two provisions tended to challenge vital elements of the administrative, legal, fiscal and economic ties between the city and the Federal Republic. The third amounted to a general clause which would have given the USSR, the GDR and the other Warsaw Pact states unlimited rights to object to any ties between West Berlin and West Germany of which they did not approve. The Soviet draft expressly stated that even ties of a 'non-governmental nature' between West Berlin and the Federal Republic were to be governed by the general provision that the city in no way belong to West Germany.

The growing Soviet readiness to compromise after the beginning of May 1971 at first implied no clear withdrawal from positions set out in the proposals of 26 March 1971. Ambassador Abrasimov continued to insist for some time that West Berlin should be completely separate from the Federal Republic. Even as regards the question of access routes, where the Soviet delegation had first shown signs of softening, the Soviet position changed only very slowly.[5] The important turning-point came when, at the beginning of June 1971, Soviet diplomats finally gave up the idea of linking improvements in transit arrangements to West Berlin with the problem of the Federal Republic's relationship to the city.[6] From then on there was a clear tendency to come to agreement on practical considerations rather than try to include these in a more broadly-based settlement. As a result, agreement on control procedure on the transit routes emerged long before it was clear how the Soviet demand for recognition of GDR jurisdiction was to be reconciled with Western claims to existing access rights.

The question of a Berlin settlement was probably discussed by the Soviet and East German party leaders when they met on the occasion of the VIII Party Congress of the SED in mid-June. Presumably they differed over the extent to which concessions should be made to the West concerning responsibility for civilian traffic by land between West Berlin and the Federal Republic.[7] Also, the East German party officials gave more emphasis than their Soviet allies to the need for a complete separation of the city from West Germany.[8] To the outside world Brezhnev and Honecker presented a picture of complete harmony. Both stressed in their speeches their mutual coordination in foreign policy, the Soviet leader making special reference to the Berlin question. While Honecker announced his readiness to normalize relations with West Berlin and hoped for progress in the Berlin negotiations, Brezhnev emphasized that the diplomatic discussions were likely to result in concrete agreement. The First Secretary of the SED demanded that the West show 'good faith' by recognizing the special status of West Berlin, separate from the Federal Republic. The Soviet party leader demanded that in creating 'normal conditions for the life of the city', there should also be 'due regard for the legitimate interests and sovereign rights' of the GDR. The formula of West Berlin as an 'autonomous political entity' was no longer mentioned.[9]

Following the SED Congress, Soviet party officials intimated to a West German correspondent that Brezhnev's statement 'in the final analysis means that the GDR will have to give up certain positions, even if its sovereignty and all its rights [are] strictly maintained'. At the same time it was hinted that this conciliatory attitude was primarily the result of efforts to induce the Federal Republic to ratify the Moscow Treaty.[10] However, despite success in points of detail, the negotiations made little progress in settling the more important issues. By the end of July and the beginning of August there was still no agreement either on responsibility for the access routes or the nature of the relationship between West Berlin and the Federal Republic.[11] However, there were signs that the USSR was prepared to undertake responsibility for safeguarding civilian ground access from harassment by the GDR, in return for a loosening of the political ties between West Berlin and West Germany.[12] A breakthrough eventually came on 11 August: the controversial questions were now discussed in marathon sessions and the Soviet delegation began to show a marked interest in achieving agreement. Official circles in Washington were certain that the haste of the Soviet negotiators was the direct result of the dialogue opened up shortly beforehand by the President's National Security Advisor, Henry A. Kissinger, with Peking.[13]

The question of Berlin had been one of the themes discussed by the leaders of the Warsaw Pact states on 2 August 1971.[14] At approximately the same time, Ambassador Abrasimov had been discussing the Berlin problem with Honecker and Stoph. Apparently some differences of opinion still persisted, as three days later General

Secretary Brezhnev and the Chairman of the Supreme Soviet, Podgorny, held further consultations with the First Secretary of the SED in Moscow.[15] The SED leaders are said to have objected above all to the Soviet intention to guarantee the smooth handling of traffic to and from West Berlin.[16]

Following the decisive ambassadorial session on 11 August, Abrasimov called on Honecker to inform him about the recent developments.[17] The following day the SED leaders gave the first hint in public that they were prepared to adopt a more flexible attitude towards the Western preferences on Berlin.[18] Discussions between the Soviet Ambassador and the First Secretary of the SED were held again on 13 August.[19] And during the following week, when the remaining controversial issues had come up for discussion, the Soviet Foreign Minister visited East Berlin for a few days for talks.[20] Official circles in Bonn were under the impression that Gromyko's presence in the GDR capital had been 'helpful'.[21] Abrasimov and Honecker met again on 20 August.[22] On 23 August the Ambassadors gave final approval to the agreements drawn up by the delegations. The leader of the Soviet delegation then called on the First Secretary of the SED and presented him with the text of what had been agreed.[23] Two days later, in an interview for the Soviet radio and television committee, the First Secretary stressed that the GDR had 'put forward concrete proposals' with regard to West Berlin and that as a result there 'should really be no serious obstacles' to a solution.[24]

Differences in Interpretation of the Four-Power Agreement

The designated date on which the four Ambassadors would sign the agreement was 2 September. The provisions of the Four-Power agreement were to provide a framework for more detailed agreements between 'German authorities' on civilian transit traffic between West Berlin and the Federal Republic, opportunities for West Berliners to visit the Eastern part of the city and the GDR, and arrangements for exchanges of territory to eliminate the West Berlin exclaves. During the preparatory talks concerning such an agreement State Secretary Bahr discovered that the East German translation and interpretation of the Four-Power Agreement differed markedly from that of West Germany at several decisive points. At his request the three Western Ambassadors found a pretext for delaying the signing; nothing should be signed until the two German governments had agreed on a translation to serve as a recognized basis for intra-German negotiations. On 2 September, succumbing to the pressures of the situation, a lower ranking East German official, acting in an official capacity, agreed to a binding German text.[25] The four Ambassadors then signed the Berlin Agreement on 3 September 1971.[26] Following the signing the GDR published a translation of the text, which contrary to previous agreement, referred to *Verbindungen* (links) – a loose term in German – instead of the stronger *Bindungen* (bonds) between West Berlin and the Federal Republic (see below).[27]

The Four-Power Agreement gave no clear indication of whether it was to apply to the whole of Berlin or only to the Western parts of the city. The lack of any agreement over this basic point of principle was glossed over by the use of neutral expressions such as 'the territory in question'. Unlike the Soviet draft of 26 March 1971, which in its general and specific sections alike had referred only to West Berlin, the general provisions of the final agreement set out principles for the conduct of both sides. It was the second part which laid down 'provisions affecting the Western sectors of Berlin'. The repeated use of the term 'Western sectors of Berlin' implied that there must be other sectors of the city. There was also a terminological distinction made between East Berlin and the GDR. During the negotiations, the Western delegations had made it clear to their Soviet partners that in their view this could have no other purpose than to extend the agreement in order to cover the whole of Berlin, even if its practical provisions only applied to the Western part of the city.[28] Yet, despite this, commentators and spokesmen both in the USSR and in the GDR declared that the Four-Power agreement applied to West Berlin only.

The USSR had declared in the agreement that civilian traffic to and from West Berlin should pass through East German territory without hindrance, and indeed that transit arrangements should be made easier and less cumbersome. Although the corresponding supplement to the agreement spoke of previous consultation and agreement with the GDR, the USSR – not the GDR – still bore overriding responsibility for the flow of transit traffic. This was underlined by a clause that in case of problems there should be consultations between the Western powers and the USSR. 'German authorities' – and those included the GDR government – were merely instructed to agree on 'arrangements for the implementation and amplification' of the Four-Power Agreement. As the arrangements were to be brought into force by the Western powers and the USSR as an integral part of the agreement of 3 September 1971 (and not by virtue of German authority), they indirectly took on Four-Power character. Despite this, subsequent Soviet and East German interpretations coincided in the view that the agreements depended on the consent of the sovereign GDR. This version was apparently a covering formula designed to bring the Four-Power agreement into line with the long-standing claim that the East German state enjoyed unrestricted sovereignty.

According to the text of the agreement, the 'bonds' (as the Federal Republic refers to them) or the 'links' (according to the East Germans) between West Berlin and West Germany should 'be maintained and developed'. The corresponding expressions in English and French (ties, *liens*) imply quite a substantial degree of integration; the Russian term (*svyazy*) could mean also technical ties – even traffic and communications links. According to the agreement, the relationship of West Berlin to the Federal Republic was made conditional on the qualification that the Western part of the city, 'as previously', should not form a 'constitutive part'[29] of the West German state, nor should it be 'governed by West Germany in the future'. The English and French terms represented a conscious limitation of the original Soviet demand that West Berlin should not form a 'part of the Federal Republic'; only in a strict and legal sense was the city prevented from being a part of the Federal Republic. Partial ties, however (which did not conflict with the supreme authority of the three Western powers), were considered in the West to be both admissible and necessary. By emphasizing that the situation, as codified in the agreement, was in keeping with past practices, it was intended to make it clear that West Berlin's relationship with the Federal Republic was to remain essentially unchanged. The Russian expression, however, allows for a more radical interpretation of separation, and implies that no political ties between West Berlin and the Federal Republic are admissible.[30]

According to the Four-Power Agreement, the Federal Republic was to 'represent the interests of the Western sectors' abroad, including among other things consular protection, treaty representation, participation in international events, etc. But all questions affecting security or status remained the responsibility of the Western powers. All this was set out in a supplement in which the three Western Powers informed the USSR that the Federal Republic was authorized to undertake responsibility for certain matters concerning West Berlin on their behalf. However, the USSR and the GDR interpreted the provisions in such a way that it was up to those states entering into relations with the Federal Republic and West Berlin to decide how far they were prepared to accept West Germany's acting on behalf of West Berlin. This was designed to prevent any firm relationship developing between West Berlin and the Federal Republic and to proceed from the assumption of two completely separate political entities.

The details of differing East European and Soviet interpretations became clear by degrees only, but they were manifest immediately in the practical realm. As the negotiations between 'German authorities' on detailed implementation and amplification of the agreement were due to begin, the GDR government declared that questions concerning transit arrangements must be discussed with the Senate as well as the Federal Government, since it was not only West Germans but also West Berliners who used the transit routes.[31] The meaning behind this was that the Federal Republic had nothing to do politically with West Berlin and that the Federal Government had no mandate to represent West Berlin's interests. On 30 September 1971 the GDR government was induced by financial considerations to conclude a postal and telecommunications agreement with Bonn which also included West Berlin.[32] West German hopes of having overcome the deadlock were, however, premature. Throughout October the East German negotiators refused adamantly to accept the West Germans as agents representing West Berlin's interests in matters concerning transit.[33]

The Agreement on Traffic between West Berlin and the Federal Republic and the Implementation of the Four-Power Berlin Agreement

There is no doubt that the GDR leaders were doing their best to rupture the ties linking West Berlin and the Federal Republic. In doing so they could count on Soviet support. But it seems unlikely that the East German leaders seriously expected the other side to give way. The Four-Power Agreement had indeed provided for a consideration reduction in demonstrative acts underlining political ties between the Federal Republic and West Berlin, but the principle of political ties as such was by no means negated. What is more, the existing *Bindungen* – or *Verbindungen* according to the GDR – were not only to be maintained, but even to be developed. Under these circumstances there was no reason for the Federal Government and its allies to yield to East German designs. In all probability this was what the East Germans intended. East Berlin had no particular desire to promote the speedy implementation of a Berlin settlement which involved the sacrifice of many of the SED's own aspirations and demands. The East German party officials were by no means alarmed at the prospect of a delay in the implementation of the Four-Power Agreement or even its abandonment. However, it was not a matter of indifference to the Soviet leaders: ratification of the Moscow Treaty, the convening of a European Security Conference and the alignment of the USA with Moscow rather than Peking all depended on the speedy implementation of the Four-Power Agreement.

During his visit to France at the end of October 1971 Brezhnev had presumably come to realize that not a single country of the Western alliance was prepared to tolerate a delay over Berlin – not even the French Government, on which the USSR had built such great hopes since de Gaulle and the development of a 'special relationship'.

Moreover, President Pompidou is said to have explained to Brezhnev that Paris would only consider recognizing the GDR after the Berlin Agreement had come into force and the two German states had achieved a settlement.[34] On 30 October Brezhnev unexpectedly interrupted his return journey to Moscow to visit East Berlin. A speech he made there cast the political changes taking place in Europe in a very positive light.[35] This was apparently a hint to the SED to modify its policy in accordance with the new prospects of détente in relations between East and West.

Brezhnev may have put his case more forcefully during his confidential talks with East German party leaders. However, it appears that the Soviet party leader's remarks initially met with little response. Consequently the visit, which was originally intended to last only a few hours, was extended to cover the next day.[36] Eventually the SED leader was persuaded to declare publicly that the GDR would 'do its best [to achieve] positive results in the talks as soon as possible'.[37] This assurance was published in detail in *Pravda* and given prominence.[38] Apparently the GDR leaders had only very reluctantly acquiesced to Soviet wishes.[39] According to the official communiqué, Honecker informed Soviet leaders about the negotiations concerning Berlin and was congratulated on the 'practical and constructive position adopted by the GDR' and for its its efforts to bring about a 'speedy conclusion of the negotiations'.[40] The effects of Brezhnev's visit became apparent immediately. The East German negotiators were now prepared to discuss the details of transit arrangements to and from West Berlin with the representatives of the Federal Government.[41]

Thus, after two months delay, the two sides could get down to real negotiations. The East German negotiators had obviously been instructed to adopt a conciliatory attitude in the detailed points under discussion. As a result, progress was made. All the same, it was some time before the GDR delegation was prepared to admit that the agreement being negotiated between the two German states formed a part of the Four-Power Agreement and was intended to implement this agreement. Other central points of dispute were West German demands for very general transit rights, and that the clause concerning misuse of the transit routes be more strictly defined. Initially the East Germans insisted that only such persons as had not contravened any GDR laws or regulations should be entitled to passage. The aim of such a stipulation was to allow GDR authorities to exclude certain categories of travellers as they saw fit. If accepted by West Germany, it could have been interpreted as a further indication of the GDR's sovereign jurisdiction over transit traffic to West Berlin. East German negotiators also tried to extend as far as possible the right granted to them by the Four-Power Agreement concerning the prevention of misuse of the transit routes. Their West German counterparts, on the other hand, were determined to ensure that only clearly-defined cases of misuse of the transit routes (such as helping GDR citizens to escape or the smuggling of propaganda material) should form grounds for East German intervention. This was to prevent retaliatory measures being used for other purposes. Eventually it was essentially the West German view that prevailed. The agreement was initialled on 11 December 1971. On 17 December it was signed.[42]

The Soviet leaders were hoping that the Western governments would be prepared to consent to multilateral preparations for the European Security Conference once a settlement had been achieved on Berlin. After the Berlin Agreement was concluded, they had tried to get preparatory talks going. Brezhnev's meetings with Chancellor Brandt in Oreanda and with President Pompidou in Paris had failed to produce the desired result. However, it appears that the Federal Republic and France did indicate their willingness to begin multilateral preparations once the intra-German agreement on Berlin had been concluded. The Soviet leaders' expectations were confirmed when, at the November 1971 session of the NATO Group of Four, the French, West German and – reluctantly – British representatives showed readiness to go along with Soviet wishes.[43] However, the American delegate raised objections and the proposal had to be shelved.

The reason why the Soviet leaders were so anxious that their ideas be accepted before the Berlin Agreement came into force was that, by September 1971 at the latest, they had come to the conclusion that the Berlin Agreement could only be put into effect after the ratification of the Moscow Treaty. Since the Federal Government was not prepared to introduce the treaty into the *Bundestag* until the settlement on Berlin had been implemented in full – for which the parliamentary process would then take many months – the Soviet Union would have to put up with a considerable delay if the Western governments were to insist not only on the formulation but also on the implementation of a *modus vivendi* in Berlin.

These problems were discussed during Foreign Minister Scheel's visit to Moscow from 25 to 30 November 1971. It became apparent that the Western states would not be prepared to participate in multilateral preparations for a conference until the Berlin Agreement had come into effect, and, conversely, the USSR was not prepared to sacrifice Berlin as its trump card before the Moscow Treaty was ratified. Influential circles in Moscow were not convinced that the Federal government was in a strong enough position to ensure acceptance of the treaty at home; on the other hand, the opposition in the West German Parliament could be expected to vote for the Moscow Treaty only if a settlement was reached on Berlin.

113

Brezhnev, Gromyko and Scheel therefore agreed that the Berlin Agreement and the Moscow Treaty should come into force simultaneously.[44] This also meant that the Soviet leaders had to accept a delay of at least six months in the multilateral preparations for the conference, and the convening of the conference itself, in order to ensure ratification of the Soviet-West German Treaty. In exchange for that, they could take credit for the fact that the CDU Chairman, Rainer Barzel, gave assurances during his visit to Moscow in December 1971 that because of the settlement in Berlin his party would not stand in the way of the Treaty.[45]

Despite this, the fate of the Moscow Treaty in the *Bundestag* hung in the balance throughout the winter. The Soviet leaders looked round for ways of influencing West German public opinion and, through it, a number of wavering members of Parliament. For example, the GDR government provisionally announced the implementation of parts of the intra-German agreement on Berlin for Easter and Whitsun to coincide with the *Bundestag's* first reading of the bill for ratification of the Moscow Treaty. Procedures for handling road traffic were expedited and improved: for the first time since 1966, West Berliners were given the opportunity of making regular visits to East Berlin and the GDR.[46] At the same time, East German representatives opened up prospects of rapid progress in discussions concerning a traffic agreement between the two German states.[47] These signs of conciliation were reportedly the direct result of Soviet influence.[48] There is no other explanation: if one bears in mind the determination with which the SED leaders had previously opposed (as they were again to oppose later) even the slightest moves towards increased intra-German contacts, and their ingenuity since the end of 1972 in getting round the concessions they were pressed into making, it seems entirely out of character for them to have adopted such a conciliatory attitude of their own free will,[49] especially since, in March 1972, the GDR had shown no desire to develop a special relationship with the Federal Republic.

The Moscow Treaty was approved by the *Bundestag* and *Bundesrat* on 17 and 19 May 1972 respectively. The Berlin Agreement, together with the supplementary intra-German agreements, was brought into force on 2 June 1972 with the signing of the final protocol. This opened the way for multilateral talks in preparation for a European Security Conference – which the USSR had been urging for so long.

References

1. Report by UPI correspondent Dederichs on 7 May 1971.
2. UPI and dpa reports on 25 May 1971; USIS report on 27 May 1971.

3. For the historical background see *Das Viermächte-Abkommen über Berlin vom 3. September 1971*, Bonn: Federal Press and Information Office, September 1971, p. 163.

4. Texts, almost complete, in *Quick*, 4 August 1971, pp. 8–11.

5. See P. Verin's call for a transit arrangement based on GDR sovereignty in *Sowjetunion heute*, No. 10 (1971), p. 30. The formulation that transit arrangements could not be worked out 'without the approval and participation' of the GDR obviously leaves room for compromise.

6. See the report by dpa correspondent, W. Marquardt, from West Berlin, on 7 June 1971.

7. See the emphatic call for acceptance of unrestricted GDR sovereignty made in July/August in the theoretical organ of the SED: P. Florin, 'XXIV. Parteitag der KPdSU', *Einheit*, No. 4 (1971), p. 659.

8. K. Kniestadt, 'Was fördert und behindert die Normalisierung der Lage Westberlins?', ibid., No. 4 (1971), pp. 723–6 and the AFP report from West Berlin on 6 June 1971.

9. Texts: Honecker's speech of 15 June 1971 in *Neues Deutschland*, 16 June 1971; Brezhnev's speech of 16 June 1971 in *Pravda* and *Neues Deutschland*, 17 June 1971.

10. See the report by J. Witsinos broadcast by *Deutschlandfunk* on 21 June 1971.

11. W. Kinnigkeit in *Süddeutsche Zeitung*, 26 July 1971; B. Conrad in *Die Welt*, 28 July 1971; UPI and dpa reports of 30 July 1971: AFP report of 12 August 1971.

12. AP report of 2 August 1971; *Frankfurter Allgemeine Zeitung*, 4 August 1971.

13. *Der Spiegel*, 16 August 1971, pp. 21 ff.: C. Kaiser in *Die Zeit*, 3 September 1971; J. Newhouse, *Cold Dawn. The Story of SALT*, New York, 1973, p. 235. Kissinger's trip to Peking, during which the surprise announcement was made of Nixon's intended visit to China, was made public on 16 July 1971. This provoked deep concern in Moscow.

14. According to the official communiqué of 2 August 1971, *Pravda* and *Neues Deutschland*, 3 August 1971. The Politburo of the SED in its report on the meeting in the Crimea on 10 August 1971 mentioned, among other things, the efforts undertaken 'for the settlement of the problem of West Berlin' (*Neues Deutschland*, 11 August 1971).

15. Text of the communiqué of 5 August 1971 in ibid., 6 August 1971.

16. According to information in Bonn: D. Cramer in *Frankfurter Allgemeine Zeitung*, 20 August 1971.

17. *Neue Zürcher Zeitung*, 13 August 1971.

18. On 12 August 1971 P. Verner dealt unexpectantly and at length with the Berlin question: *Texte zur Deutschlandpolitik*, Vol. 8, Bonn: Federal Press and Information Office, 1971, pp. 340 ff. Using similar phraseology to E. Honecker at the VIII SED Party Congress, Verner spoke of the GDR's expectations with respect to the treaty and expressed the hope that agreement could be reached soon. The remarks that the 'reactionary' circles in West Germany were in 'confusion', that 'an agreement on West Berlin could contribute to détente in Europe and prevent them [the reactionary circles] in

future from using West Berlin as an instrument in their struggle against détente', was a hint that agreement was close.

19. *Neues Deutschland*, 14 August 1971.

20. Ibid., 20 August 1971.

21. Statement by the head of the Federal Press and Information Office, C. Ahlers, as reported by D. Cramer in *Frankfurter Allgemeine Zeitung*, 21 August 1971. On 22 August 1971 the SED announced its approval of the agreement by publishing a *Pravda* article on the subject in *Neues Deutschland*.

22. Ibid., 21 August 1971.

23. Both ADN statements were published by *Berliner Zeitung*, 24 August 1971.

24. Text in *Neues Deutschland*, 26 August 1971.

25. *Südwestfunk* radio broadcast on 3 September 1971.

26. Text: *Das Viermächte-Abkommen über Berlin*, op. cit., pp. 179–93 (English version); *Le Monde*, 3 September 1971 (French version); *Mezhdunarodnaya zhizn*, No. 3 (1973), pp. 155–9 (Russian version). For the German version see *Das Viermächte-Abkommen über Berlin*, op. cit., pp. 15–29; *Deutschland Archiv*, No. 9 (1971), pp. 982–7; and *Texte zur Deutschlandpolitik*, op. cit., pp. 371–80. Supplementary documents are published in *Das Viermächte-Abkommen über Berlin*, op. cit., pp. 30–5 and *Texte zur Deutschlandpolitik*, op. cit., pp. 380–9. Declarations of the Ambassadors on signing the agreement as published in *Das Viermächte-Abkommen über Berlin*, op. cit., pp. 45–52. For an interpretation of the agreement see E. R. Zivier, *Der Rechtstatus des Landes Berlin*, (West) Berlin, 1973, pp. 113–64 (including documentation).

27. Text: *Dokumentation der Zeit*, No. 21 (1971), pp. 31–4; see also *Die Welt*, 9 September 1971 and dpa and AFP reports of 14 September 1971.

28. See the speech by Ambassador Rush to the Chamber of Industry and Trade in Berlin. *Frankfurter Allgemeine Zeitung*, 25 September 1971.

29. The linguistic and political controversy between the two German states extended to the correct rendering of 'constituent part' (*element constitutif* and *sostavnaya chast'* in French and Russian respectively), with two terms being used – *Bestandteil* and *konstitutiver Teil*.

30. There is no clear distinction made between 'constitutive part' (*sostavnaya chast'*) and the original term 'part' (*chast'*).

31. B. Conrad in *Die Welt*, 11 August 1971. See documents in *Texte zur Deutschlandpolitik*, op. cit., Vol. 9, pp. 52, 82–5 and 149–52.

32. Text of the protocol and the official Bonn statement in *Bulletin*, No. 142 (1971), 2 October, pp. 1521–3 and *Texte zur Deutschlandpolitik*, op. cit., pp. 158–67.

33. For example, *Neues Deutschland*, 19 and 27 October 1971.

34. *Stern*, 14 November 1971.

35. Text: *Pravda*, and *Neues Deutschland*, 2 November 1971.

36. H. de Kergolay in *Le Figaro*, 3 November 1971; Annamarie Doherr in *Frankfurter Rundschau*, 2 November 1971.

37. Text: *Neues Deutschland* and *Pravda*, 2 November 1971.

38. J. Herrmann in *Pravda*, 12 November 1971.

39. As reported by Annamarie Doherr in *Frankfurter Rundschau*, 2 November

1971, Honecker had a particularly long face at the farewell ceremony for Brezhnev.

40. Text: *Pravda* and *Neues Deutschland*, 2 November 1971.

41. The mass media in the GDR continued to attack the notion that West Berlin was in any way integrated with the Federal Republic, but the argument was no longer used to insist that transit matters could only be discussed if the West Berlin Senate acted in a separate negotiating capacity (see *Neues Deutschland*, 6 November 1971). See also the report of remarks by State Secretaries Kohl and Bahr concerning the stage reached in negotiations in *Neues Deutschland*, 5 November 1971.

42. Text of the agreement, supplements and interpretations in *Die Berlin-Regelung. Das Viermächte-Abkommen über Berlin und die ergänzenden Vereinbarungen*, Bonn: Federal Press and Information Office, December 1971, pp. 13–65, 104 ff., 121–40 and 145–55; and *Texte zur Deutschlandpolitik*, op. cit., pp. 320–50, 434–43.

43. G. Gillessen in *Frankfurter Allgemeine Zeitung*, 12 February 1972.

44. E.-U. Fromm in *Die Welt*, 27, 28, 29 and 30 November 1971; J. Riedmiller in *Süddeutsche Zeitung*, 30 November 1971; *Der Spiegel*, 6 December 1971, p. 23.

45. U. Engelbrecht in *Kölner Stadt-Anzeiger*, 27 April 1971.

46. Bonn declarations as published in *Texte zur Deutschlandpolitik*, op. cit., pp. 106 ff. Text of the decree of 23 February 1972, ibid., pp. 108–12. The Soviet interest in the measure was disclosed in an unusually detailed TASS report (see *Pravda* and *Sovetskaya Rossiya*, 24 February 1972).

47. The negotiations on the traffic treaty were concluded on 26 April 1971 (see documents in *Texte zur Deutschlandpolitik*, op. cit., pp. 419–24). Up to mid-February 1971 there had been no prospect of agreement.

48. *Der Spiegel*, 20 March 1972, pp. 24–7.

49. The impression is reinforced by the fact that well-informed circles in East Berlin had described such a settlement as highly unlikely to West German observers shortly before the decision was made (*Kölner Stadt-Anzeiger*, 24 March 1972). Moreover, it soon became apparent after ratification of the Moscow Treaty how much the SED leaders resented the visits from West Berliners. The provisions (which did not conform to the GDR *Abgrenzungspolitik*, or policy of 'delimitation', from West Germany and West Berlin) were interpreted as restrictively as possible. See J. Nawrocki in *Die Zeit*, 16 June 1972.

IX

The Controversy over Status and Relations between the two German States from the Winter of 1970–1971 to the Autumn of 1972

The Question of the Legal Status of the two German States

As long as the SED leaders had stressed their desire for German reunification and considered this goal to be realizable within the foreseeable future, the international status of the East German state had been of little consequence to them. Only with the gradual dissociation from these expectations from 1953–4 onwards did the issue of equality for the GDR on an international level emerge as the primary concern of East Berlin. The desire for full international recognition of the GDR emerged more and more clearly, as greater emphasis was put on the separate existence of the two German states. This theme, expressed in many different forms, became the central issue of East German policy from the beginning of the 1960s. The demand was made up of three basic elements: GDR equality with the Federal Republic; the abolition of controls and obligations ensuing from the occupation regime; and the opening up of a broad spectrum of opportunities in international affairs. In each case the target was the Federal Republic which, it was claimed, discriminated against the GDR, upheld the authority of the occupation powers in Germany and, by means of the Hallstein Doctrine, worked to prevent international acceptance of the GDR. From 1967, when the GDR began to disassociate itself from the idea of a common heritage with West Germany, and from 1969, when it rejected the concept of 'intra-German relations' between the two German states as put forward by the SPD/FDP coalition, the demand for full international recognition has carried with it the negation of the idea of one German nation.

One of the disappointments which Ulbricht and the SED leaders had to accept regarding the conclusion of the Moscow Treaty was that the Soviet Union had failed to make the East German demands a precondition for agreement with the Federal Republic.[1] However, the SED leaders were not prepared to see the GDR forfeit full international legal status. It appears that at the Conference of Warsaw Pact states on 2 December 1970 in East Berlin, the Soviet leaders felt compelled to go along with the GDR's wishes. From this point onwards they again took up the theme of international recognition of the GDR.[2] Accordingly, reporting on the Conference, Ulbricht emphasized that, as far as relations with the Federal Republic were concerned, these would consist of 'only such relations of equality' as 'are based unconditionally on the principles of international law'. This position, he added, had 'been given full recognition and support by all fraternal parties and states at the Warsaw Treaty meeting'.[3] This version also appeared in the Soviet press, as did the subsequent SED resolution stating that the 'establishment by other states of equal relations under international law with the GDR' was an indispensable prerequisite of 'European security'.[4] Also, the Warsaw Pact member-states demanded at the Bucharest Conference (18–19 February 1971) that the Federal Republic and the GDR establish 'relations based on the generally accepted norms of international law'.[5]

But more important than the strong verbal support given to GDR demands was the fact that the Soviet Union still refused to make the recognition issue a precondition for a settlement with the Federal Republic or the convening of a European Security Conference. The Soviet leaders appear to have restricted their efforts to making sure that Hungary, Bulgaria and Czechoslovakia suspend the establishment of diplomatic relations with West Germany until the problem of relations between the two German states had been resolved. However, the leaders in the Kremlin did not want to allow East German demands to constrain their own freedom of action. At the XXIV Congress of the CPSU, Brezhnev gave emphatic support to the demand for recognition of the GDR, but he failed to draw what to Ulbricht was the logical conclusion from this, namely that progress in relations with the Federal Republic should be made dependent on full satisfaction of East German demands.[6] Hortatory Soviet remarks to the effect that all states should establish 'normal relations in accordance with the norms of international law' with the GDR did nothing to change the situation.

While the Soviet leaders had no interest in providing for the political emancipation of the two German states by abolishing the relics of occupation authority, as far as the other aspects of the recognition issue were concerned they shared the same basic view as the SED party leaders. All Soviet commentaries called for unconditional equality of the GDR under international law and for its acceptance into the global network of diplomatic relations.[7] The Federal Republic was in principle prepared to grant the GDR both these demands, but insisted that these questions must be settled in intra-German negotiations. Thus, in supporting GDR demands, the USSR was not put into a position of open conflict with the Federal Republic provided it refrained from pressing for acceptance of East German demands before an agreement had been achieved between Bonn and East Berlin. However, this was precisely what the SED leaders wanted the USSR to do. In order to achieve their ends the GDR leaders could use the basic Soviet–East German similarity of views over the question of relations between the two German states as a lever. Whereas the Federal Government, since taking office in autumn 1969, had tried to establish a special 'intra-German' relationship with the GDR, both the USSR and the GDR sharply rejected this idea. Particularly after autumn 1970 the SED, with full Soviet backing, had made comprehensive 'delimitation' from the Federal Republic the central issue. There was no room for any form of national community.

Ulbricht's fall from power removed the last remaining obstacles to a complete disavowal of all previously-held ideas on all-German unity. On 15 June 1971, at the VIII Party Congress, the new First Secretary of the SED, Erich Honecker, contrasted the 'bourgeois nation' of the Federal Republic sharply and uncompromisingly with the 'socialist nation' of the GDR – a 'new type of nation', a nation whose outlook was determined by its firm anchorage in the 'world socialist system' and its continuously deepening 'integration in the socialist community of states'.[8] Within the Party ranks the explanation was circulated that the idea of unity had become obsolete as West Germany showed no signs of developing the kind of consciousness demanded by the SED.[9] On 6 January 1972 Honecker made it clear that he rejected any form of community of interests with the West Germans: The Federal Republic was 'more' than just 'foreign territory', it was 'imperialist foreign territory' (in other words, hostile).[10] In Soviet sources too the terms 'Germany' and 'German', referring to matters shared by both German states, appeared less and less frequently. The USSR, like the GDR, dropped the adjective 'German' from the previously used term 'the two German states'.

The all-important question for Honecker and the SED was whether the Soviet Union was prepared to go all out to enforce national delimitation between the Federal Republic and the GDR, thus bringing about a total separation of the two states under international law. Soviet leaders have occasionally tried, though without making any kind of political commitment, to make a show of supporting SED demands. For instance, during his visit to France at the end of October 1971 Brezhnev urged the French President to take the lead in establishing diplomatic relations with the GDR.[11] If Brezhnev's efforts had proved successful, West Germany would have lost vital support in the imminent negotiations with the GDR on the nature of their mutual relations. However, it is doubtful that Brezhnev really expected the

French to agree. He probably only wanted to demonstrate to East German party officials his support for their cause. In the spring of 1972 the East German desire for immediate and general recognition, which would have made negotiations on the matter redundant, came into conflict with Soviet interests, namely to secure the greatest possible support in West Germany for ratification of the Moscow Treaty. As a result the USSR even refrained from paying lip-service to the demand for recognition of the GDR.[12]

Once the *Bundestag* and the *Bundesrat* had ratified the treaty with the USSR, Soviet leaders began to press the East German case more strongly with the Federal Republic. They refused to take part in the Stockholm conference on the protection of the environment because the Federal Government refused to allow immediate and equal participation of the GDR, on the grounds that this would have prejudiced the status of the GDR and the forthcoming intra-German talks.[13] Presumably the initiative for the Finnish proposal of 10 July 1972 for talks leading to the establishment of diplomatic relations with both German states originated with the USSR.[14] This upset the Federal Government's calculations, according to which a settlement of intra-German relations was to precede recognition of the GDR by third parties. The USSR lent its full support to the GDR's increased efforts from June 1972 onwards to gain admission to the UN before agreement with the Federal Republic had been achieved.[15] At the end of May Brezhnev had attempted to prepare the ground for the GDR initiative in his talks with the American President.[16] In the second half of July Foreign Minister Gromyko tried to persuade the West German Ambassador to Moscow, Sahm, that it was also in the interests of the Federal Republic to clear the way now for admission of both German states to the UN.[17] In September Henry Kissinger, in his capacity as President Nixon's national security adviser, was confronted during a visit to Moscow with the Soviet demand that the GDR be admitted to the UN immediately so as not to be at a disadvantage when it came to the convening of the European Security Conference the following spring.[18] Moscow's representations came at a time of strained Soviet–West German relations.[18] Even if the Soviet leader had not been counting on achieving a fundamental breakthrough, their efforts could have had the effect of strengthening the GDR's negotiating position *vis-à-vis* the Federal Republic.

Negotiations between the two German States concerning the nature of their Mutual Relations in the Summer and Early Autumn of 1972

Relations in Central Europe obviously could not be normalized, and the GDR could not hope to achieve speedy recognition from the

West, until the two German states had come to some agreement on their mutual relations. Consequently, on 15 June 1972, State Secretaries Bahr and Kohl began talks on the nature of future relations between the Federal Republic and the GDR. On all essential points the basic negotiating positions of the two sides were clear. The Federal Government wanted a special relationship which would reflect the common German character of the two states and correspondingly differentiate the relationship from that obtaining between states foreign to each other under international law. In practical terms the aim was to link both states to the concept of one German nation and to exchange plenipotentiaries rather than follow the customary international practice of accrediting ambassadors in the respective capitals. The procedure in operation between members of the British Commonwealth could serve as a model. Furthermore, West German leaders considered it essential that the GDR recognize the continued validity of Four-Power rights in Germany as a whole, and that the agreement to be negotiated should make reference to the possibility of German reunification so as not to give it the characteristics of a partition treaty.

The SED leaders explained their own views on the subject in numerous public statements. Any idea of 'intra-German' ties with the Federal Republic, a common national community of interests or national units was strongly rejected. The only possible relations, they argued, were those based on 'peaceful coexistence'.[20] This put West Germany in the same category as other states with a social and political structure differing from that of the GDR. There was an 'unbridgeable rift' between them, resulting from the 'objective process of the historical struggle between socialism and capitalism'.[21] According to leading SED officials, the right to national self-determination, used by West Germany in support of her views on reunification, had been made meaningless by the revolutionary changes which had taken place in the GDR.[22] Consequently, relations between the Federal Republic and the GDR should be determined solely by the general principles of the inviolability of borders, renunciation of force, respect for national sovereignty and equality.[23] The essence of this argument was that relations should be regulated solely according to the norms of international law governing relations between foreign states.[24] State Secretary Kohl had tried to use the discussion about a traffic agreement between the two German states in the spring of 1972 to elevate relations indirectly to full diplomatic status, thereby prejudicing the result of future negotiations concerning the nature of relations between East and West Germany.[25]

On 23 July 1972 Foreign Minister Winzer declared to the Higher Party School of the SED Central Committee that there must be an exchange of ambassadors between the Federal Republic and the GDR. At the same time, he attacked the Western assertion that the two states were 'bound by the continuing rights and responsibilities of the four victorious powers' and therefore were 'not free' to determine the nature of their mutual relations. 'That may apply to the BRD', he acknowledged ironically, 'which ceded important sovereign rights in the Paris treaties. It does not apply to the German Democratic Republic.' Winzer stated that it was a mystery to him 'exactly which rights of the victorious powers prevented the establishment of normal diplomatic relations between the GDR and the Federal Republic'. Finally he described the 'demand that the alleged rights of the Western powers be continued' as a call for acceptance of 'imperialist supremacy'.[26] The idea of a 'Four-Power authority with respect to both German states' was rejected in other statements too. The GDR also claimed full sovereign jurisdiction, unimpeded by the authority of the occupation powers in affairs relating to relations with West Berlin.[27] Thus the SED leaders' intention was clearly to regard diplomatic relations with the Federal Republic as West German recognition of the unconditional sovereignty of the GDR and thereby to establish that there was no Four Power responsibility for Berlin.

Because of these differences of principle no appreciable progress had been made in the negotiations between Bahr and Kohl when they adjourned the talks on 5 July for a summer break. Shortly before the talks were resumed, the party leaders of the Warsaw Pact states met on 31 July in the Crimea to discuss, among other things, relations between the two German states. Following prior discussions between the Foreign Ministers of the USSR and the GDR, the East European allies were urged to adopt a policy of reserve in relation to the Federal Republic until the latter complied with East German demands. Apparently the conference participants supported the East German demand for unconditional diplomatic relations with West Germany. However, it seems that at the same time it was brought to the notice of the GDR that the USSR still placed a high value on détente and good relations with the Federal Government, and that the process of normalization which had begun would therefore not be allowed to collapse as a result of the inability of the two German states to resolve their differences.[28] On 2 August, when State Secretary Kohl resumed contact with his opposite number Bahr, he emphasized his interest in achieving speedy progress, and proposed that formal negotiations begin.[29] This suggestion was accepted by West Germany on 9 August.

The East German negotiators were quick to table a draft treaty – at the latest by 20 August.[30] The preamble declared 'the inviolability of the borders and respect for the territorial integrity and sovereignty of all states in Europe within their present borders' to be a 'fundamental precondition of peace'. The principle of sovereignty was in no way related to remaining responsibilities ensuing from the occupation regime or the existence of a German nation. The issue of the inviolability of borders was not connected with any proposal for renunciation of force, the implication being that the borders were immutable, which also ruled out any possibility of peaceful reunification by agreement.[31] According to Article 1, relations between the Federal Republic and the GDR were to be 'based on the principles of peaceful coexistence, as apply between states with differing social systems'. Article 2 repeated the principles set out in the preamble and added the principles of 'independence', 'non-interference in internal and external affairs, the right of self-determination and non-discrimination'. The SED did not interpret the right of self-determination in terms of the national aspirations of the German people, but as the right of the masses to opt for a Communist future – as they had done in the GDR. The principle of renunciation of force was not mentioned until Article 3, where it was treated as a matter of secondary importance. Moreover renunciation of force was mentioned in connection with matters 'affecting European and international security'. This can be seen as limiting its applicability, even if it was stated subsequently that all disputes were to be settled peacefully.

Article 4 stipulated that neither of the two states could 'represent [the other] internationally or act in its name'. This was not a controversial point. But Articles 5 and 7 were more controversial. For example, the parties to the treaty were to 'cease all activities . . . likely to disrupt peaceful coexistence between the two peoples', and 'discontinue measures' extending in applicability beyond the territory of the state in question and 'revoke laws and other normative acts' to this effect. The aim was to prevent the Federal Republic from doing anything which the GDR considered to be 'aggressive' and to compel the Federal Republic to renounce the legal claim to the existence of a single German citizenship. According to Article 6, the Federal Republic was to be committed unconditionally to support 'all efforts towards disarmament and arms limitation'. This could provide a possible basis for attacking the ties between West Germany and the Western alliance, using suitable disarmament proposals. According to Article 8, cooperation between the Federal Republic and the GDR was to be confined to the political sphere; there was no mention of more personal contact, communication or humanitarian arrangements.

Article 9, finally, stated that the parties to the treaty should agree that this treaty was not to affect 'bilateral or multilateral treaties and agreements, which were previously concluded by the parties in question' or those which were concluded between other states but 'apply to them'. The inclusion of such a clause was essentially a formality, but in view of the phraseology used and given the context, it acquired new significance. As far as the East Germans were concerned, the unusual reference to the continued validity of agreements which 'apply to' the parties to the treaty was a way of gaining West German recognition of the Potsdam Agreement and acceptance of the East German view that that Agreement imposed certain obligations concerning the domestic system of 'Germany', which West Germany had yet to meet.[32] Yet the Federal Republic could link the reference that previously concluded treaties would be unaffected to the Paris Treaties on the one hand[33] and to agreements between the GDR and the USSR on the other.[34] The treaties concluded between East and West Germany and the former occupying powers placed restrictions on the sovereignty of both German states. These restrictions, however, were explicitly stated only in the treaties between the three Western powers and the Federal Republic. The GDR leaders thus described the legal position in such a way that their state, unlike the Federal Republic, was not hampered by any restrictions on its sovereignty.[35]

State Secretary Bahr's instructions were that the treaty should reinforce national unity, in no way hamper a future reunification and achieve the best possible working relationship between the two states.[36] These were the main points of West Germany's negotiating strategy. The negotiators were instructed to gain acceptance for the following provisos: (i) that the treaty should be valid only until the conclusion of a peace treaty; (ii) that only plenipotentiaries should be exchanged between Bonn and East Berlin; and (iii) that Four-Power responsibility for Germany should be recognized. All this was to underline the continued existence of a German nation, despite the division, and to make sure that the establishment of intra-German relations would not be interpreted as making the division final. Furthermore, the preamble was to mention explicitly the commitment of both parties to continued national unity. The Federal Government also insisted that favourable conditions be created for personal contacts and the exchange of ideas between the two parts of Germany. Also, the humanitarian problems created by the division and the building of the Berlin Wall should be resolved. Thus, State Secretary Bahr and the members of his delegation had to induce the GDR to make concrete concessions over matters of human contact.

As was to be predicted, the GDR representatives strongly opposed the West German approach. State Secretary Kohl denied that there were any Four-Power responsibilities which could hinder the establishment of full diplomatic relations between the two states. Bahr, on the

other hand, insisted that the Germans must recognize the responsibilities of the former occupying powers concerning all-German
affairs. Kohl declared that it was pointless to try to come to an agreement on attitudes to the German nation and demanded that this issue
be dropped from the agenda.[37] However, Bahr pointed out that the
treaty would contradict the Federal Republic's Constitution, and
therefore would never gain internal approval if there were no reference
to the continued existence of the German nation.[38] One of the central
issues was whether the Federal Republic and the GDR should exchange
plenipotentiaries or ambassadors. The whole dispute hinged on
whether the special character of relations between East and West
Germany was to be emphasized or denied.[39] In addition, there was
the practical problem that, if the West German representation was
to be granted 'internal' status in accordance with the official West
German view that there existed only one German citizenship, it could
issue GDR citizens with West German passports.[40]

Other basic questions of principle were discussed, on which no
agreement could be reached.[41] The West German delegation tried to
link the inviolability of the borders, which was contained in the
preamble, with the idea of renunciation of force. This would have
meant that the borders could be changed by agreement in the event of
reunification. Furthermore, the West Germans insisted that the
renunciation of force be universal. Nor were they prepared to accept
the stipulations justifying the GDR's right to interfere in West
German internal affairs or those clauses which could have prejudiced
Bonn's attitudes towards future disarmament proposals. Bahr insisted
that the clauses on intervention be deleted entirely. Moreover, he
considered it essential that reference to Bonn's official position regarding
single German citizenship be shown to be in harmony with the treaty,
even if such a position were not accepted by the other side. The West
German representatives could only consider supporting initiatives on
disarmament in principle – in other words, subject to an assessment of
the concrete proposals. Agreement on such practical problems as
the West German demands for 'measures to alleviate hardship' could
be the subject of discussion between experts.[42]

The Final Round in Settling Intra-German Relations

The negotiations promised little hope of success even on minor
points. In fact, until the central issues were settled there was no
prospect of agreement on the rest. Negotiations reached a point of
deadlock at the beginning of October. The Soviet leaders were
becoming more and more insistent that the GDR should be accepted
into the UN forthwith, whether or not agreement had been achieved

between the two German states on the nature of their relationship.[43] The Federal Government was exposed to increasing pressures. However, the Soviet Union must have been aware that it could not so easily overcome the opposition of the Federal Republic and its allies to GDR membership in international organizations.[44] Moreover, it was in Soviet interests too that the Federal Government should come to some final agreement over intra-German relations before the West German elections on 19 November which had been made inevitable by the stalemate in the *Bundestag* since the end of April, and which could conceivably result in the return of the CDU/CSU to power in Bonn.[45] The SPD–FDP coalition, on the other hand, was desirous of crowning its *Ostpolitik* before the election by concluding a treaty with the GDR, so they could present the electorate with a successful balance-sheet. Given these circumstances, both Moscow and Bonn would welcome the speedy resolution of the difficulties besetting the negotiations between Bahr and Kohl. It seemed advisable to confer on how this could be best achieved.

State Secretary Bahr visited Moscow from 8 to 10 October for talks with Soviet leaders. On the last day of his stay Bahr had an unexpectedly long talk with Brezhnev.[46] One of the central themes of their conversation was the membership of the two German states in the United Nations. As Bahr reported afterwards in Bonn, he persuaded the Soviet leaders to adopt a more flexible attitude towards Bonn's insistence that the issue of the relationship between the two German states should be settled first. The Soviet leaders also finally agreed to join the three Western powers in reiterating their joint responsibilities for Germany, in order that it be made quite clear that these applied to both German states.[47] This was undoubtedly helped by Western determination to refuse GDR membership in the UN until the Four Powers had issued a declaration on their continuing responsibilities;[48] this was to ensure that West Berlin transit traffic would be protected by law. Bahr and the Soviet leaders seem to have discussed the problems of intra-German negotiations only in general terms, with little attention being devoted to detail.[49]

During the three days of talks between Kohl and Bahr which began on the evening of 10 October, the East Germans at first continued to be inflexible,[50] but then began to show a limited readiness to compromise.[51] The discussions turned to the West German demand that the preamble contain a reference to the continued unity of the German nation. The GDR representatives were very much against the proposal, but after much hesitation seemed willing to replace it with a reference to the need for a final peace treaty. (This would have established links between the two German states on the basis of international law.) However, the USSR, which at first seemed to have no objections, refused to agree to this and urged the GDR to make concessions over the unity formula. Bahr then suggested the following compromise for the treaty text: the parties to the treaty, despite the 'unresolved national question', would proceed from the 'realities of a divided Germany'.[52] This amounted to expressed acceptance of the division, while at the same time its unsatisfactory character would be recognized. The negotiators finally agreed on the formulation that both states accepted 'existing historical realities' and would set aside the 'differing views of the Federal Republic of Germany and the German Democratic Republic on questions of principle, including the national question'. The Federal Government saw the references to existing 'historical' realities and the 'national question' (in the singular) as sufficient expression of their common German past and of the continued existence of an unresolved German problem. At the same time it was entitled to adhere to its concept of one common citizenship for all Germans. Consequently Article 7 of the GDR draft, which had opposed this, was dropped.

As the reference to the continued unity of the German nation was not expressed in the form originally intended, the West Germans were all the more anxious that the special (non-foreign) nature of relations between the two German states be demonstrated by agreement to exchange plenipotentiaries rather than ambassadors. It was finally agreed, shortly before negotiations were concluded, to exchange 'permanent representations'. However, the GDR delegation refused adamantly to include reference in any form to continued Four-Power responsibilities. Bahr attempted instead to replace the general stipulation in Article 9 – that treaties or agreements 'concluded previously by or relating to' the two states would not be affected – by a listing of the treaties in question, or at least to add a reference to the most important of them.[53] If the Paris Treaties of 1954, on the one hand, and the agreements between the GDR and the USSR of 1955 and 1964, on the other, had been mentioned, this would have implied an indirect confirmation of Four-Power responsibilities, and further strengthened the legal basis linking the two German states to the Berlin Agreement of 3 September 1971. The West Germans were unsuccessful. The final text of the treaty follows exactly the wording of the GDR draft on this point.

Bahr could afford to concede this point because in the meantime the Ambassadors of the Four-Powers, following negotiations lasting from 22 October to 4 November, had come to an agreement on the wording of a joint declaration. In principle this represented a victory for the West. Yet the Western Ambassadors were obliged to modify considerably the formula normally used by the Western Powers and the Federal Republic. They could no longer refer to the 'rights and responsibilities of the Four-Powers for Berlin and Germany as a whole'. As was to be expected, the USSR insisted that the Four Powers had no competence with regard to Berlin as a whole, nor were they jointly responsible for the unresolved German problem. The four Ambassadors merely stated that the acceptance of the Federal Repubic and the GDR into the UN could 'in no way affect the rights and responsibilities of the Four Powers and their corresponding joint agreements, resolutions and practices'. Western attempts to include a reference to the fact that this applied until a final peace treaty was concluded failed in the face of Soviet resistance.[54]

At the end of October and the beginning of November, Bahr and Kohl made further alterations to the text presented by the GDR in August. A reference to renunciation of force was included in the preamble. This was important, because interpretation of the various provisions of the treaty itself now had to be based on the principle of renunciation of force. Thus peacefully negotiated agreement on changing or abolishing Germany's borders would not be in contravention of the treaty. As in the case of the Moscow Treaty, the Federal Republic published a letter reserving for itself the right 'to work for a peace settlement in which the German people would regain its unity through free self-determination'. In Article 3 renunciation of force was phrased in such a way that it was clearly made mandatory for the settlement of all disputes between the two states. Also, the support expressed by the parties to the treaty for the idea of peaceful coexistence between peoples and for efforts towards disarmament and arms control was formulated in such a way that it implied no prior blanket commitment. The West Germans placed high value on the numerous protocols, exchanges of letters and declarations accompanying the treaty, regulating among other things such questions as entry into the GDR, uniting of families, procedures for handling gifts and the accrediting of journalists.

Finally, there was the question of the extent to which West Berlin was to be included in the agreements. It was clear that, in accordance with the Four-Power Agreement, the city could not be automatically and unconditionally included as part of the Federal Republic. However, as the West German negotiators asserted, there were two reasons why West Berlin should not be excluded. First of all, the Berlin Agreement provided for consular representation of West Berlin's interests by the Federal Republic. This also had to apply in relations between the two German states. Secondly, the Berlin Agreement stipulated that the Federal Republic could include West Berlin in agreements on economic, cultural and other matters (provided these did not include questions of security or status). The Federal Government claimed this right vis-à-vis the GDR. Kohl refused to accept this.[55] Only after tough discussions was he prepared to compromise on this issue. It was decided to issue a joint declaration on the 'common understanding' that accompanying and subsequent treaties and agreements could be extended to cover West Berlin, 'according to agreement in each case'. At the same time the two men confirmed that the Federal Republic's permanent representation in the GDR would represent the interests of West Berlin in accordance with the Four-Power Agreement.[56] The first part of the understanding was obviously a compromise: the GDR merely consented to the possibility of including West Berlin.

It was later hinted in Bonn[57] and Moscow[58] that the whole agreement was made possible by, among other things, the exertion of Soviet influence on the GDR. This is a plausible explanation. Certainly, Soviet diplomats repeatedly intervened in the final phase of the negotiations.[59] Moreover, the USSR clearly had a keen interest in seeing the treaty on the nature of intra-German relations concluded by the beginning of November. For agreement to be achieved at this particular point in time, even if the signing did not take place until later, represented a political fact which could not easily be ignored by a possible CDU/CSU government in power after the Federal elections. What is more, the successful conclusion of the negotiations could improve the electoral chances of the ruling SPD–FDP coalition. Finally, if multilateral consultations on a European Security Conference were to begin as scheduled on 22 November, it seemed especially desirable that the GDR should be able to take its place at the conference table as an equal partner. This aim was achieved by the agreement reached on 7 November 1972,[60] and its initialling on the following day.[61] On 21 December, after the victory of the SPD–FDP coalition in the Federal elections in Bonn, the 'Treaty on the Principles Governing Relations between the Federal Republic of Germany and the German Democratic Republic' was signed.[62]

References

1. Ulbricht reportedly accused the Soviet leaders of this failure during the East Berlin conference on 2 December 1970, see H. Pörzgen in *Frankfurter Allgemeine Zeitung*, 8 December 1970. For some hints to this effect in official statements see the interview with W. Ulbricht on 8 November 1970 in *Neues Deutschland*, 9 November 1970, and the accounts by G. Hagen, 'Die DDR und der Moskauer Vertrag', *Aussenpolitik*, No. 11 (1970), pp. 662 ff. and 666–7, and G. Wettig, 'Der Moskauer Vertrag zwischen UdSSR and DDR', ibid., No. 6 (1971), p. 359. At the beginning of 1970 Ulbricht had tried to persuade the Warsaw Pact allies to make the 'establishment of diplomatic relations between the Federal Republic and the GDR' a 'basic condition of normal relations between the signatories to the Warsaw Treaty and the Federal

Republic' (comments at the international press conference of 19 January 1970, *Aussenpolitische Korrespondenz*, No. 5 (1970), p. 31).

2. For details see G. Wettig, 'Der Moskauer Vertrag', op. cit., pp. 360 ff.

3. Text: *Aussenpolitische Korrespondenz*, No. 51 (1970), p. 401.

4. *Pravda*, 11 and 13 December 1970.

5. Text: *Izvestiya*, 21 February 1971; *Europa Archiv*, No. 5 (1971), p. D124.

6. Text: *Pravda*, 31 March 1971.

7. For instance, the Soviet–East German communiqué of 18 May 1971 as published in *Neues Deutschland*, 19 May 1971, and the Prague Declaration of the Warsaw Pact states of 26 January 1972 as published in *Pravda*, 27 January 1972, and *Europa Archiv*, No. 4 (1972), pp. D106–10. See also V. Zhigulenko in *Izvestiya*, 30 April 1971; M. Podklyuchnikov in *Pravda*, 2 May 1971; B. Dmitriev in ibid., 11 May 1971; and Yu. Zhukov in ibid., 23 September 1971.

8. Text: *Aussenpolitische Korrespondenz*, No. 25 (1971), pp. 193 f.

9. F. Oldenburg, 'Das 6. ZK-Plenum', *Deutschland Archiv*, No. 8 (1972), pp. 789 ff. See also F. Oldenburg, 'V. Historikerkongress', ibid., No. 1 (1973), pp. 13 ff.; B. v. Rosenbladt, *Zur Aussenpolitik der DDR*, Stiftung Wissenschaft und Politik, SWP – S215, Ebenhausen/Isartal, May 1973, pp. 13–18 and 83–5. For the previous East German line on the national question see ibid., pp. 12 ff. and 80–3, and W. Sühlo, *Der Zusammenhang von nationaler und gesellschaftlicher Spaltung der deutschen Nation in seiner Bedeutung für die Deutschlandpolitik der DDR*, SWP – S170, Ebenhausen/Isartal, June 1970.

10. Text: *Neues Deutschland*, 7 January 1972. All formal relics of an all-German orientation were erased. For instance, the East German radio *Deutschlandsender* was renamed; The German Workers' Conference (*Deutsche Arbeiterkonferenz*) and the State Secretariat for West German Affairs (*Staatssekretariat für westdeutsche Angelegenheiten*) were dissolved.

11. See the report by the Bonn correspondent of *Die Tat*, 4 November 1971.

12. The communiqué issued at the end of Honecker's visit to the USSR from 4 to 10 April 1972 made no reference to recognition of the GDR (text in *Neues Deutschland* and *Pravda*, 11 April 1972). On 20 March Brezhnev merely attacked those circles in West Germany who rejected the Moscow Treaty and at the same time would like to weaken the sovereignty of the GDR. In his words, such an attitude was divorced from reality and could only lead to a 'dead-end' (text in ibid., 21 March 1972). Brezhnev was thus asserting that the Moscow Treaty, which failed to satisfy East German demands for recognition, was the guarantee of East German sovereignty and that acceptance of East Germany on the international scene would follow as a matter of course, and needed no (Soviet) assistance.

13. The conference began on 5 June 1972. For an assessment of the proceedings see the interview by Honecker on 7 June 1972 in Bundesministerium für innerdeutsche Beziehungen, (ed.) *Texte zur Deutschlandpolitik*, Bonn, 1973, Vol. 11, p. 49.

14. *Die Welt*, 13 July 1972 (report from Bonn); dpa report from West Berlin on 1 August 1972. For Soviet approval of the Finnish proposal see Yu. Goloshubov in *Izvestiya*, 16 July 1972.

15. On 29 June 1972 A. Norden talked to UN General Secretary, K. Waldheim, on the subject. On 1 July 1972 Foreign Minister O. Winzer was received by leading officials of the organization and for an unexpectedly long talk lasting two hours. See Winzer's statements at a press conference on 4 July 1972 in *Texte zur Deutschlandpolitik*, op. cit., Vol. 11, pp. 94–8. This UN activity was backed up by a memorandum of the GDR Council of Ministers of 15 October 1971, published in ibid., Vol. 9, pp. 183–9.

16. H. Gerlach and H. Palmer in *Kölner Stadt-Anzeiger*, 31 May 1972.

17. H.-U. Fromm in *Die Welt*, 28 July 1972.

18. H. Lathe and A. Frisch in *Frankfurter Allgemeine Zeitung*, 20 September 1972.

19. Apparently the hopes of the Soviet leaders with regard to the extent and conditions attached to economic-technical cooperation with the Federal Republic were not fulfilled. The parliamentary stalemate between government and opposition in Bonn may have disturbed Moscow and cast doubt on the value of a political commitment with respect to the Federal Republic.

20. See Honecker's statements on 7, 19 and 27 June 1972, as published in *Texte zur Deutschlandpolitik*, op. cit., Vol. 11, pp. 50, 52, 87–9 and 92, and the elaborations by Winzer on 23 June 1972 in the ADN text of 3 July 1972.

21. Speech by Honecker in Leipzig on 10 March 1972 in *Neues Deutschland*, 11 March 1972.

22. See Honecker's remarks on 7 and 19 June 1972, as published in *Texte zur Deutschlandpolitik*, op. cit., Vol. 11, pp. 50 and 88.

23. Honecker on 27 June 1972, ibid., p. 91.

24. See Honecker's explanations on 7, 19 and 27 June 1972, ibid., pp. 51, 87, 88 and 92.

25. D. Cramer in *Frankfurter Allgemeine Zeitung*, 28 March 1972; ibid., 8 April 1972.

26. ADN text, 3 July 1972.

27. Remarks by Prof. Edith Öser in the programme *Antworten* on GDR television, 5 July 1972, at 1900 hrs.

28. For the Warsaw Pact states' undertaking to adopt a reserved attitude towards the Federal Republic see the Reuter report of 1 August 1972; R. Röntgen, news and commentary on the West German radio station *Hessischer Rundfunk* 1 August 1972; Report by the *Tanjug* correspondent, A. Novačić, 11 August 1972. Reports of an agreement with respect to diplomatic relations in Germany are backed up in particular by the statement of the Politburo of the SED Central Committee on the Crimea Meeting of 2 August 1972 (*Neues Deutschland*, 3 August 1972), a report by E. U. Fromm from Moscow (*Die Welt*, 8 August 1972) and remarks by F. Ebert on Soviet television on 19 August 1972 (ADN text, 19 August 1972). Soviet interest in a successful conclusion of the negotiations is evidenced by the unusually positive evaluation of the Brandt-Scheel government in the above-mentioned SED commentary (*Neues Deutschland*, 3 August 1972) and the noticeably increased interest displayed by Kohl when talks were resumed with Bahr on 2 August 1972 (report by the dpa correspondent Wettermann from Bonn, 4 August 1972). There is also mention of agreement on joint policy with respect to the Federal Government in East German sources (*Neues Deutschland*, 3 August 1972; ADN text

of Ebert's remarks, 19 August 1972) and in one East European report (by Tanjug correspondent, A. Novačić, on 11 August 1972).

29. Report by dpa correspondent Wettermann from Bonn, 4 August 1972.

30. Undated facsimile of text in *Quick*, 25 October 1972, pp. 12 ff. On the question of the date: the draft was mentioned as a 'nine point proposal' by D. Cramer in *Frankfurter Allgemeine Zeitung*, 23 August 1972 and in the Tanjug report from Bonn, 29 August 1972. Honecker's 'concrete proposal' of 19 June 1972 (*Texte zur Deutschlandpolitik*, op. cit., Vol. 9, p. 87), may have as little to do with a draft text as the reports concerning presentation of basic positions by the two sides (*Die Welt*, 31 July 1972; *Neue Zürcher Zeitung*, 3 August 1792). It is also unusual for a draft treaty to be presented before talks have officially begun.

31. Discussion of the theoretical problems involved in discussions at the European Security Conference in G. Wettig, 'Die Vereinten Nationen und eine Normierung des Zusammenlebens in Europa', *Vereinte Nationen*, No. 3 (1973), pp. 70–2.

32. W. Sühlo, *Der Zusammenhang von nationaler und gesellschaftlicher Spaltung*, op. cit.; G. Wettig, 'Die politischen Leitsätze von Potsdam', *Osteuropa*, No. 3 (1969), pp. 173–86; similarly Ulbricht's statements at the international press conference on 19 January 1970, *Aussenpolitische Korrespondenz*, No. 4 (1970), pp. 22, 24.

33. Text: *Bundesgesetzblatt*, Vol. 2 (1955), pp. 305 ff. (in German and English); *Notes et Études Documentaires*, 14 December 1954 (in French).

34. Treaty and exchange of letters between the USSR and the GDR of 20 September 1955 (*Dokumente zur Deutschlandpolitik*, compiled by E. Deuerlein in collaboration with H. Schierbaum, Series No. III, Vol. I, Frankfurt am Main, (West) Berlin, 1961, pp. 371–7); treaty between the USSR and the GDR of 12 June 1964 (*Europa Archiv*, No. 13 (1964), pp. D325–8; *Pravda*, 13 June 1964). The Four-Power Agreement on Berlin of 3 September 1971 must also be seen in this context.

35. See Ulbricht's statements on 19 January 1970 (*Aussenpolitische Korrespondenz*, No. 4 (1970), pp. 21 and 23; and his unpublished replies to questions, put by K. Goldstein of the *Deutschlandsender* and by Lehnert, Editor in Chief of the East German newspaper *Berliner Zeitung* and the comments by Edith Öser in the GDR television programme *Antworten* (Answers) on 5 July 1972 at 1900 hrs.

36. *Neue Zürcher Zeitung*, 11 August 1972.

37. *Die Welt*, 11 August 1972.

38. *Der Spiegel*, 23 October 1972, pp. 23 ff.

39. See the GDR's call for diplomatic relations in accordance with general practice and the principles of 'peaceful coexistence'; for example, M. Kohl in an interview with ARD on 31 August 1972, *Texte zur Deutschlandpolitik*, op. cit., Vol. 11, pp. 130 ff.; M. Kohl in an interview for East German television on 13 September 1972, *Neues Deutschland*, 14 September 1972; E. Honecker in a speech given in East Berlin, *Texte zur Deutschlandpolitik*, op. cit., Vol. 11, pp. 172 ff. On the other hand, see E. Bahr, in an ARD interview on 31 August 1972, ibid., p. 132.

40. *Die Welt*, 10 August 1972.

41. Bahr's statements on 29 September 1972, *Texte zur Deutschlandpolitik*, op. cit., Vol. 11, p. 174, and on 12 October 1972, *Frankfurter Allgemeine Zeitung*, 13 October 1972.

42. Bahr's statements in ibid.

43. U. Engelbrecht in *Kölner Stadt-Anzeiger*, 6 October 1972; A. Grigor'yants in *Izvestiya*, 6 October 1972.

44. The GDR could only be admitted to the UN if neither France nor Great Britain vetoed the proposal in the Security Council.

45. For Moscow's evaluation of and views on the correlation of forces in the West German *Bundestag* see *Osteuropa*, No. 3 (1973), pp. A145–55.

46. Official bulletin in *Pravda*, 11 October 1972; *Izvestiya*, 12 October 1972.

47. E.-U. Fromm commentating on *Hessischer Rundfunk*, 10 October 1972; U. Engelbrecht in *Kölner Stadt-Anzeiger*, 11 October 1972; H. Pörzgen in *Frankfurter Allgemeine Zeitung*, 11 October 1972; D. Cramer in ibid., 2 November 1972. Following previous discussions with the Federal Government the three Western powers had tried with little success since July 1972 via diplomatic channels to persuade the USSR to issue a joint declaration confirming Four-Power responsibility for Germany as a whole. See the statements by the spokesman of the West German Foreign Office, G. Brunner, as reported in *Die Welt*, 3 June 1972; D. Cramer in *Frankfurter Allgemeine Zeitung*, 8 August 1972; *Die Welt*, 11 August 1972; D. Cramer in *Frankfurter Allgemeine Zeitung*, 23 August 1972 and 1 September 1972.

48. Above all the United States government was afraid that, if there was no simultaneous confirmation of Four-Power responsibilities, the GDR could claim that acceptance into the UN represented unconditional recognition of East German sovereignty and would thus fail to implement the obligations set out in the Berlin Agreement of 3 September 1971. See H. Barth in *Die Welt*, 9 October 1972 and 30 October 1972.

49. H. Pörzgen in *Frankfurter Allgemeine Zeitung*, 11 October 1972.

50. D. Cramer in ibid., 13 October 1972; *Die Welt*, 13 October 1972.

51. This became apparent when the First Secretary of the SED, in official statements on 20 October 1972, and contrary to previous practice, failed to use the usual phraseology when dealing with controversial points. Text: *Texte zur Deutschlandpolitik*, op. cit., Vol. 11, pp. 252 ff.

52. *Der Spiegel*, 23 October 1972, p. 24; ibid., 6 November 1972, p. 24.

53. D. Cramer in *Frankfurter Allgemeine Zeitung*, 2 November 1972.

54. Original Russian text in *Pravda*, 10 November 1972; German translation (West German version) in *Texte zur Deutschlandpolitik*, op. cit., Vol. 11, p. 325; ADN text, 9 November 1972. The Western and Eastern versions differed only in respect of the sequence in which the names of the two German states were recorded. For the background history see *Frankfurter Allgemeine Zeitung*, 23 October 1972; *Die Welt*, 23 October 1972; *Frankfurter Allgemeine Zeitung*, 24 October 1972; *Neue Zürcher Zeitung*, 25 October 1972; interview with the spokesman of the West German government, R. v. Wechmar, on *Hessischer Rundfunk*, 28 October 1972; *Neue Zürcher Zeitung*, 29 October 1972; H. Barth in *Die Welt*, 30 October 1972; *Frankfurter Allgemeine Zeitung*, 31 October 1972; *Neue Zurcher Zeitung*, 1 November 1972; *Frankfurter Allgemeine Zeitung*, 6 November 1972; *Neue Zürcher Zeitung*, 7 November 1972; *Kölner Stadt-*

Anzeiger, 10 November 1972. The USSR was interested exclusively in those occupation rights which allowed it to exercise control over developments in Germany. At the same time there was no question that the USSR would accept the view that there was an unresolved German question to be resolved at some point in the future. This was clearly demonstrated when, on the occasion of the exchange of instruments of ratification of the Moscow Treaty, the USSR refused to accept the exchange of notes between the Federal Republic and the Western powers as being part of the accompanying documents. These notes referred to the 'rights and responsibilities of the Four Powers with respect to Germany as a whole and Berlin'. By listing documents containing this formula it could be said that the Treaty could possibly at least be construed in this way. It took considerable effort to reach a compromise: the USSR accepted reference to the West German instruments of ratification, which in turn expressly mentioned the exchange of notes. See D. Cramer in *Frankfurter Allgemeine Zeitung*, 2 June 1972.

55. I. Witsinos in ibid., 27 October 1972; G. Vetter's commentary on Hessen radio, 3 November 1972; *Der Spiegel*, 6 November 1972, p. 24.

56. *Frankfurter Allgemeine Zeitung*, 9 November 1972.

57. For example in ibid., 9 November 1972.

58. E.-U. Fromm's comments on Hessen radio, 4 November 1972.

59. Among others, the name of the Soviet Ambassador to Bonn, V. Falin, is mentioned in this context. This could imply that the USSR was exerting pressure on Bonn at the same time.

60. See the official bulletins issued on 7 November 1972, *Texte zur Deutschlandpolitik*, op. cit., Vol. 11, pp. 260–4.

61. For official declarations see ibid., pp. 306–24.

62. Text: ibid., pp. 268–301 and 287. Declarations following the signing in ibid., p. 380–7. Soviet commentary in *Pravda*, 10 November 1972. Assessment of the legal implications of the treaty by W. Kewenig, 'Die Bedeutung des Grundvertrages für das Verhältnis der beiden deutschen Staaten', *Europa Archiv*, no. 2 (1973), pp. 37–46.

X

Conclusions

1. Analysis of the Interests of the USSR and the GDR

The Party leaderships in Moscow and in East Berlin have assigned high priority to the maintenance of the existing political and social order and the strengthening of Soviet hegemony in the 'socialist community'. Correspondingly, both sides make every effort to prevent as far as possible any Western political or intellectual influences penetrating the Warsaw Pact member-states,[1] and to impose strict Soviet-type discipline on them.[2] Leading party officials of both the CPSU and the SED seem to view monolithic bloc unity as indispensable. The USSR sees the universal acceptance of its own leading role at stake. The East Germans, on the other hand, regard the solidarity of the Eastern camp as essential to compensate for their exposed and, in comparison with the Federal Republic, inferior position.

Both the Soviet Union and East Germany agree that the decisive factor is to shift the global and in particular the European correlation of forces between the 'capitalist' and the 'socialist' states in favour of the latter. In the past, the degree to which progress has been made in this respect[3] has corresponded with a more and more clearly articulated desire to increase the political influence of the 'socialist community' in Europe as a whole.[4] The USSR and the GDR may differ from time to time on specific detailed priorities or methods to be employed, but in basic matters of principle they pursue congruent interests. Existing differences concern only points of detail, and while they may at any given time assume disproportionately greater importance, they have little impact on basic political unity in the long term. So, for instance, the differences of opinion between the USSR and the GDR concerning policy towards Germany over the period 1969–72 were at times considerable, but once resolved they put no noticeably lasting strain on the relationship between the two states. On the contrary, relations between the USSR and the GDR have clearly consolidated further on the basis of new conditions.[5] The conflicting interests which emerged during the process of change in attitudes towards the Federal Republic were thus only of relative and passing significance.

136

It still seems worthwhile, however, to examine more closely those spheres of interest and constellations in East–West relations which serve to illustrate the areas of conflict as well as ag eement between the USSR and the GDR. The issues raised during a period of change and transition, even though they became submerged subsequently as new patterns of interaction evolved, might surface in a new environment. Despite the congruence of basic political views between the USSR and the GDR, the fact cannot be overlooked that the two states are operating from quite different objective conditions. It would be surprising if their common ideology and shared need for discipline could neutralize all the consequences of this state of affairs.

One basic difference between the USSR and the GDR concerns their relative political potential. The USSR is a superpower with global commitments, concerned with the safeguarding of its interests on a world-wide scale. The GDR has considerably more modest political weight, and her vital interests are generally restricted to Central Europe. Up to the end of 1972, this contrast was even more sharply accentuated by the fact that very few states outside the Communist orbit had actually recognized the GDR, and that its opportunities for exerting influence in world politics were therefore severely restricted. Given this situation, the details of policy towards Germany, in so far as they do not touch on basic matters of principle, appear less important to the Soviet leaders than they do to their East German allies. The detailed arrangements for traffic between West Berlin and the Federal Republic were matters of relative indifference to the USSR, once the political framework had been set.

Because of their global interests, the Soviet leaders are not quite so free to pursue their interests in Central Europe as the East Germans would like them to be. They cannot regard aspects of policy towards Germany as the one and ultimate goal to which all else must be subordinated. On the contrary, interests in achieving goals in Central European affairs must be reconciled with interests elsewhere. What to East Berlin is an absolute necessity may be fraught with considerable disadvantages and risks for Moscow in an overall perspective.

At the same time the very nature of the respective interests of the countries in Central Europe is different. Aspects of policy towards Germany can, under certain circumstances, be used by the USSR as a lever for action in a broader context. The pursuit of regional interests is circumscribed not only by the careful consideration of interests elsewhere, but also by opportunities for adapting regional policy to serve extra- or supra-national needs. It is in the nature of Soviet interests that East European activities in Central Europe can be employed to achieve other goals than just those related directly to Central Europe.[6] Political behaviour becomes more flexible when set in a broader context. Since there is a greater number of angles to be considered, the number of postures which can be adopted also increases, and this in turn means an increase in the possible options which can be utilized in the bargaining process between East and West.

The idea that controversial aspects of the German problem should be assigned only relative importance would conflict, potentially at least, with the GDR's point of view. East German leaders see Germany's problems as directly and acutely affecting the very existence of their state. The existence of the GDR is seen primarily to depend on the state of affairs in Central Europe. Thus, the interests at stake in Germany cannot be assessed on the same level as interests elsewhere. As much depends on the situation in Central Europe developing along favourable lines, advantages in different regions cannot simply be used as adequate compensation. From East Berlin's point of view it seems quite logical to promote Soviet and East European interests in Germany, even at the expense of potentially doing greater damage elsewhere. Up to the beginning of the 1970s, intra-German national rivalry[7] and attempts to block international recognition of the GDR also served to keep the attention of SED leaders focused on the German situation, and in particular on confrontation with the Federal Republic.[8] This rigid single-mindedness has been an additional obstacle preventing the East German leaders from adjusting to elements of change in the Soviet attitude towards the Western actors in the German arena. But now that the GDR has dropped all ideas of a German nation, gained increased leverage in world affairs and come round to the Soviet idea of a normalization of relations in Central Europe, its earlier obsession with German affairs also seems to have declined.

2. The German Problem

In the second half of the 1960s Soviet and East German leaders were agreed that the greatest obstacle to the realization of their objectives was the policy pursued by the Federal Republic. Both states therefore directed their attacks in particular against 'revanchism', 'militarism' and 'neo-Nazism', trying to defame those forces in West Germany which they considered to be obstructive. Even so, the policies pursued by the two states, despite their similar terminology, were not identical. There had been indications of this during the SED–SPD dialogue, even though in this case the Party leaderships of the CPSU and the SED did coordinate their actions. In other words, their joint political strategy served to cloak their differing motivations: whereas the Soviet leaders were hoping to influence the foreign policy orientation of the Federal Republic, the SED leaders wanted to create an internal bloc effectively under SED control opposed to the CDU/CSU coalition government in Bonn.

In the former case the aim was to prime the West German state to fit in with the objectives of the USSR's European policy, in the latter the purpose was to mobilize as large a proportion of the West German population as possible against its own state. The extent to which the views of Moscow and East Berlin did differ became apparent when, at the end of 1966, a CDU/CSU–SPD government came to power in Bonn which seemed inclined to adopt a foreign policy corresponding more closely to Soviet wishes. The reaction from Soviet leaders was positive, whereas the GDR leaders saw this new constellation of forces as representing a particularly serious threat.

The SED strategy of forcing a split within the Federal Republic sprang from its obsession with German affairs. It involved creating a situation by means of change in political alignments whereby the Communists could gain increased, perhaps even decisive influence in an all-German framework. The whole idea collapsed when the SPD leaders, with the support of the party rank and file, rejected alliance with the SED. Instead the SED leaders found themselves exposed to the danger of the Social Democrats using the same national framework as a means of exerting influence on the GDR. This prospect soon induced the SED leaders, in agreement with the USSR, to treat the agreed exchange of speakers with some reserve. However, Ulbricht and his leading party officials still clung to their all-German illusions, even when the Soviet leaders had come to regard national appeals as a weapon in the hands of the adversary, which must be immobilized. The USSR was quicker to realize the danger involved, for the simple reason that from the beginning its expectations had not been motivated by national aspirations. When it became apparent that the foreign policy course pursued by the Federal Republic could not be influenced by enlisting the help of the SPD, the USSR no longer had any interest in continuing the SED–SPD dialogue. Ulbricht and the SED, however, even after they had reluctantly accepted that the whole idea was pointless, still looked for a chance to extend their influence to West German society. Not until the Social Democrats at the end of 1966 opted for government coalition with the CDU/CSU, instead of counter-alliance with the SED, were 'national' plans finally seen as hopeless.

From this point onwards the GDR leaders began to steer a radically different course. If previously their all-German aspirations had led them to pursue a policy of greater openness towards West Germany than that adopted by the USSR, they now dissociated themselves strongly from all ideas of a community of interests embracing all

Germans. It may be that leading party officials in East Berlin, following the frustration of their all-German ambitions, were quick to see the risks involved in a policy which produced no pro-Communist feeling in Germany, but exposed the GDR population to Western influences. General political trends served to magnify the fears of the SED leaders and eventually, from 1970 onwards, directed them along the path of total delimitation from the Federal Republic. The most important contributory factors were the process of détente between the Soviet Union and the Federal Republic since 1969–70 and the related efforts of the socialist-liberal coalition in Bonn to strengthen German national unity despite the division of the country and to remove the barriers keeping the people of the two halves of Germany apart. The more the Federal Republic pressed for rapprochment, the more obstinate was the resistance of the East German leaders.

There are two possible explanations for this behaviour. Conceivably the all-German aspirations of the SED were never serious, but were merely based on tactical considerations at a time when West German timidity ensured that they would not be put to the test. If this is true, it was West Germany's decision to pursue a more active national policy which forced the GDR leaders to call off their bluff. The other possibility is that East Berlin's professions of support for the idea of national unity were genuine inasmuch as they reflected aspiration for power in an all-German context. This would explain why their talk of national unity never prevented the SED leaders from increasingly striving to isolate the GDR from the Federal Republic and thereby continually reinforcing the division of Germany. The protection and even expansion of their own power base would then have to be considered as the motivating force of East German policy on this matter, not adherence to any autonomous concept of national unity.

The second hypothesis is supported by the fact that the GDR was originally designated to serve as the nucleus for a united Germany under Communist control. It would be entirely in keeping with the logic of history if this ideological mission survived in the consciousness of East Berlin party officials until such time as it came into direct conflict with the practical interests of the East German regime. Moreover, there are grounds for asserting that until 1966 the SED leaders found it useful to uphold national claims. The East German leaders could present themselves as the advocates of the interests of the whole German people and use national claims at any time as a means of exerting influence on West German society. Not until West Germany effectively took over this role with respect to all-German unity did the risks become unacceptable to the SED.

The USSR had supported the GDR in its national policy as long as this provoked no uncontrollable developments in Germany. In mid-1966, when the danger appeared on the horizon that a wave of national feeling might sweep through Germany, the Soviet leaders tried to break off the SED–SPD dialogue and thus forestall any such possibility. Six months later, when leading circles in East Berlin had come to realize the obsolescence of national appeals even in a long-term perspective, the two allies decided that the division of Germany should be consolidated in every possible way. An anti-national line was developed, according to which the division of Germany was the final, irrevocable result of historical development. Even the fact of a common German heritage was denied. The GDR and the USSR continued to support only the somewhat vague idea of the continued existence of the German people.

Ulbricht and others apparently retained this as a terminological lever to be used when, as they hoped, a new opportunity presented itself to appeal to pan-German sentiments. However, there were prominent circles within the SED which, even at that time, wanted to eliminate all vestiges of such national sentiment. This line prevailed when, at the end of 1969, the socialist-liberal coalition government in Bonn used the idea of the national unity of the German people as a political instrument for confronting the GDR with concrete demands. The more Bonn used the idea of national unity to press for increased opportunities for contact, and to insist on the possibility of future reunification, the more the SED party officials were made aware of the weakness of their position and thus felt obliged to pursue a defensive, anti-West German policy.[9]

3. Relations with the Federal Republic

The East German leaders' renunciation of their ideas on national unity facilitated their reaching an understanding with the USSR. For some time the Warsaw Pact member-states had been demanding unconditional recognition of the territorial *status quo*. This applied in particular to the legal confirmation of the border between the two German states and acceptance of the existence of the GDR. If until the end of 1966 there was also talk of the possibility of reunification of the two German states some day, this represented an extraneous element in a programme which otherwise aimed at reinforcing the existing territorial divisions between East and West in Europe. Thus the GDR's change of course from the beginning of 1967 onwards seems to have been welcomed by Moscow.

The countries within the USSR's sphere of hegemony could now be uncompromising in their demands for final confirmation of existing territorial boundaries.[10] Following the invasion of Czechoslovakia in 1968, this was coupled with Soviet attempts to gain acceptance of the view that it was the USSR's responsibility to safeguard the interests of all Warsaw Pact states. In this endeavour it could rely on East German consent. SED officials, however, were less pleased that, starting in 1970, the USSR again pressed for the adoption of a more conciliatory attitude towards advances by Bonn. Even when it was just a question of phrasing the East German rejection in such a way that the Federal Government would not break off its *Ostpolitik*, this was treated at times almost as a major concession.

Since the middle of the 1960s Soviet policy towards Germany had in essence concentrated on the Federal Republic.[11] The strategy of 'European Security', as it evolved in the spring and summer of 1966, was based on an appreciation of the importance of West German behaviour for shaping the political future of Europe. Following French withdrawal from NATO, much depended on Bonn as to whether the Atlantic Alliance could continue to exist on the European mainland or whether it would be reduced to an alliance between the USA, Canada and Great Britain only. The attacks on the Federal Republic were designed to subject the main continental European pillar of NATO to concentrated pressure.

This approach met with approval from leading SED officials, who perceived their relationship with the Federal Republic as one of inevitable enmity. However, Soviet policy in December 1966 showed that, unlike their East German ally, the Soviet leaders had no intentions of confining themselves to perpetual animosity towards West Germany. They decided according to each individual case whether pressure or relaxation would best serve to influence the foreign policy orientation of the Federal Republic in the desired direction. Thus the Soviet–East German understanding with respect to Bonn endured only for as long as the USSR saw fit to engage in a policy of confrontation.

The USSR's flirtation with the Federal Republic in December 1966 remained an isolated episode. Once Moscow had come to realize that the coalition government of CDU/CSU and SPD was not prepared to carry out the desired course alterations, the Soviet leaders once more began paying more heed to the anti-West German promptings of the SED. Complete understanding seemed to have been restored between the USSR and the GDR. However, the latent conflict generated by the possibility of a closer relationship between the USSR and the Federal Republic in the realm of foreign policy had merely been papered over, not resolved. In the spring of 1969 the Soviet leaders began making renewed approaches to the Federal Government, though this time their strategy was somewhat different.[12] The motives for this may be as much attributable to the need to shore up the façade of the 'socialist community' in the West as to the desire for rearguard defence in the quarrel with China, the need to obtain economic and technical assistance from the West, and the prospect of using détente to gain increased influence in Western Europe. Without the cooperation of the Federal Republic, these wide-ranging objectives could not be realized.

Predictably enough, this change in Soviet policy also served to revive the earlier fears of the SED. However, Soviet leaders refused to allow themselves to be deflected by the violent opposition from East Germany. In the autumn of 1969, when the new government in Bonn showed a readiness to seek an agreement with the Soviet leaders on the normalization of their mutual relations, party officials in East Berlin were powerless to prevent the USSR from responding positively. What is more, from 1970 to 1972 they could not avoid themselves being gradually drawn in as active participants in the political dialogue with the Federal Government. In the end they were even obliged to follow the Soviet example and conclude far-reaching agreements on normalization with Bonn.

SED representatives found that this policy, which obliged them to reduce their antagonisms towards the Federal Republic, was fraught-with problems. Even though the SED grudgingly accepted a settlement of several points of dispute between the two German states, they did so only with considerable misgivings – particularly since many East German demands were not met. As long as the Warsaw Pact regarded the Federal Republic as its main enemy, the GDR could portray itself as the vanguard in the struggle against the threat from West German revanchism' and, true to this self-appointed role, demand solidarity from its allies in support of GDR interests. Once this idea became redundant, the SED leaders found it much more difficult to retain the political support of their allies.

The East German leaders also considered it necessary to maintain the idea of West Germany as the main enemy because of the internal situation of the GDR. If the population could be persuaded that their very existence and achievements could only be preserved by maintaining the struggle against the West German threat, then there was clear justification for any protective measures the East German leaders saw fit to take. In this way they could minimize the GDR's vulnerability to influences coming from West German society, particularly since influences from this source did not have to surmount linguistic and national barriers. On the other hand, if this image of West Germany were dropped, there would be nothing to justify blocking contacts and communication with the other half of Germany. The SED leaders attempted to resolve the dilemma by following the Soviet example, stressing the idea of class struggle, and thereby legitimizing a policy of thorough *Abgrenzung* (delimitation). But, unlike the case of the USSR, there was one factor which, more than anything, motivated their attitude – the danger of social democratic tendencies spreading in the GDR.

For some time the Warsaw Pact member-states had been advocating recognition of the GDR by all countries, but in particular by the Federal Republic. However, there was still disagreement as to whether this demand should be a precondition to be fulfilled by the Federal Republic before détente could begin, a dialogue could be initiated or a treaty signed; or whether this was an aim to be achieved by negotiations in the process of normalization of mutual relations. The SED favoured the former alternative. Evidently they were afraid of the negative repercussions if a rapprochement came about between their East European allies and the Federal Republic prior to the recognition of the GDR. However, if the Federal Republic could be discouraged in its attempts to establish political contacts with the countries in the Soviet sphere of influence, this could only work to the advantage of East Berlin.

Soviet interests, however, lay in the opposite direction. Except for the period of immobilism from 1967 to 1968, the Soviet leaders preferred the second alternative. In December 1969 they made the Warsaw Pact adopt a decision according to which a bilateral political dialogue with the Federal Government and full diplomatic recognition of the GDR should be considered ultimate objectives. As a result, Moscow – and Warsaw – were free to conduct negotiations with Bonn and conclude agreements without being handicapped by GDR demands. The question of recognition was thus shifted to the very end of the negotiations on the normalization of relations. The Soviet leaders did, however, ensure that Prague, Budapest and Sofia delayed establishing relations with Bonn until corresponding agreements had been concluded between the two German states.

4. Attitudes towards West Berlin

As far as the Berlin question was concerned, the USSR and the GDR were in basic agreement with one another right up to the decisive phase of the Four-Power negotiations from autumn 1970 onwards. Both states demanded the legal separation of West Berlin from the Federal Republic, the right to intervene in West Berlin affairs and recognition of East Germany's sovereign jurisdiction over access. The SED leaders, unlike their Soviet counterparts, may have wanted to impose greater restrictions on the social and economic ties linking West Berlin with the Federal Republic or put greater emphasis on demands for good conduct, but these were just nuances and were of no fundamental importance. Of more significance was the fact that the GDR would have liked to extend its claims to sovereignty to cover the military transit traffic of the Western powers, but the USSR made no attempt to support this claim.

The USSR proceeded more cautiously than its East German ally. It made a point of directing its actions only against the political presence of the Federal Republic in West Berlin, making no mention of the Western presence. Thus, it appeared that only the 'illegal' ambitions of West Germany were at issue. In actual fact, the position of the Western powers was indirectly affected since, without the ties linking West Berlin to the Federal Republic, the city would hardly have survived to require protection.[13] However this strategy of moving in a gradual and indirect way involved curtailing actions against West Berlin to a greater extent than was acceptable to East Berlin. The SED leaders were impatient, and in any case were afraid that excessive caution might result in failure to achieve their objective.

One decisive aspect of the conflict was the fact that, even after the building of the Berlin Wall in August 1961, the East German leaders continued to regard West Berlin as a 'thorn in the flesh' of the GDR. The city's radio and television stations were completely outside the control of the GDR, its broadcasts reaching parts of the GDR which were beyond the transmitting range of West German stations. Many East German traffic routes converged in West Berlin and as a result had to be abandoned in some cases and replaced by arduous detours. The city was situated in the heart of the GDR and as such would naturally seem to belong to it, yet it did not. In the eyes of the population, this symbolized the fact that the USSR and its allies had been unable to gain mastery over Berlin and thus over Germany as a whole. Finally, the existence of West Berlin as an enclave made the capital of the GDR appear as a body without a head.[14] All these factors encouraged the East German leaders to advocate a policy of maximum commitment and risk in the struggle for West Berlin.

The USSR had repeatedly made clear in the course of its activity against West Berlin from April 1965 to February 1969 that measures must at all costs stop short of provoking serious conflict with the Western Powers.[15] The logic behind this is easy to follow. In the event of serious conflict over Berlin, it would be the USSR – not the GDR – which would have to make the decisive commitment. What is more, the Soviet leaders were engaged in a whole series of ventures involving them with the Western Powers, especially the United States. Thus a Berlin crisis would have had widespread repercussions and adversely affected many of the USSR's other interests. In other words, the USSR would have had to bear the political cost of any conflict which arose. As far as Moscow was concerned, West Berlin was a reality, which would have to be lived with for as long as was necessary. Moreover, Soviet leaders believed that in any case West Berlin would eventually become part of the Soviet sphere of influence, and that therefore sooner or later its present transitional phase would come to an end.[16] It was enough to take every opportunity to prevent a consolidation of West Berlin's position and to add to the problems the city already had to face. Threatening actions could even be counter-productive in that – as in previous years – they could increase Western solidarity with West Berlin and thus serve to stabilize the ranks of the opponents.

Eventually the USSR agreed to recognize the existing close relationship between West Berlin and the Federal Republic, a relationship which had previously served as the pretext for reprisals against the city. In return the Western powers confirmed the special status of the city in relation to the Federal Republic and agreed to a reduction in the political presence of the Federal Republic in West Berlin. The Soviet leaders upheld their view that West Berlin was an autonomous actor under international law entirely separate from the Federal Republic. Later interpretations mentioned only those areas where Federal presence was to be reduced, not where it was to be preserved. This provided a basis for the partial continuation of disputes concerning Berlin. The SED leaders, who has at first regarded themselves as the major loser, could draw hope from this.

5. The Problem of the Status of the GDR

The SED took every opportunity to declare that the GDR enjoyed unrestricted state sovereignty. This claim was echoed by the USSR. Apparently Soviet statements were designed to create the impression that the GDR enjoyed full status of equality with other states, thereby lending weight to East German demands for full recognition. Soviet support for recognition of the GDR did not only stem from the fact that the two countries are allies. Since the refusal by many states to recognize the GDR was based on the thesis that the SED regime was artificial and externally imposed, it also had to be taken as a direct symbol of protest against the USSR's hegemony in East-Central Europe. This allegedly revanchist attitude by the states in question was to be countered by the idea of a normalization of relations. The West was to accept the absolute legitimacy of the social and political order created within the Soviet sphere of influence. Recognition of the GDR was a key element in this programme.

However, when concrete international legal issues were to be decided, the Soviet leaders *de facto* limited GDR sovereignty while supporting it verbally. For instance, the binding declarations, issued in the spring of 1966 in support of the East German application for membership in the United Nations, upheld the continued validity of inter-Allied rights, agreed upon in 1945, on the implementation of joint measures in Germany. Admittedly these provisions also applied to the Federal Republic, but in view of the current correlation of forces (which precluded any Soviet actions against West Germany) their practical significance was limited to the relationship between the USSR and the GDR. During the talks between Gromyko and Bahr at the beginning of 1970, the USSR accepted the argument that allowance must be made for the special legal situation obtaining with respect to Germany, i.e., the continued competences of the Four Powers deriving from the occupation regime, although the USSR had no intention of accepting West Germany's interpretation of the legal basis of access to West Berlin and the special nature of intra-German relations. Instead, Soviet leaders wanted to ensure that should détente give rise to unwelcome developments in Germany, they would have at their disposal legally acceptable instruments of control.[17]

The SED leaders regarded the idea that GDR sovereignty was circumscribed by the continued authority of the occupation powers as an outrageous affront. At every opportunity, in particular at the beginning of 1970 and in the summer of 1972, leading East German officials repeatedly attacked in the sharpest possible terms Western assertions of Four-Power responsibility and, by decisively rejecting the idea of occupation rights in any form, indirectly criticized the USSR on this issue. Whereas the Federal Republic had much to gain from accepting a status of limited political autonomy, for the GDR this could bring nothing but disadvantages: it would mean jeopardizing the claim to sovereign jurisdiction over lines of communication between West Berlin and West Germany, curtailing demands for recognition by the Federal Republic, reviving the idea of the continued existence of a German nation (via Four-Power responsibilities) and assigning to the USSR a superior legal position with respect to the GDR. It was a bitter disappointment for the East German leaders that this process of normalization which they had hoped would mean the end of previous handicaps and impositions should reassert the old control mechanisms and fail to settle the German problem once and for all.[18]

SED officials also maintained that East Berlin was, without any restriction, an integral part of the GDR. The USSR supported this view verbally and advocated it in negotiations with the West. Yet despite this verbal support Soviet leaders avoided committing themselves clearly and irrevocably on this issue. Obviously, for all practical purposes East Berlin was a part of the GDR, but there still remained one or two formal provisos which could serve as a basis for maintaining that the city still enjoyed a special status deriving from the occupation regime. The East German government would have very much

147

liked to clarify the legal situation by eliminating such formal niceties, but the USSR refused.

There are two motives which could explain this Soviet behaviour. First, Moscow presumably found it expedient in its relations with the Western powers to give the impression at least that East Berlin still retained elements of its former special status.[19] Secondly, the USSR might have found it useful to be able to confront the GDR with overriding Soviet authority in its capital. But at the same time Soviet leaders were evidently concerned to prevent the West from using formal Soviet adherence to its legal position in East Berlin as a pretext for assuming or asserting indirect Soviet concurrence in the notion of a Four-Power status for the whole of Berlin, because this could have been used to claim as a matter of principle that the three Western powers also retained authority in East Berlin.[20]

6. Patterns of Coordination Between the USSR and the GDR

The political activity of the USSR and the GDR over the German question shows a considerable degree of coordination. In legal terms this is based on an understanding reached on 20 September 1955. However, the fact that the two states effectively coordinate their policies tends to have more to do with the practical interests of the parties concerned than with contractual obligations. Irreconcilable conflicts may at times totally or partly paralyse joint action, yet when mutual coordination of efforts occurs, it increases the prospects of success. This applies as much to the USSR as to the GDR when it comes to coordinating policy on Germany. At the same time coordination of policies involves a degree of mutual influence. Basically the side enjoying the superior position has a greater chance of getting its own way. This is one reason why the Soviet leaders are interested in maintaining close coordination with the GDR over policy towards Germany. The GDR leaders, on the other hand, are primarily concerned to secure for themselves the full support of the USSR as a world power in their struggle against the West. The pattern of coordination between the two states is of considerable importance in determining the relative ability of one partner to prevail over the other. Two questions are involved: (i) which issue areas are included in the coordination process and which are excluded? and (ii) Does this coordination involve merely consultation without any binding force, or does it include the actual taking of decisions?

It helps, in answering these questions, if the factual materials are divided into categories. Category A comprises all issue areas which are normally included in the coordination process. Subsequent analysis must then decide whether coordination in a particular issue area corresponds to the interests of both states equally, or whether the interests of one state prevail. Category B comprises those issue areas where coordination is sporadic and partial, but mutually agreed upon. Evaluation of this category must depend on whether coordination was motivated by mutual or unilateral interest. Category C covers all issue areas where one party coordinates the behaviour of the other. Here it must be decided how the interests of the 'injured' party are affected. Category D is reserved for those issue areas where coordination never occurs. The criterion for evaluation is whether one party benefits more than the other.

At first glance there are two focal points of coordination between the USSR and the GDR over Germany – attitudes towards Berlin and the network of East–West negotiations from 1969–70 to 1972. The USSR's interest in the former issue is easy to understand. The conflict over the future of Berlin is directly linked to relations with the West, and developments in this area in turn inevitably impinge on the USSR's global interests. Also, Berlin has always been a potential conflict area, always containing elements of risk. Moscow therefore, quite understandably, wanted to keep events under control – which included preventing the GDR from taking unilateral action. As regards the period of negotiations on Germany from 1969–70 to 1972, the various interests are less clear-cut. The Soviet leaders deemed it necessary to ensure that the GDR coordinated its actions with Moscow and did not disrupt matters by acting on its own initiative. However, it was perhaps even more in the interests of the GDR to make sure that the USSR was kept constantly aware of East German interests in the talks and negotiations conducted at the different levels. The more frequently the SED leaders were kept informed and consulted, the more effectively could they hope to gain acceptance for their own point of view. Thus the practice of mutual coordination was also an opportunity for the GDR leaders to restrict the USSR's freedom of action.

However, on closer inspection it becomes evident that no consistent coordination did take place, with regard to either Berlin or the negotiations with the West in the period from 1969–70 to 1972. In order to single out those areas where coordination always took place, further differentiation is required. Consistent coordination (Category A above) took place only in respect of actions designed to influence the domestic situation in the Federal Republic or measures of pressure or enticement *vis-à-vis* West Berlin. One example of the former case is the SED–SPD dialogue; examples of the latter are the repeated actions taken against access to West Berlin between April 1965 and February 1967, also the arrangements concerning visits to East Berlin in February 1969 and spring 1972. It is not clear whether East German harassment of the transit routes to West Berlin at the end of November and the beginning of December 1970 had been agreed from the outset between the USSR and the GDR, or whether it just had *post facto* Soviet approval. If the latter, this would have to be interpreted as a further expression of a fundamental crisis of coordination between the USSR and the GDR in the late autumn of 1970. Concerning the negotiations between both states and the West on the Berlin settlement, there seems to have been consistent coordination – at least formally. The coordination which took place both in attempts to influence internal developments within the Federal Republic and the adoption of measures against West Berlin corresponded chiefly to Soviet interests in retaining influence over important and sensitive developments in East–West relations in Germany.

Partial, mutually agreed-upon coordination (Category B) is evident in efforts to gain recognition for the GDR, and above all in the question of relations with the Federal Republic. The GDR application for United Nations membership in February 1966, the various references to the East German demand for recognition made in the documents issued by the Communist states and parties, and the differing positions adopted by the East Berlin delegation in the negotiations between the two German states on the conclusion of the Basic Treaty, were all the result of either bilateral or multilateral consultations. On the other hand, the GDR quite possibly did not consult the USSR before presenting the draft of a treaty between the two German states in December 1969. Following the signing of the Moscow Treaty, Ulbricht and the East German leaders tried unilaterally to change the situation which had arisen. Their arbitrary interpretation of the treaty as requiring the Federal Republic to recognize the GDR immediately and unconditionally was meant to extract support from their allies for neglected East German interest.

In February 1970 the Soviet Foreign Minister agreed in talks with State Secretary Bahr to certain provisos on GDR sovereignty which had the effect of limiting East German claims to recognition. This was done without prior consultation with the GDR. But the USSR could say that it complied with the requirements for consultation, since the agreement between Gromyko and Bahr was only put into writing after the SED had been persuaded to accept it. The overall picture is that, as far as recognition is concerned, the USSR – despite formally fulfilling its obligations for coordination – preserved its freedom of action. GDR attempts to do the same did not lead very far. During the basic negotiations in the summer and autumn of 1972 the East Germans again had to revert to coordination with the USSR.

The Bucharest Declaration issued by the Warsaw Pact member-states on 6 July 1966, which ruled on the political line to be adopted towards the Federal Republic, appears to have been agreed upon voluntarily. Yet, despite this, in late autumn 1966, the USSR was able to initiate a change in policy towards West Germany, allegedly based on this agreed approach. This change, however, had not been previously agreed upon with the GDR, and even provoked its violent opposition.[21] It was no mere coincidence that in this case the Soviet leaders had not considered it necessary to coordinate policy with the East Germans beforehand – the fact that the agreement of the GDR had not been sought represented no handicap whatsoever because the talks were still in the initial exploratory stage.[22] Nevertheless, the confidence of the SED leaders was severely shaken by the USSR. Once the Soviet leaders, independently of any influence from East Germany, came to the conclusion that Bonn was not prepared to go along, there was no longer any problem over which to engage in coordination with East Berlin.

Then, during the next change of course, the coordination mechanism failed once again. During the initial stages of approaches to Bonn over the winter of 1968–9, Moscow again acted independently. In March 1969 the GDR put its name to the Budapest Appeal, reflecting Soviet policy towards the Federal Republic, but this did not prevent considerable controversy breaking out over the formulation and implementation of the document. Apparently the Soviet leaders had tried to indice their allies to commit themselves to a more exact interpretation. The result was that the GDR found new ways of circumventing it.

In December 1969, as negotiations between Eastern Europe and the Federal Republic were getting under way, the Warsaw Pact member-states resolved that, subject to certain conditions (namely, that there should be mutual consultation) negotiations could now proceed on a bilateral level. The USSR formally complied with this decision: both during the talks and negotiations with the Federal Republic leading up to the Moscow Treaty, and during the Four-Power negotiations on a Berlin Agreement, there were regular discussions of the state of play with East German representatives. However, in objective terms one cannot talk of genuine coordination. Crucial points were settled between Soviet and Western negotiators before they were even discussed with the GDR. In these cases corrdination consisted of the greater or lesser degree of willingness on the part of the SED belatedly to accept the Soviet line. On the other hand the talks and negotiations the GDR Government held with the West German Government concerning regulation of their mutual relations and arrangements for transit traffic were, apparently without exception, discussed beforehand. This would seem to be suggested by the events surrounding the two meetings between Brandt and Stoph in the spring of 1970. It is also corroborated by what has come to light concerning subsequent consultation. Soviet diplomats appear to have participated directly in the decisive final phase of the struggle for the conclusion of the Basic Treaty.

Overall the impression was gained that partial coordination took place whenever the USSR had a vested interest in holding negotiations. Negotiations conducted by the USSR or the GDR were subject to mutual coordination in a number of ways. East German leaders had to seek prior approval of their actions, whereas the Soviet leaders only belatedly sought GDR sanction for their own activities. Bearing in mind that the Soviet leaders could promote their policies on different levels with different negotiating partners, while East Berlin officials were only able to deal with the Federal Government and possibly also the West Berlin Senate, the USSR was in an almost overwhelmingly superior position to that of the GDR. For if ever the East Germans refused to go along with Soviet policy, Moscow could use the negotiations on the different levels to present them with a *fait accompli*, which sooner or later the GDR would have to accept. Only if the USSR had had to depend on prior East German approval of its actions would it have been possible to prevent such a state of affairs. From 1967 to 1968 the SED seems to have entertained illusions along these lines.[23] However, subsequent events showed that the USSR was not inclined to let this happen.

There are really no examples for the imposition of coordination by one of the parties on the other (Category C). But perhaps this category should include several occasions when the USSR acted to induce the East German leaders to desist in the future from making inflammatory statements on Berlin.[24] An example of the absence of coordination (Category D) concerns fundamental attitudes towards the national question. It appears that on this issue the USSR left matters to the GDR. Although the SED's slogans on national unity had long ceased to fit in with Soviet objectives, Soviet spokesmen and commentators only ceased referring to the GDR's role in an all-German context after the SED officials themselves had dropped the idea. The reason for this may have been that national ideology is accepted to be the sole concern of the German Communists, as long as the practical consequences of this do not clash with Soviet policy towards Germany. Another example in this category is that the Kremlin rulers claimed for themselves the exclusive right to rule on questions relating to GDR status. They defend their claim by reference to the fact that the occupation statutes do still have some validity, although the USSR has tried as far as possible to avoid mentioning this in public. In the relationship with the GDR the occupation rights did represent a valuable source of power to the USSR.

7. Results of Coordination between the USSR and the GDR

The pattern of coordination between the two states is such that the results display a clear asymmetry. As far as the USSR is concerned, mutual coordination takes the form of *post facto* consultation with a minimum of East German influence. The purpose of this is to gain East German support for Moscow's line. The SED leaders, on the other hand, when they submit their policy to coordination, invite Soviet representatives to play an active role in the actual taking of decisions. The GDR's freedom of action is particularly restricted when it comes to policy on Berlin and developments of an all-German nature. It enjoys relatively greater freedom of action when it comes to the regulation of relations with the Federal Republic, but nevertheless the overall direction of policy is determined by Moscow.

The critical points in the process of political coordination between the USSR and the GDR in the exploratory phase came when the Soviet leaders, looking at the situation in broader perspective, set aside more narrowly conceived criteria of success in the controversial aspects of policy towards Germany, or assigned only relative importance to the concept of confrontation in Central Europe. But now that the GDR has been forced to accept the changed situation and, following the conclusion of the bilateral agreements, the USSR has less occasion to accede to West German wishes, this source of tension between the USSR and the GDR can only be expected to play a minor role, at least for the foreseeable future.

As a result of their inherently weaker position, East German leaders must constantly be on the look-out for ways to strengthen their influence in Moscow. By stressing their loyalty and devotion to the bloc leader and using their economic power in support of Soviet objectives, the SED leaders hope to make themselves indispensable. Also, the relative stability of the GDR within the Soviet sphere of influence, personified in his time particularly by Ulbricht, has been useful to the USSR. Thus, the GDR hopes that the USSR will see the value of taking into consideration the broad interests of this important ally. These interests, it should be added, are portrayed as being vital also for effective continuation of East German policy. The GDR also tries to increase its value by carrying out tasks delegated to it by the Soviet Union in different parts of the world.[25]

Another way of getting the USSR to protect East German interests is by influencing Moscow's perception of the international situation and its policy objectives. If the SED leaders manage to influence their Soviet ally in the assessment of Western intentions towards the 'socialist community', or gain acceptance of operational consequences stemming from an agreed course of action, they have scored a success.

This method was used very successfully by Ulbricht and the SED during the first months of 1967 in holding the USSR to a strictly anti-West German line.

Admittedly this result was facilitated by the fact that the Soviet leaders themselves had already abandoned hopes of effecting a change of attitude in Bonn, which had been the original motive for establishing political ties with the Federal Government in the first place. However, GDR influence had an effect which was not negligible: it consolidated and radicalized the anti-West German line in Moscow for an extended period of time. In the summer of 1969 and during the negotiations of 1970 and 1971, when the USSR was striving for a settlement in Germany to further higher objectives, Ulbricht and the SED leadership were rather unsuccessful in their efforts to influence Soviet perceptions. Another way for East Berlin to exert influence on Moscow is to draw attention to the less obvious aspects of a given situation. Apparently SED officials have often managed to draw the attention of their Soviet counterparts to the significance of details, which from a distance may have appeared relatively unimportant, but which were of considerable interest to the GDR.

At times, the results of this strategy of cooperative influence have been highly unsatisfactory to East Berlin. The SED leaders would then cautiously make use of their potential for obstructive counter-measures. Whenever the GDR perceives a threat to one of its vital interests and the USSR is relying on East German cooperation, passive resistance and carefully concealed sabotage can be used as political weapons. These were precisely the tactics adopted by the GDR leaders when faced with Soviet proposals concerning the issuing of border passes in February 1969 and the scheduled meeting between Brandt and Stoph in March 1970. East German behaviour during the negotiations leading up to an agreement on West Berlin transit traffic in September and October 1971 was presumably aimed to a large extent at blocking or at least delaying a Berlin settlement.

As a last resort, during the coordination crisis of 1970–1, Ulbricht used the argument that Chinese accusations would gain credibility if the USSR failed to follow East Germany's line. East German opposition to Soviet policy towards the West received additional weight in view of the fact that the SED could in part count on support from within the CPSU. However, in the long run Ulbricht's audacity helped prepare the way for his own downfall. Once Brezhnev and his supporters had regained the upper hand within the Soviet Party, they decided to remove the no longer trustworthy SED leader as soon as the opportunity presented itself.

The USSR and the GDR achieved greater successed by coordinating their policies on Germany than either could have achieved on its own.

Admittedly the results were more to Moscow's liking that East Berlin's. Apart from a short interlude in the winter of 1970–1 (which the USSR could use to test Western resolve) the USSR's freedom of action was never seriously impaired. There was also never any serious prospect of a break between the USSR and the GDR – not even over specific issues. To that extent it can be maintained that there are no 'antagonistic contradictions' in relations between the two states. The tremendous preponderance of the USSR in terms of power and ideology acts as an efficient brake on the GDR, particularly since she finds herself in an exposed position *vis-à-vis* the West. Beyond that, the SED leaders have taken the view that a growth in Soviet power in relation to the West inevitably consolidates their own position and increases their chances of success.

Confident of East German dependence, the Soviet leaders are free to conduct relations with the West without too much regard for the GDR and without having to worry too much about the psychological effects on their ally. Since the SED leaders are hardly in a position to change the course of events, the USSR is not unduly concerned if, from time to time, the East Germans give vent to their deep displeasure. At times East German resistance can even benefit Soviet policy. The course advocated by East Berlin sometimes appears to the USSR's counterparts in the West as the greater of the two political evils, making Soviet proposals appear in an advantageous light. Thus East German intransigence can, in certain circumstances, have the effect of increasing the persuasive force of Soviet proposals in the West, thereby also increasing their chances of success.

References

1. This was particularly evident during the discussion of point three on the CSCE agenda (contacts, exchange of information and ideas in Europe). See G. Wettig, 'Die Sowjetunion und die Europa-Konferenz', *Osteuropa*, No. 6 (1973), pp. 415–18; J. Riollot, 'Brezhnev and the Free Flow of Ideas and Information', Radio Liberty, *Research Bulletin*, RL 29/74, 30 January 1974. For the Soviet point of view see *Osteuropa*, No. 7 (1973), pp. A465–77; M. Slavyanov and N. Yur'ev, 'Soveshchanie po bezopasnosti i sotrudnichestvu v Evrope', *Mezhdunarodnaya zhizn*, No. 2 (1974), pp. 18–20. The SED view is dealt with in B. v. Rosenbladt, *Die Auseinandersetzungen mit der Konvergenztheorie in der DDR*, Stiftung Wissenschaft und Politik (Ebenhausen/Isartal), SWP-S, April 1970.

2. It is not coincidental that in 1968 the SED leaders were particularly fervent in supporting the liquidation of all traces of the Czechoslovak heresy.

3. The often unsatisfactory results of East–West negotiations have only played a minor part in the East European record of success. Evidently the

manifestations of crises in the Western world, in particular domestic upheavals, conflicts between Europe and the U.S.A., slowing down of the process of European integration and economic vulnerability, are held to be more important. On this see the elaborations by B. Ponomarov on 18 January 1974 at the Lenin Conference in Moscow in *Pravda*, 19 January 1974.

4. M. Mackintosh, 'Moscow's View of the Balance of Power', *The World Today*, No. 3 (1973), pp. 108–18. This is the aim behind the all-European Security body which is to be created by the CSCE and is said to be an institutional alternative to NATO in the realm of collective security.

5. There is an unusually high degree of unity of perception and policy in the concerted action of the USSR, the GDR and their allies with respect to West German representation of the interests of West Berlin, the ties linking the city to West Germany, the evaluation of the judgement given by the Federal Constitutional Court and the outflanking of the Basic Treaty in order to block West German influence on East German society in 1973.

6. Naturally Soviet actions in other parts of the world can be made to serve objectives in Central Europe. To that extent global considerations only partially serve to restrain Soviet policy on Germany. On the other hand, it is possible that Soviet policy elsewhere can serve to reinforce policy in Germany.

7. Even before the GDR was founded, the SED since 1947 has repeatedly declared that its historical mission is to overcome the division – allegedly imposed on Germany by the West. Activities towards this end ceased after 17 June 1953, when consolidation of the GDR became the immediate goal. Even though the idea of reunification was dropped in 1955, the SED leaders for another ten years at least upheld their claim to be the only force which could reconstitute the unity of Germany. See, for example, Ulbricht's address on the occasion of the 20th anniversary of the founding of the SED on 21 April 1966, *Dokumentation der Zeit*, No. 358 (1966), pp. 1–11; see also D. Kreusel, *Nation und Vaterland in der Militärpresse der DDR*, Stuttgart, 1971; W. Sühlo, *Der Zusammenhang von nationaler und gesellschaftlicher Spaltung der deutschen Nation in seiner Bedeutung für die Deutschlandpolitik der DDR*, Stiftung Wissenschaft und Politik (Ebenhausen/Isartal), SWP-S 170, June 1970.

8. See B. v. Rosenbladt, *Zur Aussenpolitik der DDR. Die Ausgangslage für ein Nebeneinender der zwei deutschen Staates im internationalen System*, Stiftung Wissenschaft und Politik (Ebenhausen/Isartal), SWP-S 215, May 1973, pp. 12–14 and 39.

9. Here the GDR's lack of a national identity and unattractive image played an important role. This is the conclusion to be drawn from the fact that the GDR has declared itself to be a nation and denies all connection with the Federal Republic. The fact that the SED leaders saw a disproportionately greater danger to their regime in relaxed relations with the Federal Republic and increased opportunities for visits and the exchange of information than in the previous policy of confrontation created a gap between reality and the concept put forward in October 1968 by H. Wehner. According to this concept a West German decision to adopt a more cooperative attitude would bring about, gradually and voluntarily, a process of rapprochement between the two German states.

10. The discussions taking place at the Security Conference have clearly

demonstrated the USSR's strong interest in unconditional legal recognition of existing borders. This began to emerge immediately after the conclusion of the Moscow Treaty of 12 August 1970 (in which the USSR had failed to implement its demands). Whereas the treaty used the term 'inviolable' (*nerushimye*) borders, the aim of the Security Conference was, the Soviet Union declared, to make them 'unalterable' (*nezyblemye*).

11. As far as the USSR was concerned, policy towards the GDR belongs objectively in the same category as relations towards the 'socialist community'.

12. In particular the USSR did not insist on withdrawal from NATO. Unlike in 1967 and 1968 the USSR did not make fulfilment of the demands a precondition for negotiations – a clear sign that this time there was genuine interest in holding negotiations.

13. G. Wettig, 'Aktionsmuster der sowjetischen Berlin-Politik', *Aussenpolitik*, No. 6 (1968), pp. 328–30.

14. This view is stressed by D. Mahncke, *Berlin im geteilten Deutschland*, Munich and Vienna, 1973, p. 112.

15. G. Wettig, 'Ost-Berlin im Schatten der Moskauer Deutschland-Politik', *Aussenpolitik*, No. 5 (1969), pp. 267–71.

16. See the statements by the Head of the 3rd (European) Section of the Soviet Foreign Ministry, V. Falin, on 29 January 1971 in conversation with a Bonn diplomat, *Die Welt*, 12 April 1972.

17. Thus in the autumn of 1972 the USSR was prepared to issue a joint declaration with the three Western powers on the continued validity of the competence deriving from the former occupation rights, but then refused adamantly to include any reference to specific responsibilities (i.e. with respect to Germany as a whole).

18. B. v. Rosenbladt, *Zur Aussenpolitik der DDR*, op. cit., pp. 16 and 38.

19. This could be important if the USSR were to assert the role of a Berlin power along with the Western powers (the latter exercising occupation rights in West Berlin) and put the maintenance or reinforcement of Soviet authority in West Berlin on the agenda (in which case the Western powers would at least make formal claim to similar rights in East Berlin). Also the Soviet Union wanted to avoid open disagreement with the Western powers in Berlin.

20. This may explain the apparent contradiction, that the USSR was not prepared to renounce completely its rights in East Berlin, but at the same time categorically denied in negotiations with the Western powers that East Berlin was subject to Four-Power status.

21. The Bucharest Declaration included several ambiguities at crucial points, so that the participants could construe from it very different interpretations. Romania justified her actions by reference to the Bucharest Declaration, when she established diplomatic relations with the Federal Republic in January 1967, thereby inviting condemnation from the USSR, the GDR and the other Warsaw Pact allies.

22. GDR opposition was more likely to convince the Federal Government that the Soviet leaders were serious in their offers of better relations.

23. The SED leaders thought they had convinced their allies of the need to meet GDR demands (particularly those for unconditional recognition) before the Federal Republic could be accepted as a negotiating partner. If the GDR

had been successful in this, it would have been in a position to dictate the extent to which relations with Bonn were to be developed.

24. See the example quoted by G. Wettig, 'Aktionsmuster der sowjetischen Berlin-Politik', op. cit., p. 330.

25. See the example quoted by B. v. Rosenbladt, *Zur Aussenpolitik der DDR*, op. cit., p. 15.

Postscript

After the basic agreements had been concluded, a new stable pattern of relations between the USSR and the GDR emerged. During 1971 and and 1972, the East German leaders had been influenced to adapt their policies *vis-à-vis* the Federal Republic of Germany to Soviet wishes. From then on, it was absolutely clear that East Berlin could act only within the range of Soviet *Westpolitik*. Accordingly, Honecker and his colleagues could no longer pose as the unconditional antagonists of the alleged West German threat, but had to do political business with Bonn. Moreover, they were no longer able to ignore what Moscow called the 'progressive' elements of West German détente policies. To be sure, the East German leaders did their best to convince their population of the necessity to close ranks against threatening 'ideological' influences from West Germany and to apply all possible measures for the political protection (*'Abgrenzung'*) of the GDR against contacts with West Germans. But these policies were in full conformity with the intentions of the Soviet top functionaries, who were as unwilling as their counterparts in East Berlin to allow the slightest destabilization of Communist power in East Germany. It seems, however, as if the Soviet leadership at moments were less fearful about considering tiny concessions to the West German desire for more intra-German contact than was the Honecker regime. Presumably, the policy-makers in the Kremlin were confident that the East Germans were in a positions to undo small concessions by subsequent administrative counteraction, while they felt that West German hopes should not be frustrated altogether, as otherwise undesirable foreign policy tendencies might start to get the upper hand in Bonn.

Once the East German leaders had had to give up their traditional uncompromising anti-West German stand, they began gradually to appreciate the advantages which better relations with Bonn could bring. Such advantages could be realized primarily in the economic field. The West German interest both in improving the communication lines with West Berlin and in expanding contacts between the two German states provided the GDR with powerful levers to exact economic assistance from the Federal Republic. In autumn 1974 it became abundantly clear that Honecker and his colleagues had finally decided to exploit their chances. In other words, East Germany set out to follow the example of the USSR. It can be called an irony of history that this caused some rivalry between Moscow and East Berlin.

For the Soviet leaders began to realize the they were now competing with their East German allies for the limited West German resources of economic and technological assistance to the East. At the same time, there was some apprehension in Moscow lest the East Germans might draw together too closely with their countrymen in the West one day in the near or distant future. The GDR regime, for its part, resented the ruthless exploitation by its Soviet ally of its economic advantages by sharply raising the formerly fixed oil prices early in 1975. This measure entailed grave economic problems for the GDR.

The common political front *vis-à-vis* the West, however, was more co-ordinated than ever. Towards the Federal Republic the USSR and GDR demonstrated monolithic unity in the repeated quarrels over the interpretation and application of the Berlin Agreements. The negotiations at the Conference on Security and Co-operation in Europe (CSCE) revealed a degree of common policy presentation which was unusual even by Eastern standards. During the Vienna talks on a mutual balanced forces reduction (MBFR) agreement, the smaller Warsaw Pact states, with the partial exception of Romania, closely followed the Soviet line, even on the occasions when their interests seemed to be different. To Western observers it was evident that the common front presented to the West was not the result of common policy-formation: repeatedly, the representatives were unaware of the Soviet line, and then changed their views after they had heard a new Soviet statement in the conference room. So far, the East–West détente, as it is being practised, has on the whole strengthened – and certainly has not weakened – Soviet control over the smaller Warsaw Pact states. This applies particularly to the position of the USSR *vis-à-vis* the GDR.

Index